ANNAPURNA
A TREKKER'S GUIDE

ABOUT THE AUTHOR

Kev Reynolds has trekked in many different regions of Nepal, from Api in the farthest west to Kangchenjunga in the north-eastern corner of the country – plus many magnificent places in between. He has organised and led treks in remote districts and written guides to five of Nepal's most popular trekking regions. A freelance writer, photojournalist and lecturer, he has published more than 40 books which, besides his Nepal trekking guides, include a series on the Alps and, nearer to home, several books on walking in southern England.

WARNING

All mountain activities contain an element of danger, with a risk of personal injury or death. Treks described in this guidebook are no exception. Under normal conditions wandering the trails of Annapurna will be neither more nor less hazardous than walking among big mountains anywhere in the world, but trekking involves physically demanding exercise in a challenging landscape, where caution is advised and a degree of stamina is often required, and it should be undertaken only by those with a full understanding of the risks, and with the training and experience to evaluate them. Trekkers should be properly equipped for the routes undertaken. Whilst every care and effort has been taken in the preparation of this guide, the user should be aware that conditions can be highly variable and change quickly. Rockfall, landslip and crumbling paths can alter the character of a route, and the presence of snow and the possibility of avalanche must be carefully considered, for these can materially affect the seriousness of a trek.

Therefore, except for any liability which cannot be excluded by law, neither Cicerone Press nor the author accepts liability for damage of any nature (including damage to property, personal injury or death) arising directly or indirectly from the information in this guide.

Readers are warned that trekkers are sometimes badly injured by passing yaks; a few unfortunates die of hypothermia or acute mountain sickness; while some simply lose their balance and fall from the trail due to a momentary loss of concentration. Since there is no organised mountain rescue service in Nepal, such as exists in some mountain regions of Europe, if an accident occurs self-help may be your only option.

Everyone trekking in the Annapurna region should assume responsibility for their own safety and look to the needs of those with them. This includes especially porters and members of a trek crew, as well as fellow trekkers.

ANNAPURNA
A TREKKER'S GUIDE

by
Kev Reynolds

2 POLICE SQUARE, MILNTHORPE, CUMBRIA LA7 7PY
www.cicerone.co.uk

© Kev Reynolds 1993, 2003
Reprinted 1996
2nd Edition 2003
Reprinted 2008 with amendments

All photos © Kev Reynolds

ISBN-13: 978 1 85284 397 7
ISBN-10: 1 85284 397 7

A catalogue record for this book is available from the British Library.

DEDICATION

This book is dedicated to Ang Phurba Sherpa and Mingma Doma Sherpa,
and all the mountain people of Nepal, who add a special dimension
to every visit to their beautiful country

Advice to Readers

Readers are advised that while every effort is taken by the author to ensure the
accuracy of this guidebook, changes can occur which may affect the contents.
It is advisable to check locally on transport, accommodation, etc, but even rights
of way can be altered.
The publisher would welcome notes of any such changes.

Front cover: Nilgiri North, seen from the trail to Jomosom (Muktinath to Tukuche)

CONTENTS

APPENDICES

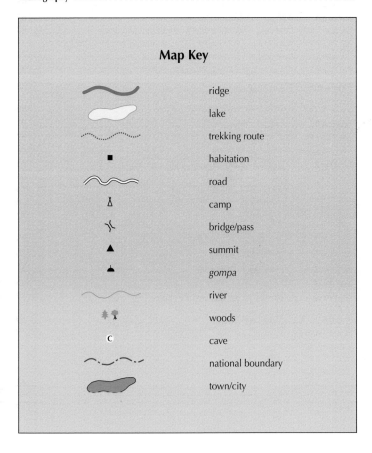

Map Key

	ridge
	lake
	trekking route
■	habitation
	road
	camp
	bridge/pass
▲	summit
	gompa
	river
	woods
c	cave
	national boundary
	town/city

The trail to Bahundanda (The Annapurna Circuit, Bhulbhule to Bahundanda)

PREFACE

I had been involved in a love affair with mountains for 30 years and trekked in many different countries before I had an opportunity to visit Nepal. But that first visit sealed my fate; I would have to return – again and again and again. Those who are about to undertake their first visit must heed the warning: you may never settle, for the Himalaya can so easily become habit forming.

Trekking in the Annapurna Himal will not only open your eyes to scenes of great beauty, but enable you to build relationships with people of another race, another culture. How you interact, both with the country and its inhabitants, will depend upon the degree of sensitivity carried with you. The rewards to be harvested will derive directly from your willingness, or otherwise, to put Western values on hold and give yourself to the multiplicity of experiences waiting there. Trekking in Nepal can be a feast. There's no need to go hungry.

While Nepal holds numerous opportunities for the trekker, this book is a guide to just one area – but what an area to concentrate on! Annapurna and its neighbouring peaks and valleys provide an arena for some of the most stimulating treks anywhere in the world. And it is my fervent hope that all who are drawn to this magnificent region, whether newcomers to trekking or old hands with years of experience behind them, will find as much magic there as I have whilst researching the trails for this book. But as you wander I urge you to treat the people and their landscapes with the respect and love they deserve. We have all heard of the Kleenex Trail; we all know a little about the environmental damage caused in the past, and the very real dangers that exist today with an ever-growing number of visitors and an expanding population. Those seemingly timeless mountains and valleys are delicate and vulnerable; no less vulnerable are the cultures of those who live in their shadow. May each one of us add nothing to the problems and dangers that exist, but instead help to alleviate them.

In the words of the King Mahendra Trust for Nature Conservation: 'While trekking, ponder your impact on the environment and culture. Teach people the importance of respecting nature and how to conserve it. By assisting in these small ways you will help Nepal enormously.'

Trail information contained in this edition reflects as accurately as possible the routes as I found them. However, each monsoon adds its own signature to the landscape. Trails and bridges may be washed away and replaced elsewhere; villages grow, tea-houses and lodges multiply, and paths become re-routed. In order to improve and update future editions of this guide I would appreciate your help in providing a note of any changes found on trek, and also welcome comments or suggestions that could be helpful to future trekkers. All notes and corrections sent to me via the publisher will be gratefully received.

A Tibetan trader sets out her wares beside the trail

It should be borne in mind that heights and distances quoted may not be entirely accurate. Different maps give varying figures and widely disparate spellings for some of the villages, mountains and passes, and until the perfect map is produced that accurately reflects the contours of the land, we must be content with estimations. Times given for the various stages on trek are also estimates only, but are offered as a rough indication of the length of each day's walking. They do not allow for tea-house delays nor photographic interruptions, but are based on actual walking time.

This guidebook could not have been written without the help and encouragement of a number of people, especially those friends who generously supplied information before, during and after visits to Nepal. Others who shared the trails, tea-houses and lodges added much to the trekking experience and, often in unsuspecting ways, provided additional notes for inclusion. I gratefully acknowledge their contributions. Firstly, I am indebted as ever to my wife for her constant support and practical help, and who, in sharing my love for Nepal and its people, joined me on my latest trek around the Annapurnas. Her company made it one of the best trips ever. In addition I'd like to thank Roland Hiss, with whom the original outline of this book was conceived, while among those who wrote in with suggestions after the first edition appeared, I'm grateful to Robert A. Pease from California, Dr Nick Ireland from Norwich and Hum Bahadur Gurung at the ACAP office in Ghandruk. My thanks to Patricia Barnett of Tourism Concern, and to Ann McLean of Empower Consultants in New Zealand for technical information about the Safe Drinking Water Scheme recently installed in the Annapurna region. My old trekking partner Alan Payne walked the Circuit with me in the early days and has since joined me on other treks elsewhere in Nepal. Thanks are also due to Steve and Debbie Wilson, Georges and Genevieve Conne and their friends from Lausanne, plus Brenda, Ruth, Tracey and Wangchu, and Rachael, Margaret and Alison who at various times shared some great days in the mountains. To Sondru Gurung of Chhomrong who rescued an 'Old Man – Very Tired' and challenged the sun with his laughter – thanks. More recently it was a privilege to have the company and friendship of Phurba Sherpa and his wife Mingma for 24 memorable days in the Annapurna region. Their presence was a daily joy, and I look forward to more treks with them in the future. I also thank my good friend Kirken Sherpa of Himalayan Paradise Trekking in Kathmandu for his hospitality, advice and help in numerous ways. Sweety Sherchan, who runs the Eagle Nest Lodge in Ghasa, deserves a special mention for her effervescent personality and some of the best lodge meals I've ever tasted, while Gunja Man Gurung at the Chhomrong Mountain View and Min Bahadur Gurung at Hotel Buddha in Ghandruk made time spent in their villages especially memorable. And lastly, the team at Cicerone Press have given tremendous support – as always – and put their combined talent and skills to my advantage. I am grateful to them all.

Kev Reynolds, 2003

Ghandruk enjoys a wonderful view of Annapurna South, Hiunchuli and Machhapuchhare

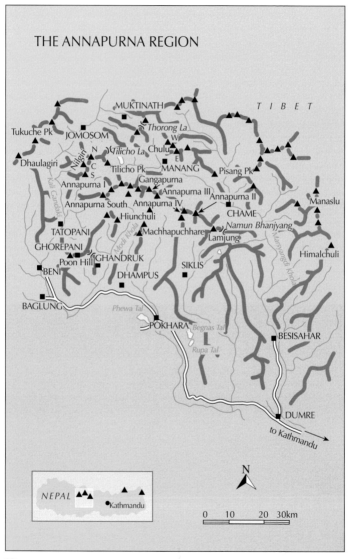

THE ANNAPURNA REGION

INTRODUCTION

Nepal is there to change you, not for you to change Nepal.

Approaching Kathmandu by air from India the plane swings eastward and suddenly, out of the left-hand window, a great bank of clouds hangs as a breaking wave of cumulus far above the brown wrinkled earth. At least, they look like clouds. Then you realise those clouds are rising out of clouds and they're not clouds at all. They're mountains – huge mountains plastered with ice and snow, a ragged barrier of fangs and domes, long white crests, abrupt faces, spurs and buttresses drawing shadow. An extensive wall like a gigantic sawblade glistening in the sunlight; a serrated, castellated horizon, fortress-like and magnificent…

The Himalaya, kingdom of the snows: dream-world for many; reality for some. Once experienced they can never be forgotten, never dismissed from memory whether one's experience of them is gained by climbing to their summits or trekking through their valleys. Once seen they become a part of you, habit forming and intrusive.

The Himalaya, of course, contain the youngest and highest mountains on earth – mountains that are still growing, and stretch in a monstrous chain from Nanga Parbat in Pakistan to Namche Barwa in eastern Tibet – a fabulous wall of mountains with 14 peaks rising above

Dhaulagiri and its icefall can be seen from Larjung (The Annapurna Circuit, Tukuche to Tatopani)

13

8000m (26,000ft). Nepal boasts eight of these giants: Everest and Kanchenjunga, Lhotse, Makalu, Cho Oyu, Dhaulagiri, Manaslu and Annapurna. Annapurna was the first of the 8000m summits to be climbed and is now the focus of some of the world's most exciting and visually spectacular treks.

Seen from the lakeside town of Pokhara in central Nepal the northern horizon, less than 40km (25 miles) away, consists of the snow-capped peaks of the Annapurna Himal. In the early morning they catch the first stain of sunrise. Hovering dreamlike, they cast their reflection in the still waters of the Phewa Tal, little more than 800m (2625ft) above sea level. Among them 12 summits rise in excess of 7000m (23,000ft), while a number of others are well over 6000m (19,500ft) high. This massive island block is moated on the east by the Marsyangdi Khola, and on the west by the deep Kali Gandaki valley. To the north, beyond the Manang Himal which forms the northern wall of the curving Marsyangdi, lies Tibet. East of the Marsyangdi rises Manaslu (8163m, 26,781ft), and to the west of the Kali Gandaki is the dramatic Dhaulagiri Himal, whose icy summit tops 8167m (26,795ft), while draining the heart of this great block of mountains is the deep shaft of the Modi Khola, at the head of which is the Annapurna Sanctuary – a miracle of ice-sculpted peaks gathered in an almost complete circle.

In addition to the mountains that dominate every scene, the Annapurna range represents one of the most ethnically and geographically diverse regions

in all Asia, and is home to 10 ethnic and caste groups.

Sub-tropical forests are inhabited by monkey and deer, raucous with chattering birds in spring. There are hillsides ablaze with rhododendron, orchid, bougainvillea and poinsettia. There are jungles of bamboo, upland pastures starred with gentians, and pinewoods reminiscent of the Alps – and beyond the rain-shadow of the Himalaya lie high, arid valleys and barren, windswept plateaux similar to those of Tibet.

This book is a guide to trekking in and around the Annapurna region. It describes the lengthy challenge of the Annapurna Circuit; the shorter, but visually rewarding, Annapurna Sanctuary trek; the Pilgrim's Trail to Muktinath which heads upvalley along the Kali Gandaki after first crossing the Poon Hill Danda with its famous sunrise views of Dhaulagiri and the Annapurnas. A fourth trek, shorter and less committing than these, explores the lower foothills, while suggestions for other treks and variations are also made.

Each of these will reward the visitor with stunning panoramas and an unbelievable variety of scenic wonders – from the lush vegetation of the lowlands where rice paddies terrace the foothills to the arctic-like wilderness of ice-falls and gleaming glaciers – and will surprise the newcomer to Nepal with the broad smiles and genuine open-hearted friendliness of the local people. 'Namaste' is in their eyes and on their lips, and signs over lodge doorways that proclaim 'Wel-Come' mean just that.

*Outside Tengi the trail is guarded by a chorten and a mani wall
(The Annapurna Circuit, Manang to Yak Kharka)*

If it is a dream of mountains that initially lures you to this Himalayan kingdom, it will be the valleys and hillsides populated by a wide range of ethnic groups, each united by a tradition of hospitality and cheerfulness, that ensure you do not forget it. Two hundred kilometres (125 miles) west of Kathmandu, the cultural diversity and ethnic variety is probably greater than anywhere else in all Nepal, and will surely form part of a rich and memorable experience for trekkers in the Annapurna Himal.

LANDSCAPE OF DREAMS

*If there be a Paradise on earth,
it is now, it is now, it is now!*

(Wilfrid Noyce)

Noyce reached the South Col of Everest in 1953, and four years later was a member of a small expedition given the unique opportunity to attempt Machhapuchhare. He was a poet as well as a mountaineer, and the outpouring of emotion quoted above is echoed in the hearts of many who have the privilege of gazing at these astonishing mountains. Every year tens of thousands of trekkers do just that.

Such a statistic may horrify you. You may imagine immense crowds of trekkers and their porters queueing to march through a village or to cross a narrow suspension bridge, overloaded lodges, squalid, cramped campsites and broad, eroded trails knee-deep in litter. Happily the reality is not quite like that.

The Annapurna region covers an area of more than 7600km^2 (2934sq miles), and the main trekking seasons amount to about five months of the year. Although it would be wrong to suggest

15

ANNAPURNA CONSERVATION AREA PROJECT

Enveloping the entire Annapurna region, in an area defined by the Kali Gandaki river on the west, the Marsyangdi and Dudh Khola valleys on the east, the Pokhara valley to the south and mountains running along the Nepal–Tibet border in the north, the Annapurna Conservation Area Project was formally established in 1986 with its headquarters in Ghandruk, under the auspices of the King Mahendra Trust for Nature Conservation – a non-governmental organisation charged with the task of trying to integrate community development with nature conservation. From the outset it was apparent that the success of the project depended heavily on the co-operation of local people, for according to ACAP: 'Our way of conservation is not a separation of people from nature. It is the empowerment of people as nature's protectors.'

The ACAP management team began a programme of education and practical support through the training of lodge owners in matters of hygiene and sanitation, in reducing dependance on forest timber and in maintaining cultural pride. Communities have been involved in schemes aimed at developing the local infrastructure and income sources in environmentally sensitive ways – by the use of kerosene for cooking instead of wood fires, for instance, and solar panels to heat water. Local Tourism Management Committees fix lodge prices and encourage basic menus with local specialities, while the rich cultural heritage of the region is also fostered and protected. Information centres have been established in several villages throughout the region to promote that heritage.

Through money raised from trekkers via the issue of entry permits, ACAP has funded the building of bridges by local people, the maintenance of schools and health centres, reforestation projects, sanitation schemes, alternative energy sources and safe drinking-water stations. The Project is now widely acknowledged as one of Asia's most successful conservation programmes. For further information visit the headquarters building in Ghandruk, where a promotional video showing ACAP in action is screened three times daily during the main trekking seasons, or write to ACAP, PO Box 183, Hariyo Kharka, Pokhara (email: acap@mos.com.np)

that there is no difficulty accommodating everyone in the peak season, there's time and space enough to swallow most of the crowds.

But clearly with so many visitors the potential for environmental damage is enormous, and over the years people-pressure has brought various problems, among them deforestation, pollution and cultural decay. However, thanks to the Annapurna Conservation Area Project (ACAP) a programme of conservation measures was begun, with the aim of repairing damage caused in the past and preventing further environmental and cultural decline in the future.

All who visit this magical region, whether on a brief once-only stroll through the foothills or on a lengthy trek or climbing expedition, should treat both the landscape and those who live in it with sensitivity and respect.

ANNAPURNA TREKS

This was the Himalaya, our promised land, and from now onwards we would carry this vision with us wherever we went.

(Maurice Herzog)

North of Pokhara the country is, indeed, a promised land, and the four main treks described in this guide provide ample opportunities to capture that vision in all its glory. Each has its own special appeal and its own rewards.

The Annapurna Circuit

This is *the* classic trek, one of the great walks of the world – a three-week journey that makes a gigantic loop round the Annapurnas along something like 190km (118 miles) of ancient trails. The ethnic and cultural diversity experienced throughout this journey is well known, but it's matched by an astonishing variety of vegetation, climate and unfolding landscapes that reward each day's journey.

Beginning to the east of Pokhara, in the little roadhead town of Besisahar, the trail heads north along the valley of the Marsyangdi Khola to reach Manang in six or seven days. Although this first part of the journey may take no more than a week, Manang is a world apart from Besisahar. A Tibetan-style village of flat-roofed houses and a forest of prayer flags, Manang stands at over 3500m (11,483ft) in the rain-shadow of the Himalaya, with a view across the valley to the northern wall of the Annapurna Himal. Time off in Manang will aid acclimatisation, and there are many interesting sites to visit before continuing upvalley for the climb to the Thorong La, the crux of the trek at 5416m (17,769ft). Under snow-free, calm conditions the only difficulties for an acclimatised trekker lie in the distance to be covered between Phedi on the eastern side and Muktinath on the west. But in snow or extreme cold the Thorong La is a major obstacle; never should the seriousness of its crossing be underestimated.

Once over the Thorong La the route descends to the upper valley of the Kali Gandaki, known here as the Thak Khola, by way of the pilgrim site of Muktinath, and continues as a long southerly trek passing between Dhaulagiri and the western slopes of the Annapurna massif – through the deepest valley on earth. This section of the walk gradually trades arid, Tibetan-like landscapes for scenes reminiscent of the Alps, but on a much larger scale. Then, below Tatopani, the Kali Gandaki is left behind in order to cross the terraced slopes of the Poon Hill Danda at the saddle of Ghorepani, before making the final descent of an ever-wrinkled land on the way to Pokhara. An alternative to this final section is to continue alongside the Kali Gandaki below Tatopani all the way to Beni.

The Annapurna Sanctuary

The Sanctuary is the name given by J.O.M. 'Jimmy' Roberts to the central core of an almost complete circle of peaks he first explored in the spring of 1956. It is a fabulous amphitheatre whose sole access route is through the narrow, steep-walled and heavily vegetated gorge of the Modi Khola. It was in the heartland of this Sanctuary that the only expedition ever sanctioned to attempt Machhapuchhare had its base in 1957, and from where Chris Bonington's expedition climbed the South Face of Annapurna in 1970. It makes a natural and rewarding objective for a trek setting out from Pokhara, and will require a bare minimum of seven days for the round-trip, depending on the actual route chosen.

Near the head of the Modi Khola's gorge the trail crosses an area threatened by avalanche, and under certain conditions the route is impassable. It is particularly hazardous in winter and early spring, but heavy snowfall at any time of the year can close the Sanctuary for several days.

Although lacking in cultural interest beyond Chhomrong, it is a spectacular walk, rather more demanding than some trekking companies like to suggest in their brochures, but somewhat less strenuous than the Annapurna Circuit outlined above.

There are several variations on the approach to Chhomrong. From Pokhara the shortest, and traditional, route heads roughly north-west to Dhampus on a foothill ridge among terraces of rice, millet or barley, and with glorious views to the mountains. The way into the Modi Khola continues via Landruk and on to Chhomrong after a descent to, and steep climb from, the river. Two or three days of narrow, helter-skelter trails lead through the gorge, finally emerging to the wonderland that is the Sanctuary. This is a spectacular cauldron of ice-coated mountains rimmed by (among others) Hiunchuli, Annapurna South, Annapurna I, and the graceful fish-tail peak Machhapuchhare – one of the most beautiful mountains in the world. In the Sanctuary itself there are two lodge areas offering accommodation: Machhapuchhare Base Camp (3700m, 12,139ft) and Annapurna Base Camp (4130m, 13,550ft), the latter a cold, often windy place, which provides an incredible 360 degree panorama of mountain majesty.

The Pilgrim's Trail to Muktinath

The original Annapurna trek, this is a linear route along the valley of the Kali Gandaki, where the only possibility of varying the route back to Pokhara lies near its southern end. But it is a beautiful walk nonetheless, with several interesting side-trips possible. It is a trek that charts an ever-changing series of landscapes and a steadily evolving range of vegetation, and experiences the riches of cultural diversity for which the region is noted.

Basically the trek reverses the second half of the Annapurna Circuit either by starting at Beni or crossing the Poon Hill Danda near Ghorepani, the two routes joining at Tatopani. Thereafter the Pilgrim's Trail follows the course of the Kali Gandaki upvalley through Jomosom and on to Muktinath, making a round-trip of at least two weeks. Jomosom has a STOL (Short Take-Off and Landing) airstrip with flights to and from Pokhara – weather permitting.

As with both the Circuit and Sanctuary treks, the Pilgrim's Trail is well suited to those travelling without tents and porters and relying entirely on lodge accommodation. The Thakalis who live in the Kali Gandaki valley are among the most adept hoteliers in Nepal, and the lodges they've provided along this trail offer some of the best facilities for trekkers in all the Himalaya.

The Ghandruk Foothill Trek

This short four-day trek remains in the foothills, but enjoys spectacular high mountain views and several welcoming villages. It is just one possibility of many loop-treks and circuits that could be made in the foothill country north of the Pokhara valley, and other suggestions are also given.

With easy access by road from Pokhara, the trailhead at Naya Pul quickly puts you on track for Ghandruk, a large but attractive Gurung village that faces Annapurna South across terraced fields. From there a helter-skelter trail leads to Chhomrong at the entrance to the Modi Khola's gorge, from where Machhapuchhare shows its distinctive fish-tail summit. The return to Pokhara continues along steeply terraced hillsides, unspoilt villages and wonderful views, and ends with a short bus or taxi ride out of Phedi.

The garden at the ACAP headquarters in Ghandruk, provides lovely views of the big moutains (The Ghandruk Foothill Trek, Section 1)

TREKKING AND TREKKING STYLES

Happiness is most often met by those who have learned to live in every moment of the present; none has such prodigal opportunities of attaining that art as the traveller.

(T.G. Longstaff)

For Longstaff's 'traveller' read 'trekker', for trekking is more than just travelling; trekking is taking part, being actively involved in a journey of discovery. Whereas the modern traveller is too often dependent on third-party schedules and mechanical aid, the trekker chooses to go where wheeled, mechanised transport is either rare or completely unknown, and where walking is the only way to get from A to B. In such activity an almost constant sense of awareness becomes not only possible, but is highly desirable.

In the heavily populated Annapurna region trekking is no real wilderness experience, for there are villages almost everywhere, and the well-walked trails have been used for generations by local people carrying on trade with neighbouring villages on all sides of the range. But while it may not be a wilderness experience in any meaningful sense, trekkers gain by daily contact with the Nepalese and Tibetan mountain folk who populate the valleys, cultivate the lower hills, and send their animals to graze slopes above the timber line.

Trekking comes in a variety of forms. There's the organised group trek, when several like-minded individuals

Morning at Baglungpani – a classic Himalayan viewpoint

travel under the auspices of a commercial tour operator (adventure travel company) and generally sleep in tents. There's independent trekking, where two or three friends forego the company of porters or guides, travel light and use tea-houses and lodges throughout – often referred to as 'tea-house trekking'. And there's a third course, a cross between independent and group travel, where a porter-guide is employed to carry some of the trekker's gear and guide him along the trail using lodges for overnight accommodation. Few regions of the Himalaya offer better facilities to accommodate trekkers of all persuasions than that of Annapurna.

The choice of trekking style will depend upon many considerations, such as cost, personal experience, availability of friends with whom to undertake a journey, the amount of time required to organise and carry out the trek, selection of route, etc. The following paragraphs therefore discuss options available, giving particular regard to the Annapurna region.

Trekking with a Group

This is the main choice for those with more money than time, who dislike the hassles of organisation, who get frustrated with bureaucracy, or who have limited mountain experience and want a degree of security. Trekking with a reputable adventure travel company does away with almost all pre departure worries and trek concerns. All that's required is to read the brochures and all dossiers carefully, sign the form, make out your cheque and let someone else take care of the arrangements.

On a group trek porters carry all camping equipment, food, kitchen stores, personal baggage, etc., leaving the trekker to shoulder just a light rucksack containing a few items likely to be required during the day. Although more and more groups these days are using lodges here, traditionally nights were spent in tents. Meals are prepared and served by a staff of trained Nepalese cooks and kitchen boys, latrines are dug by paid staff, tents erected and dismantled for you, and sherpa guides ensure that you do not get lost along the trail. A *sirdar* takes overall responsibility for the smooth running of the trek, but usually a Western leader also accompanies the group to liaise between trekkers and the local staff. This leader often has an understanding of any health problems likely to be encountered and has charge of a comprehensive medical kit.

An organised group trek is a very sociable way to travel, particularly for those who have no like-minded friends with whom to share an active holiday. Daily you will be walking with people you may never have met before, and many lasting relationships develop from on-trek introductions. On the downside, sometimes the disparate make-up of a group can lead to a personality clash, although groups are usually of sufficient size (10–14 is normal) to enable you to avoid close contact with anyone you might not get on with. Each year hundreds of trekkers resolve to undertake new journeys with a tour operator they've learned to trust. Adventure travel companies regularly advertise in the outdoor press, and several organise promotional evenings in the winter to show slides of a variety of treks, and prospective customers have an opportunity to meet and question trek leaders.

Organised parties generally need to keep to a pre-determined route and maintain a fairly strict schedule, which can be frustrating if you see an enticing side valley you'd like to visit. On the other hand, since each day's stage is limited by the distance a heavily laden porter can cover, the journey is made at a fairly leisurely pace, thus allowing plenty of time to enjoy the scenery and indulge in photography along the way.

Whilst group travel tends to insulate its members from interaction with local people, trekking for two weeks or more in the company of Nepalese guides, cooks and porters gives a marvellous opportunity, for those so inclined, to build a relationship that can be immensely rewarding for all concerned.

On an organised trek the day begins with a mug of tea brought to the tent at around 6 o'clock, closely followed by a bowl of hot water for washing. Breakfast is eaten soon after; in the foothills this will be taken outdoors around a table with views of the distant mountains. In higher, colder country, a mess tent will be used.

The day's trek starts early, around 7.30am, when the light is pure, the air cool and birds active. The·crew breaks camp and the army of porters pack their *dokos* (large conical baskets) or

otherwise arrange their loads, and set off along the trail. Sometime during the morning's walk the kitchen boys will rattle past and set up their cooker in a pre-selected spot for lunch, which may be eaten any time between 11.00am and 1.00pm, and usually consists of a hot meal with plenty of liquids.

The afternoon's walk finishes around 4pm, giving the chance to write journal notes, read a book or chat with other members of the group while camp is being set up and the evening meal prepared. This meal is usually finished by 6.30 or 7pm, allowing plenty of time to rest, read, talk or listen to the songs of the crew beneath a starlit sky.

Independent Tea-house Trekking – the Lodge Option

For those who enjoy, or who at least are not averse to, making all arrangements, such as booking flights, organising visas, permits and hotels in Kathmandu, buying bus tickets for the journey to Besisahar or Pokhara, route-finding on trek, and choosing meals and lodges – independent tea-house trekking is the answer. It can be an immensely rewarding way to travel, but it is essential to adopt a flexible attitude of mind and be ready to adapt to a variety of circumstances. There'll be no-one to blame when things go wrong, for every decision made is your own. But it is also the cheapest way to trek in Nepal.

Tea-house trekking is the most popular option in the Annapurna region, for there are lodges offering food and shelter

Julu East Lodge, on the way to Yak Kharka (The Annapurna Circuit, Manang to Yak Kharka)

practically every hour along the way on each of the treks described in this book, thus enabling you to travel with a minimum amount of equipment.

On the heavily trekked routes there are very few traditional tea-houses left, although the term 'tea-house trekking' remains in common usage. In less-trekked parts of Nepal a tea-house may be little more than a simple shelter offering refreshment to passing travellers, while a *bhatti* is a very basic hotel. But the *bhattis* that have developed for foreign trekkers in the Annapurnas now offer standards of luxury (in Nepalese terms) undreamed of in the recent past, although these standards mostly fall short of what would be commonly accepted in the West. Variously advertised as guest-houses, inns, hotels or lodges, *bhattis* are family-run businesses that are undergoing steady improvement with the encouragement and practical

assistance of ACAP. The service they provide may not be four-star, but it's well intentioned. Patience and understanding may sometimes be needed, but on completion of a tea-house trek, you'll probably discover that some of your happiest memories focus on the lodges in which you stayed.

In the area covered by this guidebook most hotels or lodges consist of a kitchen, dining area and an assortment of twin-bedded rooms. A few have dormitory accommodation too. The best have en-suite bathrooms and even flush Western-style toilets, but these are by no means the norm as yet, while general standards of decoration and cleanliness fall way below that expected, or taken for granted, in the West. As a generalisation, washing facilities are fairly basic and in some cases little more than a stand-pipe out in the yard, with only cold water on offer. Whilst the majority advertise 24-hour hot showers, these 'showers' invariably consist of a bare room or outhouse with luke-warm water provided. At best the bathroom will have just a nail or two on which to hang your towel or clothes.

Although standards are improving, some lodge toilets are still primitive enough to make you dread an upset stomach. These are mostly of the 'squat' variety with a basket or tin provided in which to place used toilet paper for the lodge owner to burn later.

Bedrooms are small and bare – little more than a cell in size – furnished with two firm but narrow beds, and occasionally brightened by a colourful poster tacked to the wall. There is no other furniture or floor covering, and the beds have only a thin foam mattress covered by a cotton sheet, and a hard pillow that may be as comfortable as a sandbag. Walls are invariably one plank thick and are not soundproof.

On environmental grounds lodge-keepers are being encouraged by ACAP to shun wood fires and use kerosene burners for cooking on. Apart from the obvious impact on the environment, in those lodges where cooking is still prepared on an open fire woodsmoke sometimes finds its way through the floor boards of bedrooms located directly above the kitchen area.

Despite electricity in practically every village, dining rooms are usually poorly lit, but in the best of them a convivial atmosphere is easily created – especially in the higher regions where a brazier of hot coals is placed beneath the dining table as a form of central heating.

Lodges offer a wide choice of meals. Trekkers who arrive expecting a limited offering of *daal bhaat* three times a day will be pleasantly surprised by the size and variety of lodge menus – although it should be stressed that not all items listed will necessarily be available. Although meat dishes are rarely on offer, pizza and apple pie are not uncommon, and Swiss-style *rosti* is just one of many different potato dishes to appear on lodge menus, so you can vary your diet between Western and traditional Nepali food if desired. One thing should be made clear though; many *bhattis* have an over-ambitious choice of meals available, but only one fire or burner on which to cook. It follows then, that if the lodge or tea-house is busy and trekkers order a wide range of meals, you can find yourself waiting literally hours to be served. Not only can this be frustrating (particularly if you're hungry after a long day's walk), it also means that more fuel than necessary is being used in the kitchen. Try to assess what your fellow trekkers are ordering and follow their lead.

The standard procedure on arrival at a lodge is to enquire of the owner if there are vacancies. After being allocated a room, request a padlock to secure the door. Before darkness falls discover the location of washing and toilet facilities, for although practically all lodges have some form of electricity, the lights do not always work. After ordering meals or drinks, enter the details in a book provided especially

The Musk Deer Valley Resort, Khobang (The Annapurna Circuit, Tukuche to Tatopani)

DAAL BHAAT

Daal bhaat is the staple diet of Nepal, and is usually eaten by locals twice a day – in the mid-morning and early evening. It consists of a huge amount of cooked rice (*bhaat*) flavoured with a small bowl of lentil soup (*daal*) and, where possible, a few curried vegetables (*tarkari*). Many Nepalis also chew a few uncooked chillis with their meal. Unless prepared and served by the same cook at an identical time, it would seem that no two *daal bhaats* are alike. Order two meals of *daal bhaat* in the same lodge on consecutive days and you're likely to have very different, but equally tasty, dishes. In reasonably 'up-market' restaurants in Kathmandu or Pokhara patronised by foreigners, you might also find side dishes with a choice of vegetables, Bombay potatoes and pieces of chicken, but even a basic *daal bhaat* in a trekker's lodge can be delicious and very filling. It makes an inexpensive meal, and is the only item on a lodge menu where you're likely to be offered a second helping at no extra charge.

for this purpose, and pay at the time of departure. Prices are exceedingly modest by Western standards, and the cost of a room so low that the lodge-keeper relies on selling meals and drinks to make a reasonable living. It is unacceptable practice to book a bed at one lodge and eat in another. Meal charges have been standardised in each village by the local lodge management committee, so there is no point in haggling over prices. If you bear in mind that all goods must be carried on the backs of porters or on mules, you'll appreciate that prices increase in proportion to the lodge's distance from a road.

On the descent to the Kali Gandaki, Dhaulagiri is on show practically all the way

Independent travellers on a tea-house trek enjoy a much more flexible routine than those on an organised group trek, and are able to vary their route according to taste. Even more so than on a group trek, it is an extremely sociable way of journeying among the mountains, although there is a danger of mixing only with fellow Western trekkers and so missing out on the chance to enrich your travels by a closer contact with Nepalese villagers. But for those who wish to learn more about local people, customs and villages along the route, opportunities abound. However, the best way to enjoy cultural interaction is with the third method of trekking, that is, with a porter-guide.

Trekking with a Porter-Guide

This can be extremely rewarding and enlightening, for the best Nepalese porter-guides quickly become your trusty friends and companions who will provide a daily insight into the ways of the people whose country you are travelling through. The camaraderie and companionship can increase the pleasures of your trek multi-fold. A porter-guide will carry some of your gear, make sure you keep on the correct trail and act as a link between yourself and locals met on the path. Those who are really familiar with the region you're journeying through may suggest diversions to side-valleys or to interesting villages off the route of most Western trekkers. They can teach you much of value, and if you are sensitive, keen to learn and prepared to treat your companion as a friend rather than a servant, your experience will be the more profound. There is the additional assurance that you are providing welcome employment, too, and it is worth remembering that the role of porter is by no means a demeaning one, for it has long formed a major source of employment – and a respectable one at that – throughout the hill regions of Nepal.

The hiring of porter-guides can be arranged in Kathmandu, either privately or through one of the many trekking agencies based in the city. For greater flexibility it is sometimes possible to hire one along the route, either for a day or two or for the duration of the trek. If you choose the latter course, enquire of your lodge-keeper for a reputable local man – preferably one who speaks a modicum of English, unless you have a reasonable command of Nepali. Porter-guides hired in Kathmandu will invariably speak some English; many of them are educated Sherpas or Tamangs. Payment is usually based on a daily rate, plus food and lodging, or a higher wage with the requirement that the porter provides his own food. Make certain that your porter or porter-guide clearly understands the arrangement before you begin the trek. At the end of the trek it is customary to give a tip, and this is usually based on a day's pay for each week of employment.

Once you hire a porter-guide, of course, you assume employer's responsibility for his well-being. Nepali law states that all trekking porters should be insured, have provision for security, personal protective equipment including clothing and shoes adequate for the weather conditions, and that the employer is responsible for the rescue of the porter(s) when required.

So far as the Annapurna region is concerned, your employee must be clothed and equipped to be able to cope with below-freezing temperatures if your proposed route reaches high altitudes (the Thorong La, for example, or anywhere in the Sanctuary). If hired through a reputable Kathmandu agency, a porter-guide *may* be reasonably well equipped, but you must check that this is so before setting out. If you take an inexperienced man from the sub-tropical lowlands, it's quite likely that he'll be ignorant as to the degree of cold likely to be encountered in the upper part of the trek, so you need to satisfy yourself that he has adequate footwear and warm clothing. If he does not, it is up to you to supply them.

In Kathmandu you can borrow decent water- and wind-resistant clothing for porters through the Porter Assistance Project run by the Himalayan Explorers Connection (HEC) in association with the International Porter Protection Group (IPPG), whose clothing bank is located next to the KEEP information centre in Jyatha on the edge of Thamel. Clothing for porters is supplied to independent trekkers and small trekking agencies on payment of a modest refundable deposit. For more information about HEC try www.hec.org (e-mail:members@hec.org). IPPG details can be found on www.ippg.net (e-mail: info@ippg.net).

The easiest and most lightweight form of trekking with a porter-guide relies on the use of lodges for accommodation. Once you decide to camp, of course, you enter a more complicated style, with a leaning towards the organised trek. The more equipment taken, the more porters you must employ to carry it. In Kathmandu there are plenty of agencies that can supply the manpower and equipment necessary for this.

One final point: trekking alone is not recommended for reasons of safety and security. In the event of an accident a companion can be invaluable in providing immediate help or arranging rescue. And sadly, although the populated hill-country remains virtually crime free, Nepal has not escaped certain aspects of Western 'civilisation', and theft is no longer unknown in the hills. Regrettably a few solitary trekkers have been mugged and one or two have even disappeared on lonely sections of even the busiest of trails. If you prefer not to travel with an organised group and have no friend to trek with, do consider hiring a porter-guide.

PORTER EXPLOITATION

Some trekkers are under the impression that porters are superhuman, able to carry massive loads, are unaffected by altitude and can sleep out in sub-zero temperatures with no ill-effect. This is nonsense. In fact Nepalese porters are victims of four times as many accidents and illnesses than Western trekkers, and some appalling incidents of exploitation and abandonment by employers have been reported.

In October 1997 a commercial trekking group set out to cross the Thorong La. Having almost reached the pass, Shyam Bahadur Nepali, a 24-year-old porter with the group, became unwell. Unable to carry his load he was given his wages, dismissed and left to descend alone to Manang without adequate clothing for the conditions. Somehow he managed to reach Letdar where he was given food and a blanket by the owner of a half-built lodge. Next morning he collapsed with advanced mountain sickness (AMS), but received no treatment until 5pm when an American climber arrived who, recognising his plight, administered the appropriate medication. Shyam's condition improved slightly, and Rps3000 was collected from trekkers and local people to pay two porters to carry him down to Manang. By the time they set out with Shyam in a converted *doko*, it was dark and snow was falling. Just an hour short of the HRA health post, Shyam collapsed and died, and for three days his body lay beside the trail…

In another incident, porter Kul Bahadur Rai became affected by altitude sickness while carrying a heavy load for a trekking group. Forced to continue by the trek leader until he could go no farther, he was then dismissed and left to descend alone. After slipping into a coma, Kul awoke to find himself in hospital where his frostbitten feet had to be partially amputated.

Though extreme, these examples are symptomatic of a major problem of porter exploitation by some unscrupulous tour operators and independent trekkers. Both the International Porter Protection Group (which was set up by Dr

Jim Duff after Shyam Bahadur's death) and Tourism Concern are trying to address this problem and have issued guidelines.

What can you do as a trekker?

Independent trekkers who hire a porter should adhere to the follow recommendations.

- Ensure adequate clothing is available for porters' protection in bad weather and at altitude: footwear, hat, gloves, windproof jacket and trousers, sunglasses and access to a blanket or sleeping bag (and mat if camping) above the snowline.

- Provide the same standard of medical care for porters as you expect for yourself.

- Never send sick porters down alone. Have someone go with them who understands the problem and speaks their language.

- Provide sufficient funds to cover the cost of a porter's rescue and treatment.

Members of a group trek can do the following.

- Before booking your trek ask tour operators what policies they have in regard to porters' working conditions, and let them know it is important to you that your trip does not exploit its trek staff.

- Travel only with an operator that has policies on porters' rights (Tourism Concern publishes a list of UK trekking companies with such policies: www.tourismconcern.org.uk).

- While on trek note the treatment of porters, their clothing, size of loads, where they sleep at night, etc.

- On return from Nepal tell your tour operator if you thought they were treated badly – and report this to Tourism Concern.

- Just as importantly, tell your operator if the porters were treated fairly, and let them know that this was crucial to your enjoyment of the trek. If every trekker were to show their concern for the treatment of porters and other trek staff, the trekking industry would be forced to define and improve its policies.

WHEN TO GO

The greatest drawback to climbing in monsoon conditions, greater even than the bad visibility, is the high temperature.

(H.W. Tilman)

Bearing in mind what Tilman had to say with regard to climbing during the monsoon, trekking in the Annapurna region is possible at any time of the year, although conditions vary greatly from season to season. The most popular period covers the post-monsoon months of October and November when lodges are at their busiest, with March and April (spring pre-monsoon season) coming second.

Spring (pre-monsoon): March–May

During March and April the average daytime temperature in the foothills north of Pokhara hovers around the lower 30s Celcius, but high mountain views are often restricted by haze or cloud by late morning. Rain showers and storms are not uncommon, although the northern part of the region is drier and usually enjoys greater clarity. From mid-March to the end of April rhododendron forests, especially those of the Poon Hill Danda near Ghorepani, and around Tadapani, provide a spectacular riot of colour. By April the high passes should be snow-free. Springtime is the prime season for bird-watchers. In May the monsoon build-up has begun, which makes the heat in the foothills unpleasant for trekking. However, conditions can be very pleasant at higher elevations.

Summer (monsoon): June–September

The monsoon usually breaks here during the first few days of June and lasts

Prayer wheels in Kagbeni (The Annapurna Circuit, Muktinath to Tukuche – Kagbeni option)

until mid-September. Heat and humidity can be oppressive in the low hills, while torrential rain and leech-infested forests repel all but the most determined of trekkers. Landslides are common, yet wild flowers are at their best and there's a dramatic quality to the scenery as swirling clouds suddenly part to reveal snow-dashed mountains. In the foothills north-west of Pokhara, Lumle receives around 5000mm (200 inches) of rain a year, but since these mountains create a rain-shadow, the northern side of the Himalayan Divide receives very little precipitation – Lo Manthang in Upper Mustang having less than 100mm (4 inches).

Autumn (post-monsoon): October–November

Understandably the most popular season for trekking in Nepal, by October the monsoon rains have fully laundered the atmosphere, visibility is crystal clear and the weather settled. In the foothills daytime temperatures are still warm, but above 3000m (10,000ft) frosts can be expected at night. Higher than this, snow can fall at any time, and those who set out on the Annapurna Circuit or intend to visit the Sanctuary should be adequately equipped with warm clothing and good-quality sleeping bags. It may be an obvious point to make, but there's a marked difference between one's tolerance of cold when moving and when resting.

Winter: December–February

From December to February days and nights turn very cold in the mountains, snowfall can be expected above 2000m (6500ft) and an attempt to cross the Thorong La can be fraught with danger (mainly from cold and a build-up of snow), while the route through the valley of the Modi Khola to the Annapurna Sanctuary must be treated with caution because of the possibility of avalanche – this danger is especially serious in late winter and early spring. Not all lodges remain open throughout the winter.

PRE-DEPARTURE PREPARATIONS

The traveller's ambition often exceeds his powers of endurance.

(Karl Baedeker)

It is an interesting observation that the highest mountains in the world attract to their valleys numerous trekkers who have never previously undertaken a multi-day walk – indeed, not even a centre-based walking holiday. That so many survive the experience to return for more says as much for the care and attention devoted to them by their trek organisers and crew as for the spell cast by the Himalaya.

Trekking demands mental preparation as much as physical fitness. Embarking upon a journey that will take two or three weeks to complete is a very different proposition to that of a fortnight's holiday based in one centre – no matter how challenging the walks. With a holiday base you can choose whether or when to go walking, but as a member of an organised group on a multi-day trek you will have a schedule to maintain and be expected to walk day after

31

Annapurna III, viewed from a chorten-topped spur high above Manang (The Annapurna Circuit)

day, rain or shine, whether you feel up to it or not. Trail weariness is no let-out. Of course, the independent tea-house trekker has greater flexibility, but there are few opportunities to 'escape' should you lose heart half-way through your chosen route. So get yourself both mentally and physically fit before boarding the plane to Kathmandu.

Consider the following scenario: of waking one morning weary from past excesses and feeling queasy from a stomach upset. Consider a cold wind and falling rain (or snow) and a trek leader cajoling you to start walking. You have about eight hours of uphill trail ahead of you before the next camp – and there's no alternative but to pull on boots and waterproofs and start walking.

High on the Annapurna Circuit there may well be extended periods of intense cold to put up with, days without being able to have a decent wash, or

several nights in a row when you've not been able to enjoy restful sleep. Maybe the diet is not to your liking or, if you're new to camping, you've discovered you don't like sleeping in a tent (it happens). On a tea-house trek you could be dismayed by the standard of hygiene or accommodation provided. There will certainly be times of confusion, times when your Western sensibilities are appalled by the different values accepted by those whose country you are wandering through. Successful trekking demands an ability to adapt to a whole range of ever-changing circumstances, to put Western values on hold and to be prepared to accept that there could be much to learn from Nepali hill culture. Learning to respect an unfamiliar culture is in itself sometimes a shock to the system.

But if you're convinced that wandering through the most dramatic scenery on earth, mingling daily with people of an entirely foreign culture, and a sense of achievement gained at the end of the trek offer sufficient rewards for the odd day of misery – then trekking is for you. If you have any doubts, forget it. Five or six days into a long walk is not the time to decide that trekking is not your cup of tea. The financial outlay required to undertake a trek in Nepal should be sufficient spur to ensure that you enjoy every moment of your time there. Don't waste it on doubts or inadequate preparation.

There's only one real way to get physically fit for trekking in the Himalaya, and that is by walking up and down hills. Jogging will help to build stamina and endurance, swimming and cycling are also of great benefit, but uphill walking with a rucksack is the best possible preparation. If hills are in short supply near your home, just walk as often as you can wherever convenient. Once you arrive in the Annapurna foothills and the trail winds away before you, you'll be glad you put in some effort at home.

Having decided to go trekking in the Annapurna Himal, put most of your well-developed Western values behind you, open your eyes and your mind to all that Nepal has to offer, and set forth with a determination to see and to understand. As has been pointed out by a number of experienced trekkers in the past, few will be content with just one Himalayan journey. The trek of a lifetime is likely to be just the first of many.

The farther one travels, the less one knows.

(Chinese saying)

Information under this heading is particularly liable to change, especially those details on air travel, as airlines come and go (no pun intended), schedules change, and routes are introduced and cancelled a year or two later. Please read this as a rough guide only and check the current situation with a variety of travel agents and airlines, getting as many quotes as possible before making a firm booking. If you plan to book a group trek with a tour operator, seek their advice first.

By Air

Several international airlines currently operate services from the UK to Tribhuvan International Airport in Kathmandu. These include Aeroflot, Biman Bangladesh, Gulf Air, Jet Airways, Pakistan International (PIA), and Qatar Air.

Flights via Biman involve a change at Dhaka; Gulf Air via either Bahrain or Abu Dhabi; Jet Airways via Delhi; PIA by way of Karachi, and Qatar via Doha.

Other flights can be arranged that require connections via India, but be warned that the bureaucracy involved in organising transit at Delhi Airport can be somewhat tedious.

Travellers coming from Tibet can get a direct flight from Lhasa to Kathmandu.

Flights out of Kathmandu are nearly always completely booked during the main trekking seasons. It is essential to reconfirm homeward flights at least 72 hours before departure time. Failure to do so may lead to your name being deleted from the passenger list. Before going on trek make a point of visiting the airline office in Kathmandu to reconfirm – it might be too late when you get back. And while you're reconfirming your flight, check the amount of departure tax you'll need to pay at the airport, and keep this sum to one side before spending the last of your rupees.

By Other Means

If you're heading to Nepal from India you will find that a combination of rail and road travel will take about three days for the journey from Delhi to Kathmandu by way of Agra, Varanasi, Patna and the border crossing at Birganj, near Raxaul. The most convenient road crossing for a direct journey to Pokhara is the border at Sunauli, near Bhairawa. Buses link Bhairawa with Pokhara via Mugling in something like nine hours. Coming from Darjeeling it is possible to take an Indian train (or bus) direct to Siliguri, and taxi from there to the border post at Kakar Bhitta, which has buses to Kathmandu or Biratnagar in eastern Nepal. Buses and RNAC planes ply the route from Biratnagar to Kathmandu.

Entering by road from Tibet is by way of Kodari, but this crossing is often closed by landslide during the monsoon.

All vehicles entering Nepal must have an international *carnet de passage*.

Travel within Nepal

Domestic **flights** are operated by the government-owned RNAC and numerous independent airlines. All flights by foreign nationals must be paid for in US dollars. Of particular interest to trekkers in the Annapurna region are the regular scheduled services from Kathmandu to Pokhara. Other flight opportunities in the region covered by this guide centre on the STOL (Short Take-Off and Landing) airstrips at Jomosom in the Kali Gandaki and Humde (Manang) in the Marsyangdi. But like all remote STOL flights, delays must be expected since weather conditions need to be settled; too many clouds in Nepal conceal mountains.

Buses daily ply the 200km (125 miles) of road between Kathmandu and Pokhara in anything from six hours upwards – depending on the number of breakdowns. Public buses used by locals offer cheap 'entertaining' travel, but these can be desperately uncomfortable and will leave you in need of a good rest before beginning your trek. Tourist buses allow more leg-room, are less crowded and are as a consequence more comfortable than local buses. There are daily services to Dumre and Pokhara, most having a pick-up point by the Standard Chartered Bank on Kantipath, a 10 minute walk from Thamel. Tourist buses are a little more expensive than public buses, but the difference will be worth paying. For trekkers setting out to tackle the Annapurna Circuit, there's a direct public bus service from Kathmandu to Besisahar which takes about six hours or

Machhapuchhare, from Pokhara

so. Public buses for Pokhara and Besisahar start their journeys from the 'new' bus park at Gongabu on the Ring Road. Reservations should be made the day before you intend to travel. There are many booking agents in Thamel.

Public buses stop at several tea-houses along the road for refreshment, at various police check-posts and, usually, at Mugling for lunch. Tourist buses often patronise more upmarket restaurants; Greenline Tours, for example, choose the Riverside Springs Resort at Kurintar, which is preferable to Mugling's basic transport cafés. Wherever you stop, make sure you eat as soon as possible and don't wander far from your vehicle, as the driver is likely to set off without much formality once he is ready. This is not the time to become separated from your baggage.

In Kathmandu **taxis** are both abundant and inexpensive, and although drivers are supposed to use a meter, they rarely do. Before taking a ride, agree a price – inevitably this will involve haggling. If you cannot face a bus ride to the start of your trek, it's usually possible to find a taxi driver willing to take you there – for a price – but you'll probably need to arrange it a day in advance, and you should insist on seeing the vehicle before making a firm commitment. At the end of your trek you will almost certainly need to ride back to Pokhara, with a choice between a local bus and a taxi. Where several taxis are waiting at a roadhead, there's usually a 'pecking order' that demands you hire the vehicle at the front of the queue – even if there's a more comfortable taxi further down the line.

PERMITS AND VISAS

*Never expect any encouragement from
the government of your country.*

(Lord Curzon)

All foreign passport holders except
Indian nationals need a tourist visa to
enter the country. Single-entry, 60-day
visas are available on arrival at
Tribhuvan International Airport in
Kathmandu or at the border. You will
need one passport-sized photograph,
and the current fee payable is US$30.
This must be paid in dollar bills.

Visas can also be obtained from
Nepalese embassies abroad (see
Appendix C for addresses). Applications
should be made direct to the Nepalese
Embassy or Consulate in your home
country. This is a straightforward process that involves minimal form filling,
the provision of two passport photographs and the payment of the appropriate fee. Postal applications should be
made at least one month before departure. The visa is valid for a period of
three months after the date of issue and
has a duration of 60 days.

In addition to a visa you will need
an Annapurna Conservation Area entry
permit, which is obtained from the
ACAP office situated below the 'Fire &
Ice' restaurant in the Sanchayakosh
building on the edge of Thamel in
Kathmandu, or at the ACAP counter
opposite the Standard Chartered Bank
on Lakeside in Pokhara. The current fee
for this entry permit is Rps2000, which
helps finance the various projects insti-
gated by ACAP. You will need to provide

one passport-sized photograph, and
after completing an application form
the permit is issued straightaway. The
offices are open daily, except Saturdays
and public holidays, from 9am to 5pm
(February to mid-November), and 9am
to 4pm (mid-November to the end of
January).

Note: If you arrive at an ACAP
checkpost without a permit you will be
charged *double* the standard fee – currently a rip-off Rps4000.

PRE-TREK HEALTH MATTERS

*Expect not to find things as at home, for
you have left home to find things
different.*

(The trekker's commandment)

First-time visitors to the Himalaya often
become obsessed with concerns about
their health. In fact there are times when
the trails of Nepal could be termed
hypochondriacs' highways.

Of course it is important to look
after your health on trek, but don't let
these concerns become obsessive. Prior
to leaving home have those preventa-
tive innoculations deemed necessary by
the health authorities, take a first aid kit
with you, adopt a sensible attitude
towards food and hygiene on trek –
then chance to luck. Trekking should be
seen as a healthy pursuit; things will not
be as they are at home, but if you
expect there to be no risk at all when
travelling in a developing country, book
a holiday elsewhere.

Pre-Trek Health

The following information has been gleaned from a number of different sources. For a start you can gain up-to-date health advice in the UK by calling the Department of Health Helpline (0800 555777). Alternatively telephone MASTA (Medical Advisory Service for Travellers Abroad) on 01276 685 040, or visit their website at www.masta.org. Another good source of information worth checking in advance of a trip to Nepal is the Nomad Travellers Store & Medical Centre, STA Travel, 40 Bernard Street, London WC1N 1LJ. See also the World Health Organisation (WHO) website: www.who.ch.

It is important to start planning your immunisation programme at least three months before the date of travel to ensure any 'new' vaccination required is in date and effective before you go.

At the time of writing Nepal makes no requirement for visitors to show proof of immunisation except for travellers coming by way of Africa or South America, when a certificate of vaccination against yellow fever will be needed. It would be sensible, however, to be 'in date' with the following:

- **BCG (tuberculosis)** – most adults will have been immunised already, but a skin test is available should you have any doubt about your immune status

- **Diptheria** – there is a moderate risk, but consequences could be serious

if precautions are not taken; immunisation is good for ten years

- **Polio** – immunisation covers a 10-year period

- **Tetanus** – make sure you're in date with immunisation, which covers a 10-year period

- **Typhoid Fever** – injectable and oral vaccines are available

- **Hepatitis A** – this is endemic across Asia, and is caused by poor sanitation and lack of hygiene. One shot of Havrix Hep A two to four weeks before travelling should protect. As for **Hepatitis B**, this is potentially much more serious than 'A' and is transmitted through unprotected sex and blood transfusions (via contaminated blood), or by means of contaminated needles and syringes. It may be possible to have a combined vaccination against both Hepatitis A and B

- **Japanese Encephalitis** – this viral infection can be contracted when passing through rice paddies where mosquito vector breeds. There is a significant risk between August and November, but immunisation is for a three-year period

- **Meningococcal Meningitis** – seasonal outbreaks occur; if travelling between November and May consider immunisation.

You might also consider the possibility of protection against **rabies**. Local information reports that 1 in every 6000 visitors to Nepal receives a potentially rabies-infected bite. Rabies immunoglobulin is not always available in Kathmandu, so you must decide in advance whether to have pre-exposure immunisation (a multi-jab course at set intervals) or take the risk. In any case avoid close contact with all animals wherever possible – even the cute and cuddly variety. Just in case.

Current advice suggests there is no risk of **malaria** in Kathmandu, Pokhara or the main trekking areas, and the risk in the Terai is low except in the east and close to the Indian border. However, precautions should be taken to avoid being bitten by mosquitoes: cover exposed skin at dusk and use repellent spray.

Anyone suffering from **lung or heart disease** should avoid treks that go to high altitudes, and is advised to consult their doctor before committing themselves to a trip to Nepal. It is in any case sensible to have a medical check before setting off on a lengthy Himalayan trek.

Since prospects of **dental care** are virtually non-existent once you begin your trek, it would be wise to ensure you have no loose fillings or even the first sign of tooth decay before leaving home. Have a dental check-up in advance of your trip, as there's nothing quite like high altitude, low temperatures and the knowledge that the nearest dentist is many day's journey away to set your teeth aching!

ON-TREK HEALTHCARE

Finding a doctor on trek can be hard; you may have to play at doctor for yourself.

(Thomas R. Gilchrist)

Although trekking should be beneficial to health by increasing vitality and providing a sense of well-being, the art of maintaining good health in a comparatively remote area is sometimes considered a bit of a challenge. It needn't be, for with a little care and forethought you should have no undue problems. Avoid complacency, and use common sense with regard to personal hygiene. Staying healthy while on trek is all about minimising risk. Carry a copy of a little book entitled *First Aid & Survival in Mountain & Remote Areas* by Dr Jim Duff and Dr Peter Gormly (TREKSAFE 2001), which is available from the KEEP office and several bookshops in Kathmandu. Full of useful information and sound advice, this 'portable doctor' should be part of your first aid kit (see 'The First Aid Kit', below, for a list of essential supplies).

Water

Trekking is thirsty work. So is living at altitude, where it's essential to consume large amounts of liquid to combat the effects of AMS (Advanced Mountain Sickness) – of which more later. But as Nepal has poor sanitation, all water must be considered suspect for drinking unless it has been boiled, comes in a bottle with an unbroken seal or has been treated with iodine (you can neutralise the taste with vitamin C tablets or powdered fruit drink). The same precautions are necessary for water supplied in hotels in Kathmandu and Pokhara, for a host of organisms active in the streams and rivers of Nepal can lay an unsuspecting traveller low with a variety of ailments – in town as surely as in the hills. Certain advanced water-filtration systems, such as the portable Katodyn filter, claim to be effective in eliminating even microscopic *giardia* cysts, so the independent trekker may want to consider carrying one of these. However, the many safe drinking-water stations located around the Annapurna region are reliable sources (see 'Minimum Impact Trekking', below) and well worth using. Tea, coffee, hot chocolate and lemon drinks bought at tea-houses and lodges should be perfectly safe, since boiling water is used.

Don't forget that the same caution in regard to purifying water for drinking should be applied to water used for teeth cleaning. On my first trek around Annapurna I listened to a monologue given by a fellow trekker on the dangers of drinking untreated water, only to see him a couple of hours later rinsing his teeth under a standpipe! I wonder how long it took for him to be suffering diarrhoea and blaming it on something he'd eaten!

Personal Hygiene

Maintaining a high standard of personal hygiene on trek should be second nature, if only to avoid gastro-intestinal problems. So whether you are using lodges or camping, try to be scrupulous in keeping hands and fingers clean, not only before you eat, but throughout the day. A pack

A mule train heads through the valley near Khobang
(The Pilgrim's Trail, Tatopani to Tukuche)

of baby wipes can be useful for this along the trail.

Kathmandu Quickstep or Trekker's Trot

Most travellers suffer a mild bout of diarrhoea at some time during their stay in Nepal. This is usually a short-lived reaction to a change of diet or an after-effect of a long-haul flight. But to be afflicted whilst on trek can be debilitating.

As suggested in the preceding section, gastro-intestinal problems can be largely avoided by close attention to personal hygiene and by not drinking untreated water. You should also be a little circumspect when choosing meals. Steer clear of salads, raw vegetables, unpeeled fruit and ice cream. Eat only food you can be sure has just been cooked and is still hot.

But should you be unfortunate and the Kathmandu Quickstep becomes the dance of the day, take plenty of liquids to remain hydrated, reduce solid food intake and avoid dairy products and alcohol. A rehydration solution, such as Dioralyte or Jeevan Jal (a Nepalese brand available in Kathmandu), is rapidly absorbed into the system and will help speed recovery. If the bug that caused the diarrhoea is not flushed out of your body and the problem persists after three or four days, break open the first aid and take Immodium.

Chest Problems

Coughs, colds and chest infections are exacerbated by smokey lodges, trail dust and the dry cold air of high altitude. The sound of locals emptying their lungs is a form of Himalayan dawn chorus, to which trekkers occasionally add an encore. Soluble lozenges will soothe inflamed throats, and catarrh pastilles are worth taking. For sore, inflamed throats, try gargling soluble aspirin dissolved in warm water – repeat at six-hour intervals.

Chest infections are usually marked by uncontrollable bouts of coughing and the release of a lot of green-yellow sputum – the latter especially first thing in the morning. Consult a qualified medical practitioner who will probably treat with a course of antibiotics.

Mountain Sickness (AMS)

Perhaps the major concern of first-time trekkers in Nepal is the fear of altitude (or mountain) sickness. Acute Mountain Sickness (AMS) is a very serious condition that can affect anyone, but being aware of the symptoms, and abiding by the rules of acclimatisation, can reduce the chances of affliction. **AMS need not affect you.** Most of us are able to adjust to living at higher altitudes, given sufficient time (acclimatisation is the process of adaptation), but individuals acclimatise at different rates. Some suffer headaches at 2500m (8200ft), while others can happily climb to twice that altitude without any discomfort other than shortness of breath. It is not possible to predict in advance who among first-time trekkers will suffer from it, or when. Physical fitness is of no apparent benefit, neither is youthfulness. In fact it would appear that young people may be more susceptible to AMS than older trekkers.

A failure to allow sufficient time for acclimatisation is almost guaranteed to bring on AMS. The best way to avoid it is to make a steady ascent to about 3000m (10,000ft), then ascend no more than about 400m (1300ft) per day after that. On the Annapurna Circuit it is not easy to follow the golden rule of 'climb high, sleep low' so it is important to make a gradual ascent, with planned rest days, in order to allow the body to adapt to reduced oxygen levels.

Another important consideration is liquid intake. At altitude it is necessary to drink at least four litres (7 pints) a day in order to avoid dehydration, and to urinate a minimum of half a litre per day – a great deal of fluid is lost at altitude through breathing. Yellow-coloured urine is a sign that liquid intake needs to be increased.

Mountain sickness can be detected in several ways. Signs to look out for are: extreme fatigue, headache and loss of appetite. Some trekkers also find that they become breathless with only minimal exercise and suffer disturbed sleep. When these symptoms develop do not go any higher until they've gone away. If they show no sign of leaving after a day or two, but instead become worse, it is important to descend to lower levels. Do not take strong pain killers or sleeping tablets, as these can mask the symptoms.

A worsening condition is indicated by vomiting, severe headache, lack of co-ordination, wet, bubbly breathing, increased tiredness and breathlessness, even at rest. Such symptoms warn of the

The Chulu peaks are briefly glimpsed from the trail to Yak Kharka
(The Annapurna Circuit, Manang to Yak Kharka)

onset of a very serious condition (fluid on the lungs or brain – pulmonary or cerebral oedema) which, if ignored, can lead to lack of consciousness and death within 12 hours. The only cure, if acted upon in time, is to descend at once (in the middle of the night if necessary) until symptoms decrease and finally disappear completely. An improvement is often experienced after just 300m (1000ft) or so of descent. But it is imperative that the patient should not be left to descend alone.

As with all health concerns, it is important to be aware of potential dangers, keep them in perspective and not to allow your worries to devalue the pleasures of the trek. Keep alert to symptoms, act upon them if they occur and, time and energy willing, continue with your trek when signs of improvement indicate that it's safe to do so.

Remember: do not go too high too fast, and descend promptly if ill.

If you've been to altitude before and did not acclimatise well, speak to your doctor before going on trek, and he may prescribe half a tablet (125mg) of Diamox (*acetazolamide*) to be taken every 12 hours on the way to altitude to combat mild AMS. Diamox does not mask the symptoms of AMS, so if you still get them, it's essential to act accordingly. Many people taking the drug experience mild tingling in hands and feet – these are not signs of developing AMS. You should notice increased urine output, though, as Diamox is a diuretic and is used to reduce fluid retention.

Medical Care and Evacuation

A **medical aid post** run by volunteers from the Himalayan Rescue Association (HRA) is situated in Manang. Two doctors are in attendance during the main trekking seasons, and each afternoon they give a lecture on AMS with lots of useful advice. This is well worth attending. The doctors are also available for medical consultations. A fee is charged for consultations, but not for attendance at the lectures, although a donation will be most welcome.

There are **hospitals** at Besisahar, Jomosom, Baglung and Pokhara, and **medical posts** at Ghandruk and Tatopani in addition to the one mentioned above in Manang. For emergency evacuation there are STOL airstrips at Humde, below Manang, and at Jomosom in the Kali Gandaki, but flights are dependent upon good weather conditions and should not be relied upon. Evacuation from more remote areas of the Annapurna region is difficult to organise and extremely expensive to carry through. Rescue takes time, there is a scarcity of radio communication and a shortage of helicopters available. Rescues will only be attempted when a guarantee of sufficient payment has been made. Independent trekkers stand little or no chance of having a positive response to a call for airlift evacuation from any remote region unless they've registered in advance with their embassy in Kathmandu and can show proof of rescue insurance.

THE FIRST AID KIT

*You should be able to repair yourself in the event of an
injury or accident, at least enough to survive until help arrives
or you stagger to the nearest road or habitation.*

(Chris Townsend)

All trekkers, whether travelling independently or with an organised group, should
carry a personal first aid kit, the very minimum contents of which should be:

- Elastoplast or similar dressing strips
- Blister prevention and treatment
- Bandages (cotton gauze and elastic)
- Aspirin and/or Paracetamol
- Throat lozenges and cough pastilles
- Thermometer
- Iodine tablets (for water purification)
- Sun cream
- Imodium (Loperamide) or similar for diarrhoea relief
- Lip salve

- Rehydration solution (Dioralyte or Jeevan Jal)
- Antiseptic cream
- Antibiotic (Ciproxin or as prescribed)
- Tiniba (to combat *giardia*)
- Emergency dental kit
- Safety pins
- Knee supports
- Scissors
- Sterile gloves
- *First Aid & Survival in Mountain & Remote Areas* (see 'On-Trek Healthcare')

Also recommended is a pack of sterile needles for use in emergencies where
injections are necessary, in order to reduce the risk of accidental transmission of
HIV (AIDS) and Hepatitis B viruses through contaminated equipment. MASTA
(see Pre-Trek Health Matters section) produces a sterile medical equipment pack
that contains syringes, sutures and dressings as well as needles.

Most medicines are readily available without prescription in Kathmandu. But
you should not rely on the diagnostic advice of pharmacists; where doubts occur,
seek medical assistance. Make sure you have all you might be expected to
require in the way of medical aid before setting out on trek.

EQUIPMENT CHECK-LIST

A superabundance of luggage infallibly increases the delays, annoyances, and expenses of travel. To be provided with enough and no more, may be considered the second golden rule of the traveller.

(Karl Baedeker)

It is perhaps as well that many airlines have a free baggage allowance of only 20kg (44lb), since there is a tendency by some group trekkers to take far too much clothing and equipment with them, knowing that by having porters they'll not have to carry it all themselves whilst on trek. Independent trekkers, on the other hand, will recognise the need to keep the size and weight of their rucksacks to a manageable limit. The following check-list covers the requirements of

Clothing
- boots and spare laces
- light shoes/trainers
- down jacket
- fleece or sweater
- shirts x 3
- socks x 3
- trekking trousers (or long skirt for women)
- waterproof jacket/poncho/umbrella
- overtrousers
- underwear (including thermals)
- gloves
- woollen hat/balaclava
- sunhat

Optional
- camera and plenty of film
- insulation mat (Karrimat or similar)
- plastic bags*
- binoculars*
- notebook and pens
- altimeter*
- gaiters

Other essential items
- rucksack (day-sack only for members of an organised group trek)
- kitbag (group trekkers only)
- trekking poles
- sleeping bag (4 seasons +)
- sleeping-bag liner
- water bottle (min. 1 litre capacity)
- headtorch, batteries and bulbs
- mending kit*
- first aid kit
- penknife*
- sunglasses
- suncream (factor 15+) and lip salve
- towel and washing kit
- money belt
- map*
- whistle
- toilet paper and lighter
- passport and ACAP permit
- small padlock (to secure kitbag for group trekkers, or lodge bedroom)
- guidebook*

most trekkers following routes described in this book. Starred items (*) can be shared between members of a group.

Note that a kitbag (holdall) and not a rucksack is used on group treks where porters carry the loads. Porters usually carry more than one trekker's gear, bound together with string or rope and held with a *namlo* or tumpline round the forehead. Several trekking companies supply kitbags for their clients, but they can also be bought from outdoor retailers. Make sure you buy one made of tough material and with a robust zip. The small rucksack included in the list is for group trekkers in which to carry their daily essentials.

It's useful to have a complete change of clothes waiting for your return from trek, and most Kathmandu hotels have a storage facility for this. Make sure your left luggage (in a small holdall) is secure and clearly marked with your name and expected date of return.

MAPS

The World is a country which nobody ever yet knew by description; one must travel through it one's self to be acquainted with it.

(Lord Chesterfield)

All maps stir dreams in the mountain addict. So it is when faced with the prospect of trekking in the Annapurna Himal, but as the above quote suggests, most of the available maps,

Dawn light brightens the Annapurnas on the climb to the Thorong La (The Annapurna Circuit, Thorong Phedi to Muktinath)

45

Twenty minutes below Muktinath, Jharkot stands on a spur of land overlooking the Jhong Khola *(The Annapurna Circuit, Muktinath to Tukuche)*

though perfectly adequate for day-to-day travel on the clear, well-trodden trails, do not properly suggest the wonders of these mountains. But stir dreams they most certainly do, and it's good to have a reasonable map with you if only to name the walling mountains and to check on your progress along the way. However, not all maps agree on the spelling of village names, and altitudes quoted vary from sheet to sheet; on some sheets certain villages are marked on the wrong side of a river and some are not shown at all, while a single tea-house may be depicted in letters as large as those reserved for a major settlement.

But none of this really matters. The important thing to remember when orienting yourself in Nepal is the name of the next village along your trail. Simply

ask directions from the first person you meet, and off you go. If the maps do not match the standard of those you're used to at home, see that as an advantage; confusion only adds to the adventure.

In recent years there's been a marked improvement in the quality of mapping in all the major trekking districts, and several reasonable sheets are now available for the Annapurna region.

Annapurna (at a scale of 1:100,000) is an excellent topographic map published by Nelles Verlag of Munich. Probably the most accurate available at present, this was produced in 1993 and may be ordered from Stanfords in London. It is sometimes on sale in Kathmandu bookshops.

Annapurna Trek is the title of a series of seven topographical maps produced at 1:50,000 by the Survey

Department of HM government of Nepal with aid from the Finnish government. Published in 2001, and with contours at 40m intervals, these maps are the most up-to-date at present, but they're not always easy to read and may be considered too detailed for day-to-day trekking. If ordering from Stanfords in London, the appropriate sheets are headed Nepal Topographical Maps and numbered: 44, 45, 49, 53, 54, 57 and 58.

Around Annapurna (1:200,000 scale), published in Nepal by Nepa Maps as an imprint of Himalayan MapHouse Pvt Ltd (e-mail: maphouse@wlink.com.np), is a double-sided laminated sheet – *Pokhara Valley* at 1:40,000 on the reverse – that is more than adequate for most trekking purposes. Contours are shown at 100m intervals, and altitudes are fairly accurate. A profile of the Circuit is given. Each of the main routes described in this guide is marked, and being waterproof the map should end the trek without too much deterioration.

Around Annapurna (1:125,000) is another useful sheet published by Nepa Maps at a larger scale than the above and covering the same area.

Annapurna Trekking (1:135,000) has been produced in the USA by National Geographic Maps/Trails Illustrated (www.trailsillustrated.com, www.nationalgeographic.com) as one in a series of Adventure Maps for Nepal. Contour intervals are at 100m, trekking routes are outlined with a black dotted line, and though quite thin the sheet is supposedly waterproof

and tear-proof. Less accurate than the Nepa map mentioned above, it is nevertheless useful to carry on trek.

Annapurna Conservation Area (1:125,000) published by ACAP. A contour map with major trekking routes marked; informative text is printed on the reverse.

Nepa Maps publish several sheets in a series concentrating on individual treks. Those relevant to the area covered by this guide (and available from the Himalayan MapHouse shop in Thamel, Kathmandu) are:

- *Ghorepani Ghandruk* (1:50,000)
- *Pokhara to Khudi* (1:50,000)
- *Annapurna Base Camp* (1:50,000)
- *Tilicho the Hidden Lake* (1:125,000)
- *Tatopani* (1:50,000)
- *Royal Trek* (1:25,000)
- *The Siklis Trek* (1:50,000)
- *Panchase Trek* (1:125,000)
- *Muktinath Jomosom* (1:75,000)
- *Upper Mustang* (1:80,000)
- *Mustang the Forbidden Kingdom* (1:125,000)
- *Pokhara City Map* (1:15,000).

Also published by Nepa Maps is an astrological sheet titled *Deep Sky of Nepal* which you may wish to have with you on trek, since a Himalayan night sky is about as magical as you're ever likely to see outside of the desert regions, and it's a useful aid to identifying many of the stars on show.

MINIMUM IMPACT TREKKING

Take nothing but photos, leave nothing but footprints, kill nothing but time.

(much-quoted slogan that has become the wilderness mantra)

Each trekker has an impact on the country through which he travels. On its own that impact may be minimal, but since the Annapurna region attracts upwards of 50,000 visitors a year, the effect on both the environment and the lives of those who live there is greatly increased. Whether that effect is positive or negative lies in the hands of each of us. Awareness and responsibility by all visitors are essential to the future success of trekking in Nepal.

Litter: The most obvious visible sign of negative impact, and perhaps the easiest to control, is litter. Happily the problem is less acute than it used to be, for huge improvements have been made in recent years thanks to media publicity, including the outdoor press, which has gone to the lengths of naming and shaming major culprits, and to the education of locals. Yet litter still remains an eyesore, and some of it is a potential health hazard and/or a danger to animals – both wild and domestic. It's incomprehensible why anyone drawn to the Himalaya by its promise of dramatic beauty would spoil those scenes by discarding litter. But it happens. Carry out what you carry in. As

THE ACAP SAFE DRINKING-WATER SCHEME

In face of a mounting litter problem caused by literally thousands of discarded plastic mineral water bottles, ACAP, with New Zealand development assistance, has installed a chain of safe drinking-water stations around the Annapurna Circuit. These not only discourage use of plastic bottles, but make safe drinking water available to local residents and trekkers alike.

Water is purified by a process of ozonation, an internationally recognised method that is highly effective against all water-borne pathogens, including *giardia*, bacteria and viruses. The small-scale ozonation units are made in the USA, installed with official New Zealand development assistance, operated by trained local Mothers' Groups, and maintained by technical staff at the beginning of each trekking season. The cost of filling your own water bottle from one of these safe drinking-water stations is cheaper than buying bottled water that has been portered in, and the profit remains within the ACAP area for community development and conservation projects.

Safe drinking-water stations are located in the following villages: Tal, Bagarchhap, Chame, Pisang, Humde, Manang, Letdar and Thorong Phedi on the Marsyangdi side of the Thorong La, and at Muktinath, Kagbeni, Jomosom, Marpha, Tukuche, Khobang, Lete and Ghasa in the Kali Gandaki valley.

for empty food packaging, tins and drinks cans discarded by some trekking groups and climbing expeditions on leaving a campsite, the old Boy Scout method of burn, bash and bury is effective if undertaken with care on a sparingly used site. Spent batteries are a different matter because they're toxic waste and need to be disposed of properly – take them back home with you to a suitable disposal facility. Toilet paper? Carry a lighter, and if you get caught out during the day, carefully burn the paper when used.

Don't pollute water sources: Use the toilets provided at lodges and tea-houses, but if defecation is unavoidable in the wild, stay at least 50m (160ft) away from water sources, and bury your faeces in a hole dug with a penknife or small trowel carried specifically for that purpose – failing that, cover with stones.

Don't use bottled water: Abandoned plastic mineral water bottles have been a major problem in the past. In the year 2000 it was estimated that tourists discarded more than 200,000 bottles in the Annapurna region alone, but with the introduction that same year by ACAP of a 'Safe Drinking-Water Scheme' with top-up stations in more than a dozen villages, the demand for bottled water and consequent potential littering has been greatly reduced. A list of these safe drinking-water stations is found in the box on page 48. But to satisfy the need for uncontaminated drinking water elsewhere, trekkers are urged to carry

iodine-based purifying tablets or a small bottle of tincture of iodine (see the section 'On-Trek Healthcare' above for further details). Note that ACAP has outlawed the sale of bottled mineral water between Chhomrong and the Annapurna Sanctuary.

Firewood: On group camping treks meals should be cooked on kerosene stoves rather than wood fires, and campfires banned in order to reduce the demand for timber that in the recent past has been responsible for destroying large areas of forest. Members of group treks could lobby their trek leaders and tour operators to provide kerosene cookers for their porters too. In the Modi Khola gorge and in the Annapurna Sanctuary there is a total ban on wood fires, but there's a kerosene depot in Chhomrong. When using lodges limit your demand for a hot shower to those establishments that use solar panels or back-boilers for water heating, and be considerate when ordering meals. If you place your order for an evening meal on arrival – and keep it simple – the lodge owner can prepare a number of dishes at the same time, thus minimising the amount of fuel used.

Stay on the trail: As a way of limiting erosion, avoid taking shortcuts, and when trekking through agricultural land be careful not to damage crops, irrigation ditches, terrace retaining walls or the low earth embankments built around rice fields to help retain water.

49

Sadhu, Durbar Square, Kathmandu

CULTURAL INTERACTION

This morning, despite the cold outside, two … middle-aged women … are wearing short shorts to maximise the amount of skin exposed to the tanning rays of the sun. It is not against the law, but it is culturally insensitive in Nepal to reveal female legs like this.

(Andrew Stevenson – Annapurna Circuit)

Many visitors discover to their surprise that interaction with local people becomes a highlight of their trekking experience in Nepal. Those that do so have usually managed to rise above the cultural divide and become sensitive to the ways of their hosts. Those ways, customs and beliefs may be very different to one's own, but they deserve to be honoured and respected. To do oth-

erwise will not only devalue your experience, but add to cultural erosion which, like erosion of the land, can have a serious negative impact on the local population.

Unfortunately few tour operators provide any guidance as to the mode of dress or behaviour their clients should adopt in order to avoid causing offence when travelling in Nepal. Revealing clothes and behavioural free-for-all may be acceptable in the 'enlightened' West, but are inappropriate in a country where Hindu customs and traditions are the rule or where Buddhist principles guide a way of life. Young Nepalis in particular are influenced by the behaviour of the apparently wealthy foreigners who trek through their villages, so it is important to ensure that that influence is not a negative one. As self-invited guests in their country, we have a duty to fit in with Nepal's cultural heritage, not dismiss it; to respect the beliefs of the local population (you don't have to share them) and not attempt to change them.

When it comes to cross-cultural interaction we are all, to some extent, innocents abroad, and in the most unsuspecting of ways are guilty at times of causing offence – although Nepalis are such generous hosts that they will rarely reveal their displeasure. The following guidelines are therefore offered as a form of cultural code which may help when preparing to visit the Annapurna region and act as a daily reminder along the trail. For an in-depth and highly readable background to the cultural interface of the country, read Stephen Bezruchka's *Trekking in Nepal*, in which he says: 'Nepal is not only a place on the map, but an experience, a way of life from which we all can learn.'

Affection: Avoid public displays of affection, for these cause embarrassment and are frowned upon.

Begging: Discourage children who beg for school pens, balloons, money or candy, for this only leads to a culture of dependency. On the other hand, giving donations to schools, health centres or other worthwhile community projects will help Nepalis help themselves.

Dress: Be modestly clad, for a state of undress is unacceptable in both sexes. Women should avoid wearing revealing blouses, and shorts are also taboo. Choose instead a long skirt or slacks. Men should always wear a shirt and preferably long trousers.

Food: Avoid touching food or utensils that Nepalis will use, and never give or take food with the left hand – this is considered unclean as it's used for washing after defecating. If cutlery is unavailable, only use the right hand to eat with.

Haggling: Whilst haggling is part of the trade culture of Kathmandu and Pokhara, do not haggle over prices in tea-houses or lodges on trek. Prices listed on menus have been set by the local lodge committee.

The hearth: If invited into a Nepalese house, remember that to many hillfolk the hearth is considered sacred. Neither discard rubbish into your host's fire, nor sit next to it unless specifically invited to do so as this is the place of honour.

Legs and feet: As feet are considered less clean than other parts of the body, the soles of your feet should not be pointed at a Nepali, nor should legs be outstretched so that they need to be stepped over by others.

Monasteries: When visiting monasteries (*gompas*) remove your shoes before entering and leave a donation before leaving. In respect of local culture and beliefs, please refrain from smoking or noisy behaviour in or near a sacred site.

Photography: Be discreet when taking photographs of local people. Try to imagine how you would react if a complete stranger pointed a camera lens directly at your grandmother's face. Take

MAKING CONTACT

Try to learn a few words of the local language (see Appendix E). The effort will be appreciated by villagers, porters and lodge owners – if only because of the few easy laughs you inspire. Keep a sense of humour and your sense of perspective, and be prepared to learn from your hosts. You won't regret it.

Meeting villagers on the trail can be a highlight of a trekker's day, but permission should always be sought before taking their photograph. These two women asked first! (Bhulbhule to Bahundanda)

Prayer walls: Always pass to the left of prayer walls (*mani* walls), *chortens* and other Buddhist symbols, and turn prayer wheels in a clockwise direction.

Smile: Retain your sense of humour, act with patience and friendliness towards others – and smile. The Nepalese smile a lot. That warmth should be reflected back.

Touching: Avoid touching Nepalis on the head.

Wealth: When handling money be discreet; do not tempt locals into envy by making an obvious display of the contents of your wallet. Keep a few small-denomination rupee notes handy for paying bills along the way. Don't leave valuable items unattended.

Finally, the word 'Namaste', given with hands pressed together, is the universal greeting of Nepal; it means 'I salute the God within you'. Use it with a smile – and mean it. From such simple beginnings may grow a flower of understanding.

time to build a relationship with your prospective subject, ask permission before taking their photograph – and respect their right to refuse.

NEPAL – FACTS AND FIGURES

There can be no other country so rich in mountains as Nepal.

(H.W. Tilman)

Rectangular in shape and measuring roughly 800km by 240 (500 miles x 150), Nepal is bordered in the north by Tibet (China) and elsewhere by India. Although it contains the world's largest collection of 8000m (26,000ft) peaks, mountains form only the northern part of this beautiful country. In the south lies the tropical belt of the Terai – an extension of the Gangetic plain, little more than 150m (500ft) above sea level – while the broad central region is one of fertile hills rising from 600 to 2000m (2000– 6500ft) in altitude. The subtropical Kathmandu valley is included in this central strip, as are neighbouring valley basins.

Nepal is the world's only Hindu monarchy. Officially some 89.5% of the growing population of about 24 million are said to be Hindu while just 5.3% practise Buddhism. Yet **Hindu** and **Buddhist** co-exist in remarkable harmony, and their faiths appear to merge compatibly in so many different ways that it is not always easy to separate them. When trekking in the higher valleys of the Annapurna region one sees more evidence of Buddhism than of any other faith, and since Buddhists are mostly patient, tolerant and understanding of outsiders, one has several opportunities to visit *gompas* (monasteries) and to photograph symbols of their faith along the way.

The official **language** of the country,

The trail to Tengi passes a new stupa, around which an old woman, bent like a fishhook, makes her slow kora (The Annapurna Circuit, Manang to Yak Kharka)

Nepali, is derived from Pahori, which comes from northern India and is spoken by some 58% of the population. But with about 60 ethnic groups within the country, and something like 50 'mother tongues' in use, you can see that there are almost as many languages in Nepal as there are races, and as many dialects as there are villages. To complicate matters further, in the Kathmandu valley the original language is Newari, which uses no less than three different alphabets. Fortunately for the Western trekker English is widely understood in Kathmandu, Pokhara and in most lodges along the popular trails, and most Sherpas and Tamangs, who generally make up the crew of organised treks, also speak a modicum of English – while the more educated among them often learn a smattering of other European languages too. But an attempt by trekkers to speak some Nepali will reap many benefits.

Although Nepal is counted among the world's **poorest nations** in terms of per capita income, the sense of hopeless poverty that is so prevalent in a number of other Eastern countries is not apparent here. Over 80% of the population depends for its livelihood on **agriculture**, much of which is subsistence farming among the intricate terraced fields of the Middle Hills. This subsistence farming, of course, falls outside the cash economy, so although statistics show an average annual income of around $210, and more than half the children of Nepal are thought to be undernourished, the reality is partly

masked as far as the hill country is concerned. Some 17% of land is under cultivation and about 30% covered by forest, but because of improved health care and a fast-growing population, Nepal's self-sufficiency in food production during the 1950s has deteriorated to a situation of grain deficiency and a serious reduction in forests. As a result Nepal faces dire economic and environmental problems which only considered development can arrest.

Foreign development aid projects continue to pour money into Nepal, although a number of these projects are of questionable value. In his book *Travels in Nepal* (1988), Charlie Pye-Smith provides an interesting commentary on the question of foreign aid in the late 1980s, and this is a theme taken up by other writers with a concern for the way some governments have influenced development along lines that are not entirely appropriate for either Nepal's geography or culture.

Tourism is a major source of income (only 5% of labour is employed in industry), and accounts for about 30% of Nepal's essential foreign exchange earnings, yet a large proportion of that income goes out of the country again to pay for foreign goods.

International telecommunications are good. Kathmandu and Pokhara have plenty of communication centres from which you can make a direct call to almost any country in the world. A few villages in the Annapurna region also boast telephone facilities, but these are not always working. Look for signs advertising ISD/SDD services. **Cyber cafés** can be found in the tourist areas of Kathmandu and Pokhara, where you can send and receive faxes and e-mails and also make international phone calls at a modest rate. Local calls can often be made free of charge from your hotel.

Nepalese currency is the Rupee (Rps) which is made up of 100 Paisa. Banknotes are printed in the following denominations: Rps1, 2, 5, 10, 20, 25, 50, 100, 500 and 1000. The Rupee is a 'soft' currency and has no value when taken out of the country. Travellers cheques and 'hard' currency can be exchanged at Tribhuvan Airport, Kathmandu, and at a number of banks which are open daily (except Saturday) from 10am until about 2pm. Always collect your exchange receipts, as you'll need these should you wish to change remaining Nepalese currency back to 'hard' currency at the end of your trip. Numerous hotels have money-changing facilities, and in tourist areas of both Kathmandu and Pokhara you'll find plenty of 'no-commission' money-changing kiosks.

ONLINE INFO

There's no shortage of information about Nepal available on the Internet, and the following sites may be worth consulting in advance of a trip:

- **www.nepalnews.net** for up-to-date news

- **www.nepalnow.com** another news site worth checking

- **www.info-nepal.com** not only gives information in regard to latest news and travel, but contains many other features including development issues, politics, culture, etc.

- **www.visitnepal.com** contains a number of features of interest to the first-time visitor.

- **www.south-asia.com/dotn/ index.html** is the website for the Nepalese government's tourism department – lots of good information about the country.

- **www.kmtnc.org.np** gives details about the King Mahendra Trust for Nature Conservation

- **www.bena.com/ciwec** for advice on altitude sickness and other medical problems associated with Nepal; this is the website of the CIWEC medical centre in Kathmandu.

- **www.fco.gov.uk/travel** is the official site of the UK Foreign and Commonwealth Office, with regularly updated information and advice for travellers.

- **www.mnteverest.net/trek.html** has an index of Nepalese trekking companies.

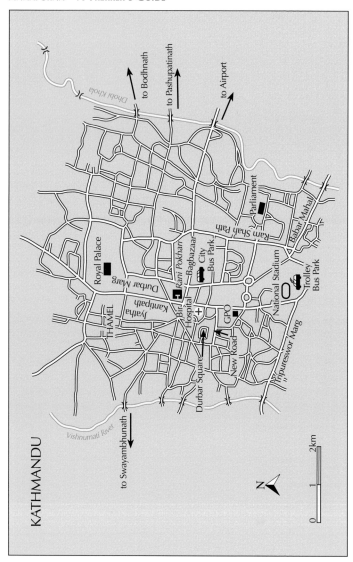

KATHMANDU

Nepalese **time** is GMT + 5¾ hours (15 minutes ahead of Indian Standard Time); 10¾ hours ahead of New York, 4¼ hours *behind* Sydney. Nepal has no daylight-saving.

Postal services are best dealt with in Kathmandu at the General Post Office located at the junction of Kantipath and Kicha-Pokhari Road. The office is open daily (except Saturdays and public holidays) from 10am to 4pm. Always ensure that stamps on postcards, letters or parcels are franked by the counter clerk at the time of posting. There is always a queue at the special counter in the post office reserved for this. Several villages on the trails around Annapurna have post offices of some description. Postcards and letters may be sent from these, but again make sure that stamps are franked at the time of posting – but don't be surprised if they never reach their destination. The same warning is valid in regard to handing postcards or letters to hotel staff to post on your behalf.

The **Poste Restante** service at the GPO in Kathmandu is reasonably efficient, but is largely a self-service affair, so it would be prudent not to have anything of obvious value sent there. Mail is usually kept for two months. Be prepared to show your passport before collecting mail.

TIME IN KATHMANDU

And the wildest dreams of Kew are the facts of Kathmandu.

(Rudyard Kipling)

The first-time visitor to the East may well experience culture shock on the drive from the airport to a hotel in the heart of

Local shop in a Kathmandu back street

Swayambhunath, the monkey temple of Kathmandu

Kathmandu. Yet once that shock subsides it is not difficult to see through the turmoil of its apparently insoluble problems to discover that this is one of the world's most magical capital cities. It's not only a springboard to Himalayan adventures, but a brimming complex of sites and cultures that would take a lifetime to unravel and several generations to understand.

After weeks spent among the mountains it's a great place in which to sample a change of menu, too, for there are dozens of restaurants to satisfy every appetite at a price easy to afford. There are hotels and guest houses of varying standards of comfort, and enough shops and street traders offering a thousand and one 'bargains' to consume the last of your money before heading for home. Hotels range from the classy and comparatively high-priced, such as those on Durbar Marg with 24-hour room service, satellite TV, sauna and swimming pool, to a host of unpretentious lodgings that would suit the budget-conscious backpacker, tucked away in Thamel back streets or on the former hippy hideout of Freak Street on the south side of Durbar Square. Low-priced accommodation can also be found away from the tourist traps in Patan, Bodhnath and Bhaktapur.

STREET-BOY SCAMS

Like most cities Kathmandu has its share of beggars, touts and rip-off merchants looking for new ways to part tourists from their cash. A novel scam tried by street children involves a bright-eyed child approaching a tourist with the opening line: 'What country you from?' Once contact has been made, he'll keep your interest with a string of questions or entertaining items of information before telling you he's not after your money. 'But my baby sister is hungry/dying/sick. If I could get some milk powder, my mother could feed her.' He'll lead you to a convenient shop in the neighbourhood where you buy him a tin of dried milk. He's full of gratitude and you part feeling good for having added to your karma. But as soon as your back is turned, the boy returns to the shop with the milk, where the owner pays him a percentage of its cost and the tin goes back on the shelf to await the next scam victim!

In truth, Kathmandu wears many different faces. It's an enigma, a kaleidoscope of colour, of smells, of noise. It's chaotic and apparently anarchic – yet somehow the city works, and a crazy kind of order prevails. There are people everywhere, of course, for like every capital city it evokes a corrupting promise of instant wealth for those brought up beyond its realities. Poverty cannot be ignored. Slums fester on the city's rim and on the banks of its rivers, while those who have made good build their houses among gardens of bougainvillea on the outskirts and surround them with high walls or fences. The cramped alleyways and broad modern streets throng with activity. Traffic streams in an endless honking procession through the daylight hours along the main highways. Bicycle rickshaws and taxis bounce and weave through the narrow lanes, somehow managing to avoid collision with the crowds of traders, the bustle of porters, tourists and beggars, and the occasional cow. The city *is* dirty – but it is improving. A dull cloud of pollution hangs over the valley, yet below it there's often unrestrained gaiety. Despite all its problems, Kathmandu is exciting, vibrant and lively, but in common with neighbouring Bhaktapur and Patan, a number of its most interesting and historic sites have a pay-as-you-enter policy.

Thamel, the ever-popular tourist district in the north-west of the city, is the quarter seen by most visitors – some to the exclusion of all else. But Thamel is not typical of Kathmandu, it's simply representative of itself. Here will be found a plentiful supply of budget accommodation, a selection of restaurants catering to all tastes, cafés and fast-food outlets, as well as bookshops, map-shops, specialist trekker's foodstores,

With good reason Swayambhunath is known as the monkey temple

suppliers of climbing and trekking equipment, and outfitters of every kind. Should you arrive in Kathmandu to discover that your airline has sent your baggage to Khartoum, do not despair, for in Thamel you can buy or hire every item of equipment you'll need on trek.

For much of its history Kathmandu profited by having control of the important trade route between India and Tibet, which enabled taxes from this trade to finance the Newari artisans in creating a unique architectural elegance, not only in the capital, but in neighbouring cities like Lalitpur (Patan) and Bhadgaon (Bhaktapur). It is this architectural elegance, and a wealth of religious and cultural sites, that makes Kathmandu so extraordinarily appealing today. 'There are nearly as many temples as houses, and as many idols as inhabitants', wrote W. Kirkpatrick in 1811, and while there are certainly

more houses and inhabitants in the 21st century than there were in the 19th, there's no shortage of places to visit, either in Kathmandu itself or in neighbouring Patan and Bhaktapur. The following suggestions merely scratch the surface, but for more detailed information, background history and as a pointer to the full glories of the valley itself, readers are directed to the *Insight Guide: Nepal* (APA Publications), which is highly recommended.

Kathmandu

Durbar Square is a must. Containing more than 50 important monuments, shrines and temples as well as the home of the Kumari (the living goddess) and a huge former royal palace, it offers a superb roofscape of exotic shapes. Intricate wooden carvings adorn every building, with erotic figures, faces, patterns and religious symbols etched by the

Cloth dyes, Pashupatinath

Durbar Square, Bhaktapur

metre on struts and beams and around doorways and windows. Early morning is the best time to visit, for this is when street vendors are setting out their wares, porters gather to await employment, the faithful scurry to various temples for their first devotions of the day, and the place comes alive with streams of light, colour and movement. By mid-morning the square is crowded with foreign visitors and touts, and on nearby Basantpur Square, between Kumari Chowk and Freak Street, rows of identical *kukuri* knives, carved Buddhas and bangles are laid out from one end to the other in the ultimate flea market.

Kumari Chowk is where the pre-pubescent living goddess spends most of her years of reign until menstruation casts her back to mortality. The building has an accessible inner courtyard bounded by exquisitely carved pillars,

doors and windows – but you need to duck your head when entering.

To the north of Durbar Square, midway between the square and Thamel, and secluded from the busy street of Shukrapath, stands the biggest *stupa* in central Kathmandu. **Kathesimbhu** is a colourful gathering place for Buddhist monks, tourists and the children of a neighbouring school, who use the surrounding space as a playground.

Just 2km from Thamel, on the western side of the Vishnumati river, the 2000-year-old *stupa* of **Swayambhunath** looks down on Kathmandu from its lofty hilltop perch. Around the base of the hill hundreds of prayer wheels are interspersed with small 'shrines', and colourful prayer flags add to the scene. The main entrances to the site on both east and west are guarded by large Buddhas. On the Vishnumati

61

side a long flight of 365 steps leads to the crowning *stupa* through trees where monkeys play, while from the top a fine view looks out over the valley. More prayer wheels encircle the *stupa*, and to one side there's the *gompa*, or monastery, of Shree Karma Raj Mahavihar which visitors are free to enter. Inside hundreds of butter lamps cast an orange light, while the sound of drums, gongs and trumpets accompanies each devotion. If you visit in the early morning to catch sunrise over the valley you'll experience a full *puja* centred on the open-faced building beside the *gompa*, as Newari musicians and chanting devotees begin their day with prayer and procession and the singing of religious songs. As well as the *gompa* and large *stupa*, the crowded summit of the hill has a gilt-roofed temple built in honour of the smallpox goddess, Harati, and numerous small shrines, statues and symbolic votive monuments.

North-east of Kathmandu city centre **Bodhnath**'s 40m high (130ft) dome makes it the largest Buddhist *stupa* in all Nepal. Seen from afar it marks the country's centre of Tibetan culture, and pilgrims are often found making a *kora* here – measuring their length upon the ground on a circuit of the stupa. *Gompas* and pilgrim rest-houses cluster around, and at the start of the Tibetan New Year *lamas* take part in colourful ceremonies. Masked dances are performed for the public in a nearby field, while other dances take place in a monastery courtyard. One of the best places from which to study the site

is the rooftop restaurant Stupa View – especially at dusk with the sound of monks chanting, when haunting music drifts from houses that ring the *stupa*, and butter lamps glow in the gathering darkness.

The Bagmati river twists round the eastern side of town below **Pashupatinath**, the country's largest Hindu shrine. Being a tributary of the Ganges, the Bagmati is considered sacred by devotees who gather each day for ritual bathing in the fetid water. Overlooking it all is a temple complex whose entrance is forbidden to non-Hindus, but on the east bank a series of terraces lined with identical *chaityas* (in appearance a little like small *stupas*) provides viewpoints from which to study not only the gilded temple opposite, but also riverside activities below. In the river women do their laundry, while Hindus fast approaching death are carried from nearby *dharmsalas* (rest-houses) and lain on stone slabs with their feet in the water until all life has drained from them. Nearby *ghats* are used for cremation, the ceremonies carried out in full public view.

Patan

South of Kathmandu, and divided from it only by the Bagmati river, the once independent kingdom of Patan (Lalitpur – the 'City of Beauty') is said to have been founded in the third century BC by the emperor Ashoka and his daughter Carumati. Primarily a Buddhist town it has around 150 former monasteries, but there are also many Hindu temples and shrines and scores of exotic secular buildings, so many in fact that it would take weeks of concentrated study to properly visit each one.

This 'town of a thousand golden roofs' has its own **Durbar Square** with the one-time royal palace facing a complex of Newari-crafted architectural splendours. The palace itself has three main courtyards open to the public, each one displaying the skills of generations of woodcarvers. Nearby the beautiful **Hiranyavarna Mahavihara** (Kwa Bahal, or 'Golden Temple'), which dates from the 12th century, is guarded by gleaming lions, the buildings embellished with silver doors, gilded copper roofs and bronze Buddhas.

On the south-western edge of Patan many Tibetan exiles have settled in the quarter known as **Jawalakhel** and established a thriving carpet factory there, visited by many tour groups.

Like Kathmandu, Patan is a bustling town with a vibrancy all its own. But it's much less frenetic than the capital, and a number of regulars to Nepal prefer to stay there rather than in Kathmandu itself. It's a town of artisans, with metalwork a speciality, and the narrow alleyways and side-streets ring to the sound of hammer or file on copper and tin. Once you've absorbed as much spiritual and architectural wonder as you can, it's worth strolling round the tiny workshops where craftsmen pick out ornamental filigree with hammer and punch, or spending an hour or two haggling for bargains with the street vendors in the bazaar.

Bhaktapur

Also known by its former name of Bhadgaon, this handsome town of about 50,000 inhabitants lies 16km (10 miles) to the east of Kathmandu. Described in 1928 by Percival Landon as 'willingly remote from her neighbours, and one of the most picturesque towns in the East', Bhaktapur is reached by frequent trolley-bus service from Kathmandu. A taxi ride is less 'ethnic' and more expensive, but is likely to be more comfortable and certainly a lot quicker than the trolley-bus journey. Although badly damaged in 1934 by the same earthquake that so devastated the capital, it nevertheless retains much of its medieval character and has some of the valley's finest buildings. Restoration work has been made possible largely through a German–Nepalese development project that has so far helped to preserve some 200 buildings without destroying their essential character.

Some of the best of Bhaktapur is seen in its **Durbar Square** which is entered through a gateway. At once you are faced with an open and uncluttered approach to an impressive collection of temples and monuments. At least two large temples were completely destroyed by the earthquake, but those that remain are set out with sufficient space to enable the visitor to study them from different angles without being confused among other crowding buildings. It is this sense of spaciousness that contrasts Bhaktapur's Durbar Square with those of Kathmandu and Patan, and once you manage to free yourself from the guides touting for business, it's worth studying its many facets at leisure. One of the most startling objects of attention is the brass-made **Golden Gate** through which access leads to the former royal palace, whose west wing now houses the National Art Gallery.

Whilst Durbar Square is the main focus of attention, a short 100m stroll down a narrow street leads to **Taumadhi Tole**, a smaller yet more lively square surrounded by fine old Newari houses and dominated by the pagoda-like **Nayatapola**, Bhaktapur's tallest temple, which dates from 1702 and stands on a five-stepped pedestal guarded by a succession of stone wrestlers, elephants, lions, griffins and goddesses. A very fine view of this, and the rest of the square, can be obtained from one of the balconies of Café Nayatapola, which is itself a splendid building.

The oldest quarter in Bhaktapur is located east of Durbar Square where **Tachapol Tole** (Dattrataya Square) has two old, but not especially elaborate, temples and a slender pillar-statue of Garud. Take particular note of the magnificent carvings adorning so many buildings, especially around the windows and doorways. The art of wood-carving has reached the very height of perfection, with the famed **Peacock Window**, hidden away down a side-alley, being the most celebrated piece of work in the Kathmandu valley.

Once you've visited all the main sites, which will no doubt take several trips to Nepal to achieve, a random exploration is worth tackling. Avoid the

known places and duck into the mystery of back alleys previously unvisited, for there you will discover the old Kathmandu, Patan or Bhaktapur, whose heart and soul belongs to the Nepal that is slow to change, where lives are lived beyond the camera lens. There you will find that urban, workaday Nepal has an appeal all its own.

ABOUT THIS GUIDE

In a hundred ages of the gods I could not tell thee of the glories of the Himalaya.

(Skanda Purana)

In common with other books in the Cicerone series of guides to the major trekking regions of Nepal, this volume has not been produced in order to encourage even more trekkers to explore the trails of this Himalayan wonderland, but in the hope of adding something to the experience of those already committed to going there. Being forewarned about the nature of the route and the seriousness of some of the trails is one way of reminding trekkers that in order to make the most of every step along the way it is essential to be both physically and mentally prepared. 'The art of Himalayan travel', said W.H. Murray, 'is the art of being bold enough to enjoy life now.'

In truth, a detailed route guide to the Annapurna region is hardly necessary. The majority of trails are so well travelled that it's almost impossible to get lost. But an idea of how long it's likely to take to trek from one village (or region) to the next, and what to expect in the way of accommodation or services when they arrive, is something that many trekkers find useful when planning their journey. Times quoted, however, will not agree with every trekker's pace, but are offered as a rough guide only. After a day or so along the trail, it should be evident just how much our times vary, and you can take this differential into account when deciding how far to walk each day. Remember: **times quoted in this guide refer to actual walking time only**; they do not take into account rest stops, photographic interruptions or refreshment delays.

Altitudes quoted in the text of this guide are not always in accord with maps or other guides of the region, for different maps and publications give wildly varying measurements. Where published altitudes are undisputed I have used them, but in those instances where there seems to be no general agreement, I have quoted readings from my own altimetre used during my latest trek. I make no claim for its accuracy.

In the following pages of text the main treks have been broken into sections of several days, with each multi-day section divided into sub-sections, rather than manageable day-sized stages. This is to avoid concentrating

PRE-TRECK CHECK

- Obtain your ACAP entry permit in advance from Thamel (Kathmandu) or Lakeside (Pokhara).
- Don't trek alone. If you have no companion – hire a guide.
- Register your personal details and route plan with your embassy.
- Be adequately insured.
- Carry a first aid kit and know how to use it. Make sure you have any medication you are likely to need.
- Be aware of the dangers of high altitude sickness – and watch for signs among those with you.
- Follow the Minimum Impact Code.
- Watch where you're walking, and remain alert.
- Register at check-posts – this increases your chance of rescue in case you need help.
- Respect local culture and customs: don't wear revealing clothes and avoid public demonstrations of affection.
- If staying in lodges, choose those that use alternatives to wood for cooking and heating.
- Discourage begging, and encourage fair dealing.
- Treat villagers, porters and guides with respect.

High Above Manang there are many viewpoints from which to study Annapurna III
(The Annapurna Circuit)

attention on specific villages as overnight halts, to the detriment of others. There are now so many trekkers' lodges throughout the Annapurnas that it is invidious to single out any particular hotel or village in which to stay, for it is often in the quieter, less well-patronised places that the most rewarding experiences are gained.

Wherever possible, the names of lodges passed on the treks have been given. But lodge names sometimes change – as do the names of villages – and new lodges are being built year by year. Villages grow in size, and new villages appear where before there may have been just a single lodge or teahouse. Reading the accounts of travellers who journeyed through the Annapurna region just a couple of decades or so ago will clearly illustrate this growth. Please bear this in mind as you make your own journey.

TREK 1
THE ANNAPURNA CIRCUIT

In such country there is no monotony.
(H.W. Tilman)

TREK SUMMARY	
Distance:	190km (118 miles)
Time:	15–21 days
Max. altitude:	5416m (17,769ft)
Start:	Besisahar
Finish:	Beni or Naya Pul
Trekking style:	Tea-house (lodge accommodation) or camping

Widely acknowledged as one of the world's classic treks, this tremendous route makes a long horse-shoe loop of the Annapurna Himal. Preferably tackled in an anti-clockwise direction to give a somewhat less demanding approach to the Thorong La than would be required from the west, the trek links the valley of the Marsyangdi Khola with that of the Kali Gandaki. The Thorong La (5416m, 17,769ft) is the crux; if conditions are unfavourable for its crossing the Circuit cannot be completed.

Whilst the trail along the Kali Gandaki had been an important trade route for centuries, probably the first Westerner to see it was the Swiss geologist Arnold Heim, who flew through the valley in 1949 in a Dakota and brought back some unique photographs of the mountains. The following year members of the successful French expedition to Annapurna I, under the leadership of Maurice Herzog, explored the Kali Gandaki and made their base at Tukuche. By remarkable coincidence, at the very same time Bill Tilman was leading a small party through the Marsyangdi to Manang, from which they made an attempt on Annapurna IV. (Tilman's party included Jimmy Roberts, who later explored the Annapurna Sanctuary and who was to become the 'father' of trekking in Nepal when he established his Kathmandu-based company Mountain Travel in 1964 – see box, p179.) Gaston Rébuffet was possibly the first European to cross the Thorong La during the French expedition's reconnaissance, whilst a few days earlier he, along with Herzog and Marcel Ichac, had traversed the Tilicho La which also links the two valleys.

In 1956 the Tibetan scholar David Snellgrove came into the valley of the Kali Gandaki on completion of a long journey through Dolpo. He visited many of the villages through

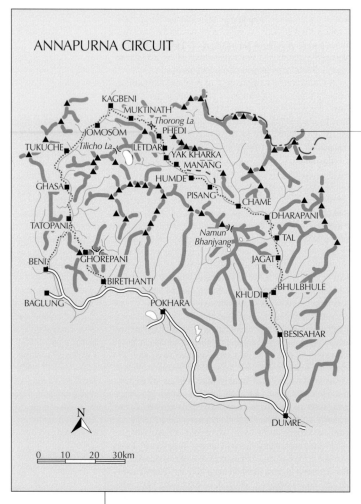

which the Circuit now travels, studied their *gompas*, then continued upvalley to Mustang before returning to Kagbeni and Muktinath. He then crossed the Thorong La and descended to Manang, and progressed through the Marsyangdi as far as modern-day Dharapani. There he left the Marsyangdi to follow the Dudh Khola north-eastward to the Manaslu Himal and eventually to Kathmandu. His book *Himalayan Pilgrimage* contains many interesting descriptions of the landscape, villages and customs of the area at the time.

By the 1960s a combination of political difficulties, mainly stirred by the Chinese invasion and occupation of Tibet, effectively put the region out of bounds to foreign visitors. But in 1977 the Nepalese government at last lifted restrictions on the Manang valley, and for the first time the Annapurna Circuit became a reality for adventurous trekkers.

The route followed by the vast majority of trekkers today, and that which is described here, begins in Besisahar, which is linked by a spur road cutting north from Dumre on the Kathmandu–Pokhara highway. Two alternative, but less travelled approach routes, start either in Gorkha to the east (one of the standard routes in the early days, taking 3–4 days to reach Bhulbhule) or at Begnas Tal, which lies south-west of Besisahar, giving a three-day trek to Khudi. Neither of these approaches has many lodges, and where they do exist they are pretty basic. Anyone planning to trek one of these routes is advised to hire a guide because the ways are not always easy to find. In that lies some of their charm.

The trail through the Marsyangdi valley is always clear on the ground, although confusion might arise at one or two minor path junctions where there are no obvious indicators as to which alternative is the one to take. Whilst the ACAP authorities have erected a few signposts indicating the route to Manang, there will be no other signs or waymarks, apart from a few marker posts in snow-covered areas on the way to the Thorong La – in this alone the Himalayan trekking experience proves to be very different from that of European mountain regions.

There are dozens of villages on the Circuit, and even more tea-houses spread along the trail. Lodges are in plentiful supply and there's no shortage of good campsites for organised parties. Mountain and valley views are constantly changing and are never less than magnificent; the initial stages wind among rich terraces of vegetation, but these soon give way to the rugged narrows of the Marsyangdi's impressive gorge. This in turn leads to the stark landscapes of the Manang valley in the rain-shadow of the mountains.

The route crosses and recrosses the river countless times. Most of the suspension bridges are sturdy and with good handrails on both sides, which is comforting when you see (and hear) the river furiously thrashing through its bed below.

On reaching Manang it is advisable to spend a couple of days there to aid acclimatisation, then take two short days to walk up to Thorong Phedi in preparation for the 985m (3200ft) ascent to the pass. In clear conditions and with no snow lying, the only difficulties experienced in crossing are caused by the altitude, and in the actual distance to be covered between Phedi and Muktinath on the far side. In snow, or with poor visibility or a strong wind blowing, the Thorong La gives a very demanding day. At no time should the potential seriousness of its crossing be underestimated. It is essential that all members of the party, including porters, have clothing adequate to cope with sub-zero temperatures on the approach to the pass.

From Muktinath the route descends easily to the bed of the Kali Gandaki and then works its way south between Dhaulagiri and the Annapurnas, through countryside which contrasts markedly with that experienced on the eastern side of the Thorong La. Lodges and tea-houses are as numerous here as in the Marsyangdi.

Below Tatopani the trail forks, with one route continuing alongside the Kali Gandaki as far as the roadhead at Beni, while the other leaves the river valley for a relentless climb among lush vegetation to Ghorepani astride the Poon Hill Danda. From there outstanding views are to be had of the big mountains through whose gateway you have recently passed. Beyond Ghorepani a long descent leads to Birethanti and Naya Pul, for a taxi or bus ride out to Pokhara, while those with sufficient time and energy could add a few days to their trek by breaking away from Ghorepani to visit the Annapurna Sanctuary.

Do not be tempted to hurry this route. The scenery, vegetation and cultural diversity experienced along the way are so rich that it would take several treks around the Circuit to absorb their full impact. Actual trekking time for the basic Circuit is 14–15 days, but it is important to add to these acclimatisation days in Manang (two recommended) and at least one rest day in the Kali Gandaki valley. At the very minimum you should allow 18 days for the circuit, but where possible make more available in case your crossing of the

Thorong La is delayed by bad weather. The Annapurna Circuit is generally considered a three-week trek, but as has been said of other mountain journeys, the connoisseur will always take longer.

PROLOGUE
Kathmandu – Dumre – Besisahar

Distance:	175km (109 miles)
Time:	6–8hrs
Transport options:	Bus (Kathmandu to Besisahar direct, or Kathmandu to Dumre)
	Bus, truck or jeep (Dumre to Besisahar)

Under normal circumstances (breakdowns permitting) it is quite feasible to leave Kathmandu by bus in the morning and arrive in Besisahar the same afternoon, with sufficient hours of daylight left to trek upvalley as far as Khudi or Bhulbhule.

As mentioned in the Introduction, public buses bound for Besisahar depart from the new bus park at Gongabu on Kathmandu's Ring Road every day during the main trekking seasons. Up to seven buses a day service this route, and all leave in the morning. Seats need to be reserved the day before travel.

Tourist 'express' buses destined for Pokhara, which are more comfortable than those used by locals but do not visit Besisahar, can be taken as far as Dumre (but you pay the full Pokhara fare). These tourist buses leave Kathmandu from outside the Standard Chartered Bank on Kantipath around 07.00hrs. Seat reservations are essential, and tickets may be obtained at least a day in advance from various agents in Thamel. Baggage is carried on the roof. When passing your rucksack to the man loading it, make sure to inform him that your destination is Dumre, rather than Pokhara. On arrival in Dumre you can change to either a public or a 'local' tourist bus for the last 42km (26 miles), pay to ride on the back of a truck, or hire a private jeep. It is also possible to take public transport from Pokhara to Besisahar. Three buses a day travel along this route.

The journey by public bus can be nerve-racking, for some of the drivers (though not all) are suicidally reckless as they career along the winding road, horns blaring, and overtake on blind corners or on the brow of a hill. These buses can be heavily overcrowded, and although some passengers choose to perch on the roof among the luggage, this is illegal and you are advised (on safety grounds) to avoid the temptation to join them. The drivers of tourist buses are usually less frenetic at the wheel, and the vehicles better maintained than public buses.

Leaving Kathmandu the journey runs along the Tribhuvan Rajmarg heading west and rising steadily to the Chandragiri pass on a ridge that forms a rim to the valley. From there it then spirals down a series of hairpins into a fertile, sub-tropical region with snow-capped summits of the Ganesh and Manaslu himals at first seen to the north. The Tribhuvan Highway then breaks away to the south, while the way to Dumre follows the Prithvi Rajmarg heading west. Built with Chinese aid in the early 1970s this road winds along the bank of the Trisuli – Nepal's most popular rafting river – where mountain views are lost behind the foothills. The road is regularly disturbed by landslips caused by the heavy monsoon rains, and at various points along the way traffic may be held up while essential repairs to the road are carried out.

Public buses make one or two halts for refreshment at wayside tea-houses, but these do not always have adequate toilet facilities, and passengers have little option but to stand in a line beside the road to water the vegetation. Tourist buses, on the other hand, are more discriminating with regard to refreshment stops. The grubby little township of **MUGLING** (about 110km (68 miles) from Kathmandu), with its wide main street lined with basic 'transport cafés', is the standard lunch stop for passengers of public buses. But you're advised against straying too far from your vehicle during the break, as some trekkers have found themselves stranded in the town while the bus carrying their luggage trundles off in a cloud of dust and smoke.

About 25km (15 miles) beyond Mugling, **DUMRE** (440m, 1444ft) is not the place in which to spend a night unless you've been delayed getting there and have no way of moving on. It's a busy, dusty and noisy bazaar whose main street is lined with warehouses, shops and lodges run by Newars, the original inhabitants of the Kathmandu valley. Until the road was extended north, porters used to begin their journeys to far-distant villages from here, taking weighty supplies on their backs along the well-padded trails of the Middle Hills. Most goods are now carried by truck to the roadhead at Besisahar, from where porters continue the process of distribution into the hill country.

The direct Kathmandu–Besisahar public bus spends little time in Dumre, but trekkers who make the journey by tourist bus need to change here. If you intend to take a local tourist bus for the onward route to the trailhead, obtain a ticket from the Chhimkeswori Hotel. Alternatively, take a public bus or one of the open-backed trucks that regularly trundle along the newly paved road on the west bank of the Marsyangdi. Neither leaves town until it is full to overflowing with passengers, so you may have a long wait. An alternative is to hire a jeep. This offers a faster and more comfortable journey with the certainty of a seat, but is considerably more expensive than the truck ride – you should agree a price before leaving Dumre.

The paved road crosses the Chundi Khola outside Dumre and pushes north along the west bank of the milky-blue Marsyangdi, through a fertile countryside lush with rice paddies. There are one or two check-posts and a few villages lining the road, their houses overhung with bougainvillea and hibiscus, and with bananas growing nearby. On occasion the road may be broken by streams that burst their banks in the monsoon, bringing down rocks and vegetation, but that being said, the bus journey is likely to take something like 2–2½hrs to reach **BESISAHAR** and the trailhead.

BESISAHAR (823m, 2700ft) is a small township which serves as the administration centre of Lamjung District. In clear conditions, Lamjung Himal and Annapurna II can be seen from the edge of town. There are more than a dozen trekkers' lodges strung alongside the main street, together with an assortment of shops, a bank, telecommunications centre, post office, school and a hospital. There's even a cinema at the southern end of town, and the district jail nearby. A little over halfway down the street, on the left-hand side, the first ACAP check-post of the trek is located, and before heading off along the trail you should sign the register and have your entry permit inspected there. It should be possible to hire porters or a porter-guide for the journey ahead, if required, before leaving Besisahar.

SECTION 1
Besisahar to Manang

Distance:	76km (47 miles)
Time:	6–7 days
Start altitude:	823m (2700ft)
High point:	Manang, 3540m (11,614ft)
Height gain:	2717m (8914ft)

Beginning in the low foothill country the first day or so of the trek journeys through a richly vegetated landscape before entering a series of abrupt gorges that provide access to the upper Marsyangdi, on the northern side of the main Himalayan chain. In terms of vegetation, scenery, architecture and religious observance, Besisahar and Manang are worlds apart, but therein lies much of the charm of the Annapurna Circuit.

Dictated by the severity of the terrain in this section of the route, the trail is a helter-skelter, frequently rising and descending, and crossing and recrossing the river many times. There are numerous villages, groups of lodges and tea-houses, and in addition to fellow trekkers there will no doubt be plenty of local travellers and porters sharing the trail. It would be difficult to lose the way.

The first day or so should be taken steadily. With more than two weeks of trekking ahead you'll need to adapt to the rhythm of the trail; slip into a comfortable stride and absorb the whole experience of this magical land. There will be patches of sub-tropical forest along the way, terraces of agriculture stepping the hillsides, lush vegetation typical of the Middle Hills of central Nepal, insect-seething trees, and views upvalley to Himalchuli, Ngadi Chuli (Peak 29) and Manaslu, the world's seventh highest mountain. Above Bhulbhule will be seen the first of many fine waterfalls spraying down the valley walls.

This foothill country is largely populated by Hindus – Brahmins, Chhetris and Gurungs – but north of the high mountains villagers originally migrated from Tibet; they have distinct Mongoloid features, keep yaks and practise Buddhism. Traditionally, Brahmins are the Hindu priest caste and Chhetris the warrior caste, although along the Marsyangdi the latter are mostly farmers, while Gurungs have their own religious practices that can be either Hindu or Buddhist. Gurungs are noted shepherds, peasant farmers and Gurkha soldiers; they make up the majority of the population in the Annapurna region and are found mostly in the middle range of hills where a number have made a successful transition to the role of businessmen.

ANNAPURNA CIRCUIT – Section 1

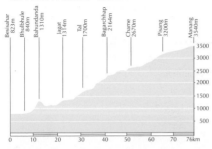

At the northern end of Besisahar's main street a dirt road extends upvalley. This was apparently created to aid the building of a hydroelectric plant at Ngadi, but construction work never started and the road has foundered on the west bank of the Marsyangdi at a point a little north of Ngadi. Much of the way to Khudi makes use of this dirt road, but as no bridges have been built to take it across the many tributary streams, there is no wheeled traffic. The first part of the trek therefore makes for easy walking.

Besisahar to Bhulbhule (2–2½hrs) ▶

On the outskirts of Besisahar descend to the Puwa Khola, a side-stream crossed by a causeway of stones, and go up the opposite slope to rejoin the dirt road. This contours round a hillside spur and soon comes to **CHANAUTE**, a small village of orange-walled houses. Passing the village continue along the road and about 40mins from Besisahar pass a solitary lodge, Hotel Himalchuli View. In another 20mins the road is interrupted by the Bhoran Khola, a river draining the western hills. This may be spanned by a bamboo bridge, otherwise it will be

The Boran Khola, between Besisahar and Khudi

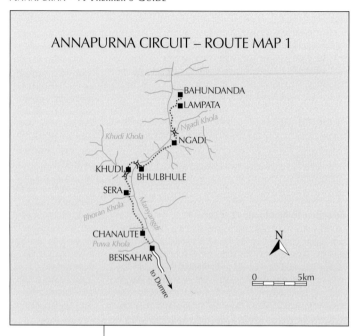

ANNAPURNA CIRCUIT – ROUTE MAP 1

Note: An alternative trail climbs above the west bank of the Khudi Khola to reach the Gurung village of Ghanpokhara, high on the ridge at the southern end of the Telbrung Danda. Another curves south and south-west to cut across country to Begnas Tal and Pokhara.

necessary to use stepping stones to cross. Just beyond the river stand the few tea-houses of **SERA**, then there's a Rural Training Centre on the right. About 30mins later go through a grove of trees, and soon after come to another Hotel Himalchuli View and enter the Annapurna Conservation Area. A noticeboard pleads: *Step gently in this fragile land and take care of nature.*

The dirt road now contours above the first major tributary, the Khudi Khola. Leave the road and take a descending path which soon crosses a suspension bridge. ◀

KHUDI (790m, 2592ft, 1hr 30mins) is a small but tightly packed Gurung village whose houses are roofed with either thatch or tin. In addition to a few lodges and tea-houses, it also has one or two shops and a post office. Near the bridge on the right is the Riverside Restaurant & Lodge. The path climbs a steep flight of stone steps to the Memory Guesthouse, where you turn right to the Kemix Guesthouse.

Just above the last lodge rejoin the dirt road on the village outskirts and turn right. With the Marsyangdi flowing below, views ahead now include Ngadi Chuli and Himalchuli, both of which received early attention from Japanese expeditions.

After passing a school and a forest nursery, about 20mins from Khudi come to a line of houses, tea-houses and the Friendship Guesthouse strung alongside the road. A few minutes later reach the first group of tea-houses and simple shops of **BHULBHULE**, which has been built on both sides of the Marsyangdi. Leave the road and take a path on the right by the Thorong La Guesthouse.

BHULBHULE (840m, 2756ft, 2–2½hrs). Descend to the Everest Guesthouse, and beyond a few shops and tea-houses cross a long suspension bridge to the east bank of the Marsyangdi, where the main part of the village overlooks the river. Below the bridge to the left there's a good campsite. On the right is the fancy-looking Hotel Arjun. The literal translation of Bhulbhule is 'the place where water springs from the ground' – the spring is found not far from the path. The village here consists of two lines of buildings with a paved street between them. ACAP used to have a check-post here, but that was relocated to Besisahar in 2002. However, there are one or two simple shops, a bakery and a tailor's. The first lodge on the left is the Heaven Guesthouse, then Hotel Manang next door, followed by the Manakamna.

Bhulbhule to Bahundanda (2½–3hrs)

Through Bhulbhule continue upvalley among low terraced fields, with the big snow mountains teasing far ahead, and in 5mins pass below an attractive ribbon of a cascade which falls into a pool on the right. Just beyond it the trail forks. Unless the river is high take the lower path – the upper trail is the one to use during the monsoon. The two converge a little later.

About 20mins from Bhulbhule pass through a small settlement that consists mostly of tea-houses, and 15mins later come to River View Lodge. Cross a side-stream by way of a simple bridge leading to Hotel Sunam, where once again the trail divides. Take the left fork, and in a further 30mins come to a village set among terraces and divided by another stream.

NGADI (930m, 3051ft, 1hr 5mins). At first there are several picturesque lodges with neat gardens: Sky High Guesthouse, Seasons Lodge and Trekkers Lodge. Then come Hotel Pisang Peak and the Hikers Restaurant & Lodge. The village street is paved and lined with shops and yet more lodges: Himalaya Restaurant & Lodge, Annapurna Lodge, the Marshyandi, Kamala and Hotel Mina. After these you cross the side-stream on a bamboo bridge to the next part of the village, which has shops on either side of the paved street.

Beyond Ngadi the path goes alongside rice fields leading in 10mins to a group of buildings that guard the entrance to a big steel suspension bridge over the Ngadi Khola, which flows out of a major tributary valley. (There's a campsite below the bridge on the left.) Over the bridge there's another campsite and a few simple tea-houses.

Beyond the Ngadi Khola the trail continues along the steep east flank of the Marsyangdi's valley crossing a small landslide area, and about 40mins from Ngadi tops a rise at the Sital Danda, where there are a few tea-houses. On the

NGADI CHULI

The Ngadi Khola drains a large portion of the Manaslu Himal. At the head of the valley looms the south face of Ngadi Chuli, flanked by Himalchuli and Manaslu. Dr Harka Gurung, author of *Vignettes of Nepal*, was born in a village within the valley of the Ngadi Khola, and he writes of the fine views to be had of those mountains from the upper valley. Seen from various places on the early stage of the Annapurna Circuit trek, the 7871m (25,923ft) Ngadi Chuli was first approached from the west by Japanese climbers in 1961, but they failed to find a practical route up their chosen peak. Two years later the mountain was attempted from the east, and in 1969 another Japanese team tried the south side of its East Ridge, but they too failed to reach the top. In 1970 a possible first ascent was made by H. Watanabe and Lhakpa Tsering via the East Ridge. The two were seen close to the summit before disappearing from view. They reappeared 2hrs later, descending, but then sadly fell to their deaths before anyone could ascertain whether they'd reached the top. In 1979 a Polish expedition concentrated on the peak's difficult West Buttress, and succeeded in putting R. Gajewski and M. Pawlikowski on the summit – they later expressed doubt that Watanabe and Lhakpa Tsering had achieved the first ascent. Over the years the mountain has had several names: Peak 29, Manaslu II, Dakum and Dunapurna, but Ngadi Chuli seems to be universally accepted today.

opposite side of the valley a fine waterfall is seen, and moments later you gain a first view of Bahundanda gathered in a saddle of hills ahead, perched above an amphitheatre of rice terraces. From this viewpoint you gaze across stepped fields to the milky-blue river snaking below and to big green hills leading ever higher to mountains of the Manaslu and Lamjung himals.

Rice terraces below Bahundanda

Bahundanda is nearly 400m (1300ft) above the river, and it will take about 50mins to reach it from the Sital Danda. It's a fine trail and a very pleasant walk, climbing among trees and terraced fields, and passing groups of tin-roofed houses at **LAMPATA**, after which the path steepens for a final ascent through a badly littered gully to

BAHUNDANDA (1310m, 4298ft, 2½–3hrs). Manaslu Lodge is passed on the way up to the village. The Swiss Alpen Hotel stands in the square, while the aptly named Mountain View and Super View hotels are located at the top of steps to the left of the square. One overlooks the terraced amphitheatre through which you approached the village; the other is dominated by the view north to the Manaslu Himal. The Tibetan Hotel is situated beside the path a little north of the square.

Perched on a saddle in a spur of the Nagi Lekh with lovely views both up- and down-valley, the village also has several shops, including a telephone facility, gathered around or close to the square, which is graced by a large pipal tree. The Nepali poet Madhave Prasad Ghimire was born here, and being the most northerly Brahmin village of the Marsyangdi valley, its name is said to mean 'Brahmin hill'. From it several Gurung villages can be seen to the north, south and west. The village school is located to the east, and is where groups often set up camp.

Bahundanda to Jagat (3–3½hrs) ◀

North of Bahundanda the trail descends steeply, at first eroded into deep channels, then winding through a magnificent curve of rice or millet terraces, the Marsyangdi twisting far below. At the foot of the slope the way then makes a long traverse of the right-hand hillside, undulating easily among the terraces. When you look back it is to gain a clear impression of the natural amphitheatre through which you have just descended, and of the brief gorge carved by the river to the west of Bahundanda's long spur of a hill.

About 50mins after leaving Bahundanda, the way crosses a side-stream with a small bamboo water-mill straddling it, then goes up a slope to a string of simple lodges: Greenland Restaurant, Eagle Nest Hotel and Hotel Sunrise. After these the path becomes an enjoyable belvedere, gently undulating along the hillside and leading in another 20mins to a small settlement of lodges set among low terraces of rice. This is

KANIGAON (1170m, 3839ft, 1hr 10mins). There are just two lodges here, the Shangri La and Peaceful Hotel.

Ten minutes later reach the first of several lodges in a newly created village built on a large flat shelf of land opposite an impressive waterfall.

GHERMU PHANT (1180m, 3871ft, 1hr 20mins) has plenty of accommodation in the Crystal Guesthouse, Pramila Guesthouse, Sabiwa, Hotel Annapurna, Dipak Guesthouse, New Garden Hotel, Kusum Restaurant & Lodge and the Rainbow Restaurant & Lodge. There are also simple tea-houses and one or two basic shops. The village school stands back across the fields to the right.

Despite the steepness of the terrain, terraces on both sides of the river have been created in seemingly impossible situations, turning the hillsides into vast stairways. In the post-monsoon trekking season before the harvest begins, the light plays on these terraces, each of which is outlined with a curve of shadow. Here and there a dark thumbprint of greenery tells of a tree or a group of trees, and on occasion the roof of a house can be seen above the growth. The trail brushes alongside the fields and you become absorbed into the landscape, as much a feature of it as the brightly coloured birds that dash and cry overhead.

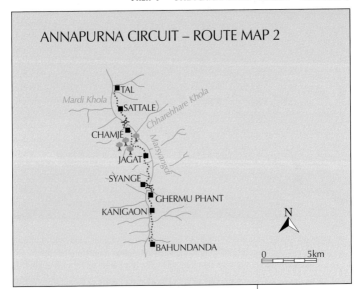

Edging fields you pass through the settlement, then descend steeply to the river, with a frontal view of the waterfall crashing in ribbons of spray whose outflow has now been siphoned off to power a small hydro scheme. Halfway down the slope pass the View Point Hotel, then River Side Guesthouse at the foot of the descent near a long suspension bridge which takes the trail across to the west bank of the Marsyangdi. Gathered on the west bank by the bridge is the small, one-street village of

SYANGE (1100m, 3609ft, 1hr 45mins). Sonam Tibetan Lodge and the Thakuri Guesthouse line the street, along with one or two shops and tea-houses. The river thunders just below.

North of Syange the Marsyangdi narrows to a gorge. The continuing trail heads upvalley, angling across the steep slope for 10mins to reach a tea-house by a pipal tree, where the valley makes a sharp bend to mark the start of the Marsyangdi's gorges. These gorges are a typical feature of Himalayan geography, for most of the high mountain regions are cleft by similarly deep

The bridge between Ghermu Phant and Syange

and narrow river valleys. All the main trekking routes in Nepal that either draw close to the highest mountains or explore the northern side of the Himalyan Divide have to pass through such gorges, often on exposed but well-crafted trails. When Tilman came this way in 1950 he found slender wooden galleries fixed across the mountainside, but the galleries, he said, 'were pretty frail, particularly the hand-rails which were better left alone or at the most touched rather than grasped. They were seldom wider than a single plank and were reached by a stone staircase or up-ended logs with footholds cut in them.' Fortunately the path to Jagat has been considerably improved since then.

After the pipal tree tea-house the path loses height, then climbs again for another 10mins to the tiny New Thorong La Restaurant and the Asia Hotel. Below the hotel on the opposite bank of the Marsyangdi there are hot springs, but the trail to Jagat ignores these and climbs on, more steeply now, among wild marijuana plants and stinging nettles, and with crags sometimes overhanging the path. At the top of the long climb you come to the Marco Polo Hotel and a first view of Jagat. It will take almost 30mins to reach it from here.

JAGAT (1314m, 4311ft, 3hrs 15mins) used to be a customs post set in a forest clearing in the days of the Tibetan salt trade that thrived for centuries until 1959 when, in the wake of the Chinese invasion, cross-border trade with Tibet ended. Although much enlarged, the village is tightly packed on a natural shelf among huge boulders and a few banana trees. There's a school, three campsites, a few shops and at least ten lodges: the Himali, Tibetan Pemba Hotel, Mont Blanc, Garden Hotel, Eco Home, the Paradise Hotel, Everest Hotel, Susma Hotel, Manaslu and the fancy-looking Lord Buddha Hotel at the northern end of the village.

Jagat to Tal (3–3½hrs)

Leaving Jagat the trail takes an easy contour to the Tatopani Restaurant, reached in 10mins, where a sign suggests it will take another 10mins to visit a hot spring down by the river. Ignoring the hot springs path continue ahead on an undulating course high above the river, and 30mins from Jagat, at a low point on the trail, there's a simple tea-house set among lush vegetation. Just beyond this, pass the Arjun Hotel and, above it as you gain height, the larger River View Guesthouse. A rather basic watermill is seen a few metres above and to the right of this lodge. ▸

The trail now levels out with views of a very fine waterfall of the Chhrehhare Khola on the eastern side of the valley; it hurtles through a narrow gully, then pours free before crashing onto a projecting rock where it then explodes in a burst of spray to the river far below. Shortly after, one arrives at

> The wooded hillside here had been swept by a landslide during research and a temporary path created, which led to the crossing of a cascade on a makeshift log bridge of questionable safety. By the time this guide is in use, it is hoped that that bridge will have been replaced by something more permanent and satisfactory.

CHAMJE (1433m, 4701ft, 1hr), a small paved village with the Tibetan Hotel and a small shop, then the Potala Guesthouse and Tibet Lhasa Hotel.

THE MARSYANGDI'S GORGE – A ONE-TIME BARRIER

For centuries the Marsyangdi's gorge represented a major obstacle for all who needed to pass either up- or down-valley. There were no proper bridges, and in places the trail consisted of little more than a series of wood or bamboo galleries tenuously fitted across the steep gorge walls. Pack animals were unable to travel between Bahundanda and Thonje at the Marsyangdi's confluence with the Dudh Khola, so all goods (salt downstream, grain upstream) had therefore to be transported on the backs of men and women. But with the construction of 'safe' bridges and the creation of permanent paths with the use of dynamite in the late 1960s and early 1970s, the series of gorges became less of a barrier, not only benefiting Western trekkers, but reducing the cost of living for villagers in the upper Marsyangdi.

Ahead the valley is squeezed into another gorge, even more narrow and dramatic than before, and the path slopes downhill among trees to reach a good suspension bridge at about 1350m (4429ft) that will carry the way over to the east bank once more.

From this point as far as the Tal levels, about 350m (1150ft) higher, the route climbs steeply in places, while the river boils and cascades among huge, cottage-sized boulders, and the valley ahead appears to be almost blocked near its confluence with the Mardi Khola which marks the boundary between the Lamjung and Manang districts. Waterfalls streak the gorge walls, and the river's thunder fills the narrows.

The trail winds among great boulders and climbs tight against the eastern cliffs at an area known as **SATTALE**, meaning 'seven storeys' – so-named because the original route depended on the maintenance of seven rope ladders stretched across the rockface. About 50mins from Chamje pass Hotel Thorong Peak, and half an hour later, on a steepish climb, reach a couple of simple tea-houses from which you have splendid views downvalley through the deep, river-cut narrows. From here it will take another 30mins to reach Tal. Continue uphill for another 20mins and, topping a rise, go through the first entrance archway (*kani*) of the trek by the

Crossing the Marsyangdi near Chamje

Sangri La Hotel and River View Guesthouse, and there before you lies a large open area of gravel flats, sandy bays and pastureland. The Marsyangdi winds in lazy curls below, soft blue and gentle. Ahead lies Tal nestling in the pastures, big mountains soaring on either side to dwarf the village into a collection of toy houses. It is very much a Shangri-La view.

Gravel flats at Tal suggest that this was once the bed of a lake

The path eases down to the pastures, rims the right-hand side of the valley, and on nearing the village you see a classic waterfall bursting out of the mountainside behind it. Pass through an older, less garish *kani* than that at the top of the rise (this one has prayer wheels embedded as if to emphasise the fact that you've arrived in Buddhist country) and enter

TAL (1700m, 5577ft, 3hrs). ACAP has installed a **safe drinking-water station** here, the first on this side of the Thorong La; there's also a check-post and information centre, a kerosene depot and a well-stocked **health post**. Tal has a range of shops and no shortage of lodges. These include the Sunrise Hotel, Dragon Hotel, Tilicho Hotel, Captain's Guesthouse, and the Annapurna, Manaslu, Thale, Potala and Himalay guesthouses, then the Tashi Delek Hotel, beyond which you cross a wooden bridge and come to the first mani wall by the Tibetan Hotel. A short distance along the trail in a peaceful location,

85

BUDDHIST SYMBOLS ON THE TRAIL

The Buddhist peoples of the Himalaya invest their lands with plenty of evidence of their faith. Walls of flat stone slabs (*mani* walls) are built along the trails, and each stone is carved with the sacred rune *Om mani padme hum*. This same prayer is printed on cloth flags hung over houses, strung across specific hillsides or flown from poles erected on passes. As the wind blows through them it distributes the prayers across the surrounding country. The *mani* prayer is written on papers and inserted into metal drums to be spun in prayer walls; other prayer wheels, as tall or even taller than a man, are filled with the same *mani* mantra, and are either revolved by a stream – the same process as a watermill – or manually turned by the devout traveller passing by. Each revolution is counted by the ringing of a bell that tells of more prayers being released. Lamas in saffron robes spin hand-held prayer wheels and thumb rosaries as they walk. On entering a Buddhist village the trail often passes through an archway (*kani*) whose walls and ceiling may be decorated with sacred paintings or lined with prayer wheels. White-painted *chortens* of various size symbolise the Buddha and stand on the edge of numerous villages, while many *gompas* (monasteries) have been built within villages along the route of the Annapurna Circuit. Please remember to pass all Buddhist structures along their left-hand side and to turn prayer wheels clockwise.

the Paradise Hotel has its own flower-filled garden and a splendid view of the celebrated Tal waterfall.

This most southerly village of Manang District, known here as Gyasumdo, is inhabited by people of Tibetan origin, and the Buddhist influence is clearly evident. Here you will find prayer flags, a white-painted *chorten*, and the first *mani* wall of the Annapurna Circuit. The village occupies the site of a silted-up lake (*tal* means 'lake') formed when a landslide blocked the gorge. It used to exude a Wild West atmosphere, with horses tethered at hitching rails or roaming free in the wide main street. But this has changed with a dramatic increase in lodge building, and the many hotels and shops now encroach on the former open spaces. However, behind the village there is still plenty of room for camping.

North of Tal the Marsyangdi's gorge closes the valley again with a deep U-shaped cleft. The gorge makes an arthritic twist on the way to Dharapani, and then curves sharply westward where the Marsyangdi digs its trench along the northern side of the Annapurna–Lamjung crest.

Tall to Bagarchhap (2½–3hrs) ◀

Leaving the village the trail passes alongside the Paradise Hotel, and shortly before entering the steep-walled gorge comes to the River Plate Guesthouse. The path is paved here as it leads past several small stone buildings, and as you turn into the gorge there's a view of high peaks in the distance towards the head of the valley.

In 30mins from Tal the trail forks near a small wall-enclosed forestry plantation. While the two options take different sides of the valley, they rejoin further upstream by the group of lodges at Karte. The east bank trail is less popular and more demanding than its counterpart. The left-hand path skirts the base of cliffs, then crosses the Marsyangdi on a steel suspension bridge (at 1720m, 5643ft) built in 1995 in conjunction with the Swiss Association for Development and Cooperation.

The trail continues upvalley, now on the west bank. About 10 minutes later you climb past the first simple buildings of **KHORTE**, a small settlement with a few basic tea-houses, whose inhabitants eke out a grim existence with just a few terraces of maize hacked out of a rough hillside. The continuing trail

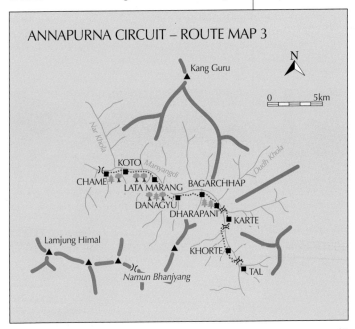

ANNAPURNA CIRCUIT – ROUTE MAP 3

remains high above the river before sloping downhill once more, and an hour or so after leaving Tal you come to the Manaslu Hotel and nearby Marsyangdi Hotel, built just above a few simple farm dwellings. Ten minutes later reach the Height Park Guesthouse, then recross the river again, this time on a 140m-long suspension bridge, to the group of lodges of

KARTE (1850m, 6070ft). The incongruously named Hotel Dorchester used to stand alone here, but now there are two more lodges, the Alpine Hotel and New World Guesthouse.

The trail continues upvalley for another 25 minutes or so. You then descend a number of steps and recross the Marsyangdi yet again by another suspension bridge. After climbing a flight of steps on the west bank and passing through a *kani* you enter

DHARAPANI (1960m, 6430ft, 2hrs), with its long string of hotels, shops, kerosene depot and police check-post. There are almost a dozen lodges here: Tashi Delek (with a campsite), Eco Himalayan Hotel, Tibet Lhasa Guesthouse, Hotel Manaslu, the Bishnu, Ganga Jamuna, Peak 29 and Trekkers Hotels, plus the Tibet Guesthouse, Machapuchhare Hotel and Tibetan Hotel.

Dharapani, a one-street village two hours from Tal

DUDH KHOLA TRADE ROUTE

At the northern end of Dharapani, where the valley forks, a second bridge crosses the Marsyangdi to the village of Thonje on the bank of the Dudh Khola. Until the Chinese invasion of Tibet in the 1950s, the valley of the Dudh Khola was an important trade route, with long strings of pack animals journeying upvalley with rice and down with salt from Tibet. Nowadays that route, or at least the section of it that crosses the 5213m (17,103ft) Larkya La, forms part of the classic Manaslu Circuit, one of the finest treks in Nepal (See *Manaslu – a Trekkers' Guide* published by Cicerone Press). The Dudh Khola, or 'milk river', rises among glaciers on the west side of the Larkya La, behind the beautiful Bimtang meadow and in view of Manaslu.

In 1950 Tilman visited this meadowland, which he called Bimtakhoti, and witnessed much coming and going of dzos (yak cross-breeds) carrying loads across the Larkya La, reporting that in the brief summer season more than 3000 animal loads were traded – the rate of exchange being 16 measures of rice to 25 of salt. David Snellgrove also travelled through the Dudh Khola valley six years after Tilman, and described how the trade had extended to include wool from Tibet, and cotton cloth, cigarettes, matches and 'other useful oddments' from Nepal. Following the Chinese occupation of their country, Bimtang was taken over by Khampa guerillas from Tibet, and their presence throughout the 1970s was a source of embarrassment to members of the Nepalese government who were fearful of upsetting their powerful neighbour in the north.

Ignoring both Thonje and the Dudh Khola, the onward trail leads out of Dharapani, and just beyond the Thonje path comes to the Kangaroo Guesthouse and another camping area. Five minutes later pass the Sisters Guesthouse on the left, just beyond which the path forks. Take the lower path, now curving westward and entering a more alpine region on the northern side of the Lamjung Himal. Climbing among fragrant pinewoods and with good views back through the Dudh Khola, the way heads over a spur and, 30mins from Dharapani, goes through a *kani* into

BAGARCHHAP (2164m, 7100ft, 2½hrs). At first glance the village has a haphazard appearance, but off the trail to the left it is an attractive place, with old flat-roofed stone houses and a fine gompa worth a visit. Bagarchhap has just a handful of lodges: the Marsyangdi Hotel, Pasang Guesthouse and the Buddha Hotel. There's also a **safe drinking-water station** and partial views ahead to Lamjung Himal and

Annapurna II. The village used to be much bigger and more compact, but on 10 November 1995, following 72hrs of heavy rain, it was devastated by a landslide. Several houses, lodges and watermills were destroyed, and 22 lives were lost. Of these 11 were villagers and 9 trekkers. A small memorial to an English trekker who died in the tragedy stands beside the trail near the safe drinking-water station.

Bagarchhap to Chame (3½–4hrs) ◀

On the way out of Bagarchhap pass through a *kani* near the Buddha Hotel and head west, now on the northern side of the Annapurna–Lamjung wall, among forests of blue pine and fir. About 30mins later top a rise and come to the first buildings of

DANAGYU (2300m, 7546ft). Also spelt Daneque, this once small settlement has grown considerably since 1995 as a number of villagers from Bagarchhap relocated here following the landslide disaster. New lodges are being built to join those already established in this strung-out Buddhist village: the New Tibetan Hotel, Annapurna Hotel, Hotel Snowland, Hotel Pearly Gate, Hotel Tibetan, Himalayan Hotel (with a camping area) and the Thakuri Lodge. Just beyond the Thakuri Lodge there's a big prayer wheel on the left, followed by a mani wall. Then comes the Dhorje Hotel, Trekkers Hotel, the Potala Guesthouse and Manaslu Hotel. This last hotel is well named, for Danagyu enjoys privileged views of the big snow peak of Manaslu back to the east.

Having at last arrived on the northern side of the high mountains the nature of the valley has changed. There are still gorges to negotiate, and vegetation is plentiful, with some lovely forests along the way, but this is very much an alpine landscape that has little in common with the lower valley. High mountains are often glimpsed from the trail, but they'll not be fully revealed for another day or so.

West of Danagyu the trail rises a little and curves into the valley's forest-clad narrows to a wooden cantilever bridge which spans a torrent draining the snowfields and glaciers of the Lamjung Himal. The unseen ridge extending eastward from Lamjung Himal is crossed by the 5560m (18,241ft) Namun Bhanjyang, and the path to it departs from the main trail here. This strenuous route is rewarded by spectacular views, but is difficult because it is often snowbound and there is no habitation for a long way on the far side of the pass. For a long time the Namun Bhanjyang was the normal way for much of the year to reach the Manang valley from the south.

Over the bridge take the right-hand path and climb over a minor spur, then continue among trees with the Marsyangdi thundering in its gorge below. A bridge of stone and concrete

MANASLU

Measuring 8156m (26,758ft) Manaslu is the world's eighth highest mountain. A beautiful ice peak whose extended massif effectively marks the eastern wall of the Marsyangdi valley, its name is said to derive from the Sanskrit *manasa* meaning 'soul'. Manaslu is therefore the 'Mountain of the soul'. Tantalizingly glimpsed from several places along the Marsyangdi, it was studied by Bill Tilman and Jimmy Roberts during their 1950 approach to the north side of Annapurna, but the mountain became the focus of a succession of Japanese, rather than British, expeditions in the ensuing years. During one of these, villagers from Samagaon in the upper Buri Gandaki effectively stopped the attempt on religious grounds. However, the summit was eventually reached from the Larkya glacier above Samagaon in May 1956 by Imanishi and Gyaltsen Norbu, members of an expedition led by Yuko Maki. In 1972 an avalanche hit a South Korean team, killing 5 climbers and 10 Sherpas, while in the autumn of 1996 a dramatic helicopter rescue saved two badly frostbitten Japanese climbers and their two Sherpas who had been avalanched on their descent from the mountain. The rescue, hailed at the time as one of the most daring to be attempted in Nepal, took place in the icefall above Camp I at about 6300m (20,670ft), where a helicopter hovered, belly-down on top of a serac with its wheels overhanging, while the beleaguered climbers scrambled aboard.

is crossed beside an impressive waterfall (another stream coming from Lamjung Himal); then you climb a stone staircase, at the top of which there's another very fine view back to the east. The trail levels for a short way before descending to a tiny settlement about 1hr from Bagarchhap. This is **TIMANG BESI**, with just two simple tea-houses.

The tiny settlement of Timang Besi on the way to Chame

Climbing again the path winds among forests of rhododendron, oak, maple and walnut, and 45mins later comes to the collection of Tibetan-style houses of

LATA MARANG (2454m, 8051ft, 1hr 45mins). The first hotel is the Tatopani Lodge, then down a slope is the very basic Hotel Moonlight (with campsite), followed by Mountain View Hotel and Hotel Annapurna.

Continue on the switchback trail, sometimes beside the river, sometimes high above it. There are one or two landslide areas to negotiate within the woods before you come to a few simple tea-houses and an apple orchard. About 50mins after leaving Lata Marang pass Hotel Marsyangdi, a large timber building in an attractive setting among pine trees near the river. Impressive rock scenery rises ahead; great faces soar above the valley and are topped with pines. Then at last you emerge from the forest to a clearing and pass through a *kani* to enter the village of

KOTO (2600m, 8530ft, 3hrs), a two-part village of flat-roofed houses and lodges, paved streets and orchards, each part separated by a 10-minute walk. The first, eastern, part of the village has the Tibet Annapurna Hotel, Chhesang Tibetan Hotel and Tashi Hotel, plus a few simple houses and walled fields.

THE FORBIDDEN NAR VALLEY

To the north of Koto, on the other side of the river, stretches the narrow forbidden valley of the Nar Khola (Phu Khola on some maps), one of the three administrative districts of Manang, which has a population of only 850 people. The valley is guarded by steep cliffs and access is severely restricted. The Nar Khola and its several tributaries drain a large block of mountains spreading to the Tibetan border. The trail, which climbs through the valley, visits the villages of Nar and Phu before crossing into Tibet by way of the high Lugu La (6260m, 20,538ft). According to Harka Gurung the trail is a difficult one that involves 18 river crossings. Through Tilman's visit in 1950, we learn of other high passes that link the Nar valley with Mustang (via the Mustang La) and with Ghyaru in the upper Marsyangdi beyond Pisang. Tilman's *Nepal Himalaya* has an enticing account of this hidden region, while Windsor Chorlten's book *Cloud-Dwellers of the Himalayas* describes the lives of the people who live in the valley.

Just before reaching the second part of Koto (or Koto Qupar, as it is more properly known) cross a stream driving two water-mills. There are more apple orchards and attractive tradition-al houses with balconies overlooking the street. Hotels include the Super View, Manaslu Hotel and the Hotel Viewpoint, next to a police check-post and beside a *kani*. There's a gompa standing just above the village.

The final half-hour walk to Chame is mostly along a broad and easy trail led by drystone walls, at the end of which stands a large gateway topped by a corrugated roof. Through this you enter the administrative centre for Manang District.

CHAME (2670m, 8760ft, 3½hrs) is a bustling place with a number of trekkers' lodges, shops and even a bank (open daily except Saturday 10.00–14.00hrs, but 10.00–12.00hrs on Fridays). The largest township since Besisahar, it has a telephone office, police check-post, ACAP information office, **safe drinking-water station**, **health post** and a post office. Overlooking the town is Annapurna II, which looks splen-did with the early morning sun on its upper snowfields. Manaslu can be seen downvalley. A long mani wall stud-ded with prayer wheels leads the way into town. Lodges include the Trekkers Holiday Hotel, the Manaslu View and Tilicho Guesthouse. More hotels are found on the north side of the river, reached by a suspension bridge on the way out of town. The large New Tibet Hotel stands in its own gar-den, and there's also the Sangso Guesthouse and New Annapurna Hotel.

Chame to Pisang (4–4½hrs) ▶

Before leaving the main part of Chame the trail crosses to the north bank of the river, turns left away from a few lodges, and goes through a *kani*. There's a settlement of old stone houses and the Ranjana Hotel, and a few minutes later you go through yet another *kani* and continue among pinewoods. Between the trees lovely views are to be had across the valley to the soaring peaks and ice-crests of the Annapurna range, 5000m (16,000ft) above the river. In 30mins you arrive in

TALEKU (2720m, 8924ft), a village of stone-built houses, a small gompa, large prayer wheel in a white-painted housing

Around Chame there is plenty of vegetation, thanks to an overflow of monsoon rains, and the area remains alpine and wooded. But as you approach Pisang, and having finally emerged from the Marsyangdi's gorge, all this begins to change. The land-scape becomes more arid and the first evi-dence of wind, rather than water, erosion leaves its signature on the valley.

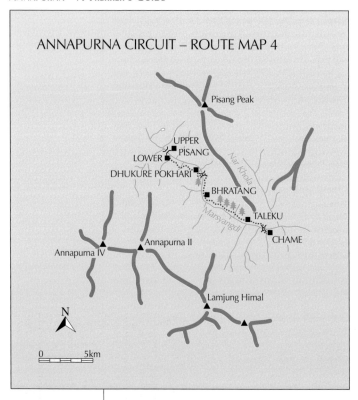

and an orchard of apple trees. There's a single lodge here, the Namaste Hotel.

Outside Teleku the trail forks. Take the right-hand option into more pinewoods, where the route now establishes a pattern for the day: alpine-like, the trail switchbacks up and down, often through pine forest above or beside the river. There is a landslide area to cross, but then the way continues as before – and always with rewarding views.

An hour from Teleku you enter a more open, level area of pinewoods and walled orchards of low-growing apple trees leading to the village of

BHRATANG (2850m, 9350ft, 1hr 30mins), a one-street Tibetan-style village with prayer flags flapping in the breeze and a long mani wall at its entrance. Accommodation is in the Raju and Maya hotels. The original village was located on the west side of the river. In 1973 Harka Gurung came through and described a camp of 27 armed Khampas [Tibetan refugees] who managed to grow vegetables 'even in this shady depth', and who commanded a bridge over the Marsyangdi, built Bhutanese-style with a timber roof. But two years later the Khampas were resettled, and Bhratang was rebuilt on the east bank to serve trekkers using a new path that was blasted with dynamite in the walls of the gorge ahead.

Remain on the east side of the river and 15mins beyond Bhratang the trail cuts through the steep rock face that walls a section of the gorge like a huge breaking wave. Half an hour beyond this you will come to a suspension bridge decorated with tattered prayer flags. Overlooking the valley now is the vast, impressive slab face of the Paungda Danda, a vast sheet of curving rock scraped clean of vegetation and towering more than 1500m (5000ft) above the Marsyangdi.

Above Bhratang the trail has been cut through a gorge

Cross the bridge at 3075m (10,088ft) and climb a series of steep zig-zags into forest. It's a wearisome stretch, but the shade of the pine and fir trees will be welcome on a warm day. For some time the forest trail leads on, passing a rather basic tea-house on the way, and about 3hrs from Chame you emerge to a view overlooking the charming, flat-bottomed Manang valley, with a group of lodges and a bakery at

DHUKURE POKHARI (3185m, 10,449ft), which is named after the small lake in the valley ahead. Chortens and a mani wall stand beside the trail that is flanked by Hotel Adlom, the Buddha Guesthouse & Bakery, and the Marsyangdi Guesthouse.

Two paths descend from Dhukure Pokhari into the valley ahead. Take the left-hand option (the alternative passes to the right of the lake), sloping down at first among pine trees, then passing well to the left of the little lake and heading across more open country where the valley is broad and flat, and dotted with stunted pines and low-growing juniper. Pisang Peak rises to the north.

Lodge children at Pisang enjoy the morning sunlight

It is obvious that this is a region denied much of the benefit of monsoon rains. Rain clouds from the south are deflected by the Annapurna Himal, and the valley makes a

fair imitation of parts of Tibet. The Marsyangdi continues to flow through, but it is not the full-bodied river seen lower down, for here it's a modest mountain stream writhing through a twist of carved brown soil.

Soon the dun-coloured houses of Upper Pisang can be seen like swallows' nests on the hillside ahead, and 30mins from Dhujure Pokhari the trail forks. If it is your intention to visit Upper Pisang, you could take the right-hand trail, which crosses the Marsyangdi on a wooden cantilever bridge then heads up the slope on the far side.

The normal route to Lower Pisang (from which the upper village can also be reached) continues ahead and soon crosses a tributary stream, then climbs a slope to a couple of tea-houses. A few minutes later the Peace Guesthouse is seen on the left, and shortly after this you pass alongside a *mani* wall which brings you into

PISANG (3200m, 10,499ft, 4hrs). Once a spartan village in a barren land, Pisang has grown into a busy place of lodges, campsites, basic shops, a post office and a **safe drinking-water station**. The first lodge past the *mani* wall is the simple but friendly Hotel Karma Beautiful, followed by Hotel Maya, the large New Tibetan Guesthouse, Hotel Utse, the Kamala Hotel, Hotel Pisang Peak and Hotel Star. On the way through the village a *kani* bears an ACAP plea: 'Step gently, nature is so fragile, please be sensitive, culture is vulnerable.' In the heart of Pisang there's a long *mani* wall with dozens of inset prayer wheels. At the western end of the village water is diverted through wooden conduits to power two small mills.

From Lower Pisang the view to the northwest shows snow-capped Chulu East, one of several so-called Trekking Peaks in the valley (see Appendix B), while another of these, the much-climbed 6092m (19,987ft) Pisang Peak, rises above and behind the upper village, from where the view is severely foreshortened and the graceful pyramid aspect, seen from Humde, is lost.

To visit the upper, original, village of Pisang cross the Marsyangdi by one of two bridges (one a suspension bridge, the other a wooden cantilever construction) accessed from the western end of the village. A clear path then winds uphill between fields and in about 20mins brings you into

ANNAPURNA II

As its name suggests Annapurna II (7039m, 26,046ft) is the second highest, but the most easterly, of the four Annapurnas. Seen from the Manang valley, it appears as a huge wall of rock and ice flanked by buttresses and topped by an extensive ridge system that rises to an elegant peak before stretching north-west for more than 3km to Annapurna IV. In 1960 a British–Indian–Nepalese Services' Expedition, led by Jimmy Roberts, established its base camp below the North Face of Annapurna IV, and from there found a successful route to the summit of Annapurna II. One of the expedition members later described the climb as a long snow slog, but intimidating on account of its length. The final section, climbed by Chris Bonington, Dick Grant and the Sherpa Ang Nyima on 17 May, involved a lengthy high-altitude traverse from a shoulder of Annapurna IV along the narrow connecting ridge, then up the summit pyramid where a 45–50° rock rib gave some serious climbing, but which brought them at last onto the snow crown in the late afternoon.

The North Face of Annapurna II was climbed in 1973 by a Japanese expedition, while a route up the South Face and Spur was made by an Australian team 10 years later.

Annapurna II dominates the view from Upper Pisang

UPPER PISANG (3300m, 10,827ft). This is an amazing place with a medieval air, spoilt only by the sagging power lines that loop across the village. Practically every building has its wand of prayer flags and stunning views from its rooftop. There's a long *mani* wall, a large prayer wheel and two *gompas*. When the harvest has been completed in the autumn, you may see locals threshing barley with long-handled flails made of wood and leather. There's much less accommodation to be had here than in the lower village, just the Manang Marsyangdi, Shanti and Annapurna hotels. But views are magnificent, especially across the valley where Annapurna II dominates. Downvalley, beyond the big wall of the Paungda Danda, snow mountains of the Manaslu Himal are seen for the last time, while to the west the upper valley is blocked by Tilicho Peak.

Pisang to Manang (3½–4hrs) ▶

The main villages of the region are Ngawal, Braga and Manang, and although they are inhabited by people of Tibetan stock, their home tongue is neither Tibetan nor Nepali, but a language also known as Nyeshang. Locals are often seen riding ponies with a rapid and seemingly uncomfortable gait; they keep yaks and yak cross-breeds, goats and sometimes sheep. Because of the altitude and the climate here, farmers manage to grow only a modest crop of barley, buckwheat or potatoes in their small fields.

Note: There are two options for the trek from Pisang to Manang, both of which are interesting and visually delightful. The first is the main valley route via Humde described below. The second is a longer, more strenuous high route which begins in Upper Pisang, makes a long contour of the northern hillside to visit two medieval villages, and eventually rejoins the main route at Mungji. This high route option is described in the section which appears after the main route reaches Manang.

The following stage is the standard route, which provides a fairly undemanding walk. It leads through the broadening valley with no overly demanding height gain, while the mountains of the Annapurna Himal grow in stature as a great wall to the south.

From the western end of the village leave Pisang by a wooden bridge over a tributary stream near a *chorten* and go up a short slope to a *mani* wall, more *chortens* and coloured prayer flags, and a lovely view left to Annapurna II. The path is broad and easy, passing a water-driven prayer wheel and winding gently uphill among pine trees. In 50mins you top a rise to gain the **NGORO DANDA** (3440m, 11,286ft), a viewpoint on a steep wooded spur descending from Annapurna II. From this viewpoint, marked by prayer flags and a simple teahouse selling souvenirs, the fascinating, broad upper Manang

Pisang is the first village of Nyeshang (or Nyesyang), the wide upper valley region which began just below Dhukhure Pokhari and which extends north-west to Manang and Khangsar. This is a much drier and more arid part of the valley than that of Gyasumdo.

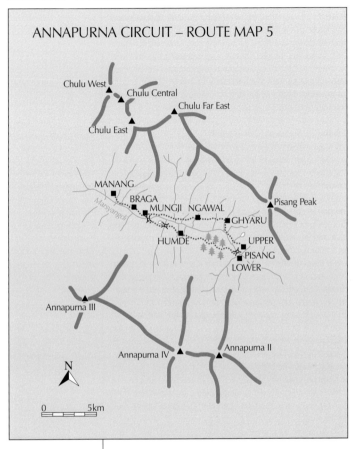

ANNAPURNA CIRCUIT – ROUTE MAP 5

Chulu West
Chulu Central
Chulu Far East
Chulu East

MANANG
BRAGA
Marsyangdi
MUNGJI NGAWAL
GHYARU
Pisang Peak
HUMDE
UPPER
PISANG
LOWER

Annapurna III

N

0   5km

Annapurna IV   Annapurna II

valley is spread out before you in all its wind-eroded glory – a strangely sculpted semi-desert with Tilicho Peak (7134m, 23,406ft) rising nearly 20km (12 miles) away as part of a great enclosing wall.

Descend from the spur into the flat bed of the valley through more pinewoods, then continue out of the woods to open country and uninterrupted views in all directions. About 50mins from the Ngoro Danda you come to

HUMDE (3400m, 11,155ft, 1hr 20mins). Also known as Ongre or Hongde, this is an important village on account of its STOL airstrip and police check-post. It has one broad main street with a handsome *chorten* and a long *mani* wall down the centre. There's a **safe drinking-water station** and a number of lodges, including: the Airport Bakery & Lodge, Maya Lodge, Hotel Buddha, Shanta Hotel, Hotel Gandaki, Jullu Peak Guesthouse, Tibet Guesthouse and the Snowland Guesthouse. The airstrip has scheduled flights to and from Pokhara (Tuesday & Saturday for tourists) and, occasionally, charters from Kathmandu, but is used mainly by the local Manangba who, contrary to appearances, have established a reputation for being sophisticated world-travellers who regularly make business trips to Asia's capital cities.

The police check-post is located at the western end of the village as you leave Humde. The trail is as wide as a jeep track and it passes wind-eroded crags before turning a corner to gain a tremendous view of Tilicho Peak once more. About 15mins later cross a tributary stream, and shortly after come to a small tea-house on the left and a shallow green lake on the right. Stretching behind the tea-house is the Sabje valley, an enticing place backed by an amphitheatre created by the curving ridges of Annapurnas III and IV. The large

After leaving Humde the trail passes this shallow lake by the entrance to the Sabje valley

building just inside this valley is the mountaineering school created for Nepalese climbers by the Yugoslav Mountaineering Federation in 1979.

While the long wall of peaks grows in stature along the southern flank of the valley, Chulu East and Chulu West (both Trekking Peaks over 6000m, 19,600ft) hog the northern slopes, and Tilicho Peak draws you on. It's a splendid walk, and so easy underfoot that you can forget the trail and simply amble along enjoying the views. About 30mins beyond the shallow green lake, the Marsyangdi is crossed for the last time on a wooden bridge below the small village of

MUNGJI (3482m, 11,424ft, 2½hrs), a settlement of low stone houses, a tea-house, the Trekkers Bakery and a single lodge, the Mount View Restaurant, set in a yak pasture below dun-coloured, wind-eroded sandstone crags. It is here that the alternative high trail from Upper Pisang rejoins the main route for the final walk to Manang.

Now on the north bank of the Marsyangdi clear and unobstructed views across the valley make the last hour of this section even more scenically inspiring than the previous 2hrs or so. The trail takes an undulating course above the river, and shortly before reaching Braga there's another wooden bridge

ANNAPURNAS III AND IV

Flanking the south-west side of the valley on the trek beyond Humde, Annapurnas III and IV are linked by an extensive ridge that was first reached by Tilman's party in 1950 on their attempt to climb Annapurna IV (7525m, 24,688ft). This is the easternmost summit of the two, a near neighbour to the more difficult and higher Annapurna II, and it received its first ascent from a German expedition led by Heinz Steinmetz just five years after Tilman was beaten back. Their route used a combination of the North Face and Northwest Ridge. Annapurna III (7555m, 24,787ft), on the other hand, was not climbed until 1961, when Mohan Kohli's Indian team managed to put three men on top by way of the Northeast Face. The mountain is guarded by monstrous icefalls, while its upper reaches bristle with gendarmes or overhang with deadly cornices. From its summit a long ridge system extends southwards. This is seen in all its glory from the Sanctuary, a beautiful ice-fluted crest that projects over the peak of Gandharba Chuli (also known as Gabelhorn) and up to Machhapuchhare.

spanning the Marsyangdi. Across it a trail heads off to Milarepa's Cave at about 4310m (14,140ft), nearly 3hrs walk away. It is said that Milarepa, an eccentric Tibetan poet who possessed magical powers, spent much of his life during the 11th century meditating in various Himalayan caves, where he lived on stinging nettles that turned his body green. A few minutes later pass through a *kani* below the fascinating village of

Below Mungji this bridge takes the trail across the Marsyangdi for the last time

BRAGA (3500m, 11,483ft, 3hrs). Also known as Bhraka, Bryaga or even Drakar, the main village comprises a number of Tibetan-style houses built in tiers against a steep, eroded cliff-face whose upper crags form turrets, pinnacles and organ pipes of rock above a 500-year-old white-painted *gompa*. A string of electricity cables sagging between crazy-angled poles makes an incongruous addition to the scene. Below the village, along the edge of a meadow, stand the New Yak Hotel, a post office, Hotel Buddha, Braka Bakery and the Himalayan Lodge, which also has a campsite and money-changing facilities. The *gompa* is one of the most distinguished on the Annapurna Circuit and is well worth visiting. In his book *Himalayan Pilgrimage*, David Snellgrove describes the *gompa* in some detail (he refers to the village as Drakar), and it's interesting to discover that what he saw in 1956 remains largely the same today.

The way continues through a *kani* and beside *mani* walls along the floor of the valley. It breaks across some fields, and goes over a stream by a watermill and up a slope to pass through a white *kani* on a hillock guarding the entrance to

MANANG (3540m, 11,614ft), the main village of the upper valley. There are, of course, plenty of lodges here, among them the Manang Hotel, Mountain Lake, Yeti and Tilicho hotels, Hotel Himalayan Singi, Marsyangdi Lodge, Hotel Moonlight, North Pole, Gangapurna Hotel, Glacier Dome Lodge and Hotel Snowland. There's a *gompa* in the heart of the village, and going from the sublime to the bizarre, a 'cinema' next to Hotel Snowland showing the latest videos. Manang has an ACAP information centre, a post office, **safe drinking-water station** at the Gangapurna Hotel, a museum, kerosene depot, telephone office and an all-important **Himalayan Rescue Association health post** run by volunteer doctors. At 3pm each afternoon during the main trekking seasons, one of the volunteer doctors on duty gives a lecture on altitude sickness. There is no charge for this and attendance is highly recommended. None but the most experienced of high-mountain trekkers should miss it.

The Manangba who live here are more closely related to the people of Tibet than they are to the Nepalese of the Middle Hills; they have similar features, customs, manners and dress, and practise a form of Tibetan Buddhism. And even the countryside in these upper reaches of the Marsyangdi has a scenic affinity with that of Tibet to the north, as opposed to the lower

Manang, a crowd of sturdy stone houses at over 3500m

section of the valley with its lush vegetation. For two centuries the Manangba have enjoyed special trading privileges, a fact which Tilman noted in his 1950 visit when he commented upon their 'strikingly independent ways and their manners'. He also reported, rather laconically: 'We found no wireless sets in Manangbhot, but a man whom we attempted to photograph retorted by whipping out a camera himself.'

High Alternative Route – Upper Pisang to Mungji (4½hrs) ▶

From Upper Pisang's long *mani* wall, with its many inset prayer wheels, take the path heading left (north-west) out of the village to contour across an open slope. Be careful not to stray onto any of the paths that climb the hillside here, for they are heading for Pisang Peak Base Camp. The correct way goes through patches of pine and juniper, and passes above a small green tarn. It then slopes down into a basin of trees in which there's another long *mani* wall. Shortly after this the trail crosses a side-stream flowing from Pisang Peak and then divides. Take the upper path, which now climbs steeply in numerous zig-zags and, as it does, views are shown ahead to the curious eroded cliffs that threaten to block the Marsyangdi way below. It's a demanding ascent of about 350m (1148ft), but eventually you come onto a shelf of hillside at the village of

GHYARU (3673m, 12,051ft, 2hrs), an astonishing medieval collection of stone-built houses, the stones simply laid one on top of another in a sometimes rather ad-hoc fashion.

This is the high-route option on the way to Manang, a fairly strenuous option too, but the rewards are tremendous, with wonderful views to enjoy. Both Ghyaru and Ngawal are fascinating villages in their own right, and vistas from them – and from the path which links them – are quite stunning. Be warned, though, that the path heading up to Ghyaru is the steepest of the route so far and will surely tax all but the fittest of trekkers – a good test before tackling the Thorong La.

Mani wall and Annapurna II, near Upper Pisang

Typically, one house appears to stand upon the jutting roof of the house below. There's an interesting *gompa* (if you can find the keeper of the key), and prayer flags slap against upright poles from almost every rooftop, while views across the valley to the northern wall of the Annapurnas are again spectacular. For accommodation there's the Yakru Mountain View Resort and the Annapurna Lodge.

Just outside Ghyaru (the name means 'goat pasture') the continuing trail takes you past a water-driven prayer wheel and a number of *chortens*. At first leading between stony fields outlined with drystone walls, it then becomes a fine belvedere of a path offering superb views all the way – the bare fluted rocks and patched forests of Nyeshang below, big ice-peaks above.

Rounding a long jutting hillside spur you come into view of the next village set across a broad, shallow slope. Gangapurna, Tarke Kang (Glacier Dome), the Great Barrier and Tilicho Peak look magnificent upvalley. About 40mins or so from Ghyaru pass through another *kani* and enter

NGAWAL (3650m, 11,975ft, 3hrs), a larger village than its neighbour and with more opportunities to cultivate a basic agriculture in the surrounding fields. The lodges here may be rather more simple than those visited on the lower valley route, but the village's location makes it a good place in which to spend a night. Lodges are: the Shanti, Peaceful, Annapurna III and Hotel Maya. Ngawal has a new *gompa* dating from 1990.

Leave the village by cutting down into a shallow scoop on a clear trail that loses much height, then slants off to the right into the bed of the Marsyangdi's valley not far from the Humde airstrip. It's possible to cross the river to Humde and join the main trail to Manang from there. Otherwise, remain on the northern side of the river and continue along the path to round a band of cliffs, beyond which you eventually join the main trail by the small settlement of **MUNGJI** (3482m, 11,424ft 4½hrs). Manang is about an hour's walk upvalley from here.

TIME IN MANANG

Above Manang there are no more large villages; indeed, apart from Tengi, half an hour's walk upvalley, there are no permanent settlements, beyond a few lodges, until you reach Muktinath on the western side of the Thorong La. The Thorong La is almost 2000m (6500ft) higher than Manang and, having reached an altitude of 3540m (11,614ft), it is now important to allow time to acclimatise before proceeding further. One or two days at least should be set aside for acclimatisation, and Manang makes a good base for this. It also provides a last opportunity to hire a porter-guide for the crossing, if required – enquire at one of the lodges for a reliable man.

From Manang you gaze across the valley to a wonderful array of high mountains. First climbed by a German expedition in 1965, Gangapurna (7454m, 24,455ft) rises directly opposite the village, with a glacier cascading down its northern flanks. At the foot of the glacier lies an icy turquoise lake. Annapurna III is the peak to the south-east of Gangapurna, and beyond that a long ridge extends to Annapurna

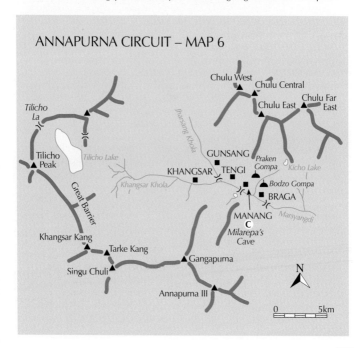

ANNAPURNA CIRCUIT – MAP 6

IV. West of Gangapurna is Tarke Kang (7193m, 23,599ft), formerly known as Glacier Dome, while Tilicho Peak (7134m, 23,406ft) stands well to the north-west of that at the far end of the Great Barrier, so named by Maurice Herzog in 1950. Below Tilicho Peak, but unseen from Manang, lies Tilicho Lake (Tilicho Tal), discovered by Herzog when he and his team were searching for Annapurna. On that occasion they had crossed the Tilicho La from Tukuche in the valley of the Kali Gandaki, and then he and Rébuffet descended to Manang, where they hoped to buy provisions. But Manang seemed then a very poor village with nothing to spare, and they returned empty-handed.

It seems strange, when Manang is now so obviously geared to trekkers, that in 1950 there was practically no spare food to be had at all there. Tilman had a similar experience to Herzog, although he at least managed to base himself in the village for some time. He found the Manangba to be inhospitable and reluctant to sell him food or to provide porters for his expedition, but deduced that their winter trading ventures abroad probably brought the villagers sufficiently lucrative rewards that money offered by the Europeans provided no real incentive for them to change their ways. Happily a very different experience will be had by today's trekkers in Manang.

For acclimatisation purposes there are several interesting sites and features worth visiting in the neighbourhood. The first is the very fine *gompa* 30mins downvalley at **BRAGA**. At least 500 years old, it is certainly the oldest monastery in the valley, in which there are numerous manuscripts, a large Buddha, rows of terracotta statues, butter lamps and *thankas*. In the upper building there's a collection of ancient knives, swords and home-made muskets. Although normally kept locked, the guardian has an uncanny sixth sense that lets him know when anyone wants to visit, and he appears from nowhere, keys jangling, to show you around.

Behind Braga, at an altitude of about 4600m (1509ft), is **KICHO LAKE**, also known as Ice Lake. A full day's acclimatisation hike is recommended here, with a good chance of sighting blue sheep (*bharal*) on the way. A sign in Braga indicates the start of the trail.

On a rocky ridge between Braga and Manang another *gompa* worth visiting is that of **BODZO** (Bhojo or Pocho), a red-walled building said to have been founded by Guru Rimpoche which contains some fine paintings. Better still, for acclimatisation purposes and atmosphere, the tiny **PRAKEN** (or Tsamkhang) *gompa* is reached in 2hrs by a steep trail directly above Manang. Set in a cave nearly 500m (1640ft) above the village, this is more like a hermitage than a traditional monastery. Views are simply stunning from here, and for a small fee the solitary lama will perform a *puja*, or blessing, to safeguard your crossing of the Thorong La.

Opposite Manang the small lake trapped below the icefall of the Gangapurna glacier makes a short but interesting excursion. **GANGAPURNA LAKE** is reached in 15–20mins, and there's a teahouse suitably located for refreshments. High above the lake the viewpoint of **PAPU CHONG** is reached by a 2–2½hr walk.

Also on the opposite side of the valley to Manang, **KHANGSAR** lies at an altitude of 3734m (12,251ft) on the route to Tilicho Lake, making it the highest permanently inhabited village in the Marsyangdi, and this may be visited by a walk of 2hrs or so. As simple accommodation may be had there, it serves as a more peaceful alternative to Manang. There are just two lodges, a *gompa* and glorious views through the valley of the Khangsar Khola to Tilicho Peak.

Gangapurna and its glacial lake

A difficult walk (not recommended for inexperienced trekkers) leads in about 5hrs from Khangsar to the **TILICHO BASE CAMP**, where there's a lodge set below a moraine bank at 4140m (13,583ft). If you plan to trek from here to **TILICHO LAKE** you will need tent and supplies, since there's no shelter to be had there. Allow at least 3½–4hrs from Tilicho Base Camp. Lying below the Great Barrier's glaciers at 4920m (16,142ft), the lake, not surprisingly, is often completely frozen – Herzog called it the Great Ice Lake. In October 1985, a group of trekkers from New Zealand was trapped nearby by heavy snowfall for over a week. Four Sherpas lost their lives in an avalanche when trying to force a way out. (See *People Within a Landscape* by Bert Willison and Shirley Bourke published by The Four Sherpa Trust/The Mountaineers, 1989.)

SECTION 2:
Manang to Muktinath

Distance:	27km (16½ miles)
Time:	3–4 days
Start altitude:	3540m (11,614ft)
High point:	Thorong La, 5416m (17,769ft)
Height gain:	1876m (6155ft)
Low point:	Muktinath (Ranipauwa), 3710m (12,172ft)
Height loss:	1706m (5597ft)

Above Manang the valley forks. The left branch is sliced by the Khangsar Khola which drains the Tilicho Lake region, while the right branch, angling a little west of north, leads to the Thorong La and is flanked by Chulu West, Central and East. This latter valley, the valley of the Jharsang (or Jhargang) Khola, is a narrow one with steeply plunging hillsides and plateau-like yak pastures (*kharkas*) on the true left bank of the river. As you journey deeper into the valley, the mountains tower overhead and protect much of the route from cold winds. With clear skies and no wind, the daytime temperature can be very pleasant, but it falls dramatically the moment the sun dips behind the mountains, and nights are often bitterly cold.

In order to acclimatise properly before tackling the Thorong La, it's advisable to take at least two days for the trek to Thorong Phedi, the base from which to set out for the pass. Staff at the HRA post in Manang advise three days: the first day's trek to end at Yak Kharka, the following day a very short stroll to Letdar, and on the third day continue to Phedi. That villagers from Manang think nothing of riding from their village to Muktinath in just one day is something else – what their horses think of it is not recorded. Since there are several fairly comfortable lodges in the Jharsang Khola's valley, and excellent views back to the Annapurnas, time here can be well spent, if taken slowly.

Crossing the Thorong La is the high point of the Annapurna Circuit, and it represents the single major difficulty to be faced. Trekkers who have not acclimatised sufficiently will either find the crossing a misery or an impossibility. In snowy conditions it becomes a very serious proposition; cold, high winds and the advanced altitude together ensure that it is not undertaken lightly. Although trekkers are known to have made the journey in unusually mild snowless conditions wearing shorts and trainers, no one should begin to contemplate setting out on the trek without adequate clothing and equipment to cope with extremes of cold. That goes for porters and other members of a trek crew too. Frostbitten toes and fingers, and even fatalities among ill-equipped trekkers and their porters, occur most years. The Thorong La is more than 600m (1900ft) higher than the summit of Mont Blanc, the highest mountain in the European Alps, and if you bear that in mind you'll get its crossing in perspective.

Manang to Yak Kharka (3hrs) ▶

An old *kani* signals the way out of Manang. From it the dusty trail heads upvalley, winding between terraced fields on the way to **TENGI** (3642m, 11,949ft), which is gained in just 30mins. The trail winds through the village, which has just a couple of basic lodges, and on the outskirts passes a long wall adorned with a row of worn prayer wheels and prayer flags.

The trail soon begins to curve north-westward into the valley of the Jharsang Khola. As it does, note the position and

Shortly before reaching Tengi you pass a new and attractive stupa, and on the approach you can just see the summit of Chulu East at the head of a narrow valley cutting into the mountains behind it. From the stupa, and from Tengi, there is a splendid view back down to Manang and across to Gangapurna's icefall.

ANNAPURNA CIRCUIT – Section 2

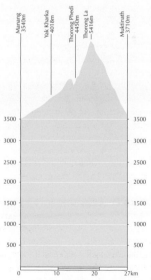

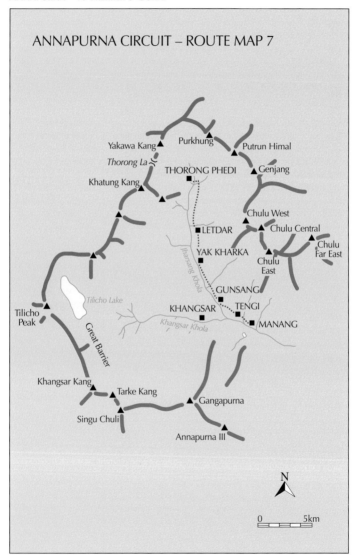

ANNAPURNA CIRCUIT – ROUTE MAP 7

The Tengi stupa, a short walk beyond Manang

shape of Tilicho Peak across to the west, for on the walk down to Jomosom from Muktinath the north side of this fine mountain will be in view. Climbing again you come to a wayside *chorten* from which there are more grand views downvalley. The route continues, and about 1¼hrs from Manang tops a rise marked by a solitary tea-house. A few minutes later come to the small settlement of

GUNSANG (3900m, 12,795ft, 1½hrs). There are two lodges here, Chulu West Hotel and the attractive Marsyangdi Hotel, which has a neat garden, carved stairway and incredible views. Just below the trail are the remains of a former settlement.

Having turned out of the main valley there are few steep ascents to contend with now, and height is gained without too much effort. Whilst the mountains ahead may lack the charisma of the Annapurna massif behind, the whole scene retains a wild kind of beauty, while the backward view is never less than magnificent. Herds of blue sheep (*bharal*) are sometimes observed on the hillsides. About 20mins after leaving Gunsang come to a small pool on the left of the trail, beside which stands the rather basic Julu East Lodge. A few paces beyond the lodge/tea-house, a stream comes down from a side-valley headed by the Chulu peaks. Continuing, in a little under 3hrs from Manang you should arrive at the scattered lodges of

YAK KHARKA (4018m, 13,182ft). As its name suggests, this is located on a yak pasture. The original lodge was an adapted *goth* (a herder's temporary shelter), but now there are several purpose-built lodges, the first being Yak Kharka Hotel. About 10mins further upvalley there's a group of three lodges: the large Gangapurna Lodge, Thorong Peak Hotel and Hotel Nyeshang. The Himalayan View Hotel stands on a rise about 15mins further along the trail. This has a wonderful unobstructed view of the Annapurna range to the south, and some of its rooms even have attached toilet and washing facilities.

Yak Kharka to Thorong Phedi (3hrs)

Beyond the Himalayan View Hotel the trail crosses a broad yak pasture, then descends into a gully to cross a side-stream on a wooden bridge. The climb out on the far side is short but steep, and it leads to the Snowland Hotel in a little under 30mins from Himalayan View. The Snowland offers the first chance of accommodation and refreshments in

LETDAR (4200m, 13,780ft), another lodge settlement on a yak pasture. The second lodge is reached by a short stroll along the trail. Hotel Churi Lattar houses a **safe drinking-water station**. Then comes Jimi Hotel and the very simple Chulu West Guesthouse. Although it is a somewhat austere place, Letdar enjoys a superb high-mountain view downvalley. The Trekking Peak of Chulu West rises above and behind the lodge after which it is named.

THE CHULU PEAKS

There are four Chulu peaks in the Manang Himal: Chulu West, Chulu Central, Chulu East and Chulu Far East. Each one is in excess of 6000m (19,685ft) and included on the list of open Trekking Peaks. Until fairly recently there was some confusion about their position in relation to one another, thanks to errors on the available maps. But cartography has improved, and most maps now give a reasonable interpretation. According to Bill O'Connor's *The Trekking Peaks of Nepal*, it would appear that Chulu West received its first ascent via the South Ridge at the hands of a Japanese expedition as early as 1952. This, and others in the group, has been climbed many times since and makes a popular ascent by a choice of routes. A base camp is usually set up in a high valley approached from Letdar. A German expedition claimed to have made the first ascent of Chulu East in 1955, but it is thought that their peak may in fact have been Chulu Far East. A British team climbed both East and Far East peaks in 1979. The Chulu massif is seen to advantage when looking back from the final approaches to the Thorong La.

From Letdar the trail winds upvalley at a comfortable gradient high above the river, but then climbs steeply for a short way. After this an easy traverse is followed until, about 40mins from Letdar, the trail forks. Formerly the route descended to the river and continued to Phedi on the west bank, but two areas of landslide and rockfall have now made this rather dangerous, and a recommended alternative route has been created by ACAP along the east flank of the valley.

Take the continuing, right-hand, path which rises steadily for another 20mins to gain a high point of about 4450m (14,598ft). This is marked by a *chautaara* (a porter's resting place) and a prayer flag, and beyond it the trail contours, then rises again to a seasonal tea-house in a remote setting about 10mins later (4500m, 14,764ft). Being the only opportunity for refreshment between Letdar and Phedi, it makes a good place to rest for a while. Ten minutes beyond the tea-house you reach the highest section of trail and gain a first view of the lodges at Thorong Phedi across the valley, a huddle of buildings on a barren slope. The zig-zag trail that climbs from Phedi towards the pass is also clearly seen.

Descend in long switchbacks to the river, which at this point is little more than a stream working through its broad and stony bed in an amphitheatre of soaring cliffs. This is the

Winter conditions in the Jharsang Khola valley near Yak Kharka

true *phedi*, which means 'foot of the hill', and is where trekkers used to camp before lodges were built a little way up the slope – some groups still choose to camp here. A simple footbridge takes you across the Jharsang Khola, then a 15min climb brings you to the lodges of

THORONG PHEDI (4450m, 14598ft, 3hrs). Here we have the New Phedi Lodge and the larger Thorong Base Camp Lodge which houses a **safe drinking-water station**. Accommodation can be at a premium during the main trekking season, especially when heavy snowfall delays departure for several days. Standards of lodging have improved greatly in recent years, but it's still a cold and somewhat bleak place, and if you've not acclimatised, it will seem especially so. Prices both for a bed and meals are much higher than at Manang and the early

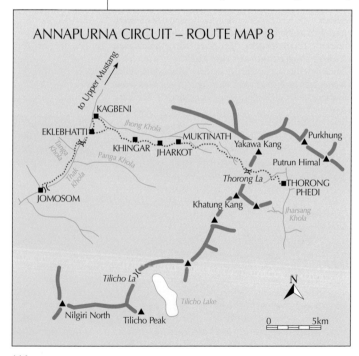

ANNAPURNA CIRCUIT – ROUTE MAP 8

stages of the trek, but this is understandable when you consider the effort involved in keeping the lodges supplied. However, the dining room of the Base Camp Lodge is light and reasonably warm, and the service is both efficient and friendly. Make sure you drink plenty of liquids and remain alert for signs of altitude sickness in yourself and those with you. Be completely honest with one another in regard to headaches, etc, and if you display any signs of AMS, do not attempt to go higher until they have disappeared. ▶

Thorong Phedi – Thorong La – Muktinath (Ranipauwa) (6–12hrs)

In settled conditions the crossing of the Thorong La is arduous only on account of the altitude, but it takes you into the very heart of the Himalaya, and exchanges one landscape for another. On the way to the pass, views of the Annapurnas become lost, although the Chulu peaks behind to the southeast look very fine. Under new snow the route can be difficult or even impossible if lying deep, but with or without snow it's likely to be cold, and the pass can be extremely windy. However, you should try to enjoy the crossing, for it's the lynchpin of the Circuit and it will no doubt be seen as a memorable event in years to come. For many trekkers this is likely to be the highest point they'll ever reach, so you should prepare yourself for it, be properly equipped, keep hydrated and don't be rushed. ▶

Generations of shepherds and cross-border traders have used this route for centuries, so the trail, though narrow in places, is clear in snowless conditions. The steepest part of the ascent is experienced at the very beginning as you set out from Phedi, where the trail climbs in long zig-zags up a slope of scree above the lodge buildings. In a little over an hour it brings you through a cleft, or minor pass, at the top of the slope, from which a good view of the Annapurnas can be had. Here stands a large new lodge, the Thorong High Camp (4760m, 15,617m), the highest in the Annapurna region. Tibetan snow cocks are sometimes seen on the nearby slopes, and their maniacal cackling echoes in the early morning.

The trail now veers leftward, traversing a steep slope of scree and shale to enter an inner wedge of a valley with a big moraine wall on the right. Cross a bridge over a stream, angle up and over the moraine, and continue to a simple tea-house

Note: There is more lodge accommodation about an hour's trek and some 300m (1000ft) above Phedi, but you should not consider this unless you're properly acclimatised and feeling both fit and healthy.

Inevitably there will be some at Phedi determined to set out at the unearthly hour of 3.00am – or even earlier. This is not only unnecessary but is potentially dangerous on account of the extreme cold generally experienced before dawn. Being exposed to such temperatures for hours at a time can easily lead to hypothermia, so make a point of setting out no earlier than an hour before sun-up. The staff at the lodge serve breakfasts about 1½–2hrs before sunrise, thereby enabling you to get away in good time and with food and warm drink to fortify you.

at about 5100m (16,732ft). This is reached 2–2½hrs after leaving Phedi. The tea-house may not be open when there's snow, while in good conditions it's sometimes possible to hire a pony here to carry you to the pass.

Beyond the tea-house the way winds among a seemingly endless series of moraine hillocks and crosses several false cols and tops. Views are constantly changing and being lost by the folds of the intervening country, with individual mountains reappearing once more from a different perspective.

The pass itself is seen nearly half an hour before you reach it, and is gained by a broad, gentle slope. Ahead the giant cairn and colourful streamers of wind-tattered prayer flags that mark the summit beckon you on. Depending upon trail conditions, individual fitness and degree of acclimatisation, the **THORONG LA** (5416m, 17,769ft) is reached in anything from 3 to 6hrs. A very simple tea-house built on the pass serves some of the most expensive tea in Nepal, and can literally be a life-saver. It's not always open, though, so do not depend on it.

Above to the south rises the glaciated peak of Khatung Kang (6484m, 21,273ft). To the north Yakawa Kang (or Thorungtse, 6482m, 21,266ft) sometimes shows itself to be a snow-free rock peak. Behind, the Chulu peaks make a splendid wall of ice and snow, but ahead to the west the countryside appears barren, a dun-coloured vertical desert dusted with snow. Far below lies the Kali Gandaki (otherwise known as the Thak Khola). Crossing the Thorong La you pass from one world to

Festooned with prayer flags, the Thorong La (5416m, 17,769ft) is the high point of the Annapurna Circuit

another, for although it is no true watershed the pass effectively separates two contrasting landscapes. On the descent to Muktinath those contrasts become increasingly evident. ▶

On the western side of the pass the long descent can be almost as tiring as the ascent, a knee-jarring effort that will take anything from 3 to 6hrs before reaching Muktinath. From the pass the trail veers right and then goes down the centre of the valley, winding to and fro along what appears to be a central spur of moraine. Caution is essential when the way is snow-covered – not simply to avoid losing the path, but because it can be extremely slippery and treacherous. It takes you down a number of moraine spurs and over open hillsides, barren, dusty and with a completely different landscape to that which you've been trekking through now drawing you on. As you lose height so Dhaulagiri begins to show itself downvalley to the south-west.

After passing a ruined yak-herder's hut, the descent continues steeply, then reaches the foot of the moraines, where you cross a stream and come to the simple lodge called Hotel Thorong La, at a place known as **CHABARBU** (c4290m, 14,075ft, *refreshments*), about 2hrs below the Thorong La. This is the only facility on the west side of the pass before you reach Muktinath.

The final descent of at least an hour from here takes you over rough pastures, descends into a narrow ravine to cross a stream – the infant Jhong Khola – and then climbs steeply out the other side. The trail then angles round the hillside and comes upon a wall surrounding the sacred shrines of **MUKTINATH** (3800m, 12,467ft), set in a grove of poplars and revered by both Hindu and Buddhist alike, for whom it is an important pilgrimage site. In a wall of one of the temples there are 108 water spouts shaped like animals' heads, while in a nearby rather run-down Tibetan-style *gompa* a flame fed by jets of natural gas flickers behind a curtain alongside more trickling water. This phenomenen is seen as the miracle of burning water. After Pashupatinath, the shrine at Muktinath is Nepal's most sacred Hindu site, and on the trek down to Pokhara you may well meet *sadhus* from far distant Indian cities who are making, or have made, their pilgrimage to this holy place, as well as lowland Nepali pilgrims making the journey on horseback, while the more affluent of devotees arrive by helicopter.

A Thorong tragedy

In snowy conditions, even the modest slopes above the pass can be dangerous. In November 1997 Jindro Martis, an experienced Czech mountaineer, led a trekking group around the Annapurna Circuit. Having reached the Thorong La, he began to ascend the slope above the pass in order to take a photograph of his group, when the slope avalanched around him. Despite the fact that he was quickly extracted from the debris, Martis had sustained serious injuries from which he died.

Autumn colours the valley near Muktinath

A few minutes beyond the walled shrine come to

RANIPAUWA (3710m, 12,172ft). More widely known to trekkers as Muktinath, Ranipauwa is the proper name for this village – Muktinath refers only to the pilgrim site, where there is no accommodation. Ranipauwa has many lodges, camp-sites, tea-houses and shops. There is a police check-post, an

THE NUN OF MUKTINATH

On his visit to Muktinath in 1956, David Snellgrove commented that there was no village at all, just a two-storeyed stone shelter for pilgrims being looked after by a 32-year-old nun. During the course of his stay, Snellgrove discovered that the nun's family came from nearby Purang, but that some years earlier her father had fallen in debt to a wealthy man from Tukuche. As he had been unable to pay off his debts, the whole family had been taken into enforced service. At the age of 20 the girl had run away to join a well-known lama. Although uneducated and with little religious knowledge, she proved adept at handling the lama's affairs, trading on his behalf and then, gradually, on her own account too until she had made sufficient money to pay off her father's creditor and so buy the family's free-dom. When Snellgrove met her she had been trading in Calcutta, and was then planning to visit Singapore – a far cry from this semi-arid valley on the northern side of the Himalayan Divide (see *Himalayan Pilgrimage* by David Snellgrove, published by Shambala Publications, 1989).

ACAP information centre with a **safe drinking-water station** adjacent, and a rest house for pilgrims nearby. The numerous lodges include Hotel Moonlight, the Mona Lisa and Hotel Nilgiri. There's the incongruously named Hotel Bob Marley, the Laligurans, Mount Kailash, Hotel Caravan, the North Pole, Royal Mustang, Hotel Nightingale and the Dream Home, which has a tremendous view of Dhaulagiri. Sunsets are often quite spectacular from the village; Dhaulagiri dominates the vista downvalley, while on the northern side of the arid Jhong Khola valley can be seen the buildings and ruined fortress of Dzong (Jhong), at one time the most important village in this part of the mountains and seat of the local ruler. The hillside above it has been savagely eroded by wind, while from the ridgetop it is possible to look down into the basin of Mustang.

SECTION 3:
Muktinath to Tatopani

Distance:	60km (37 miles)
Time:	3–4 days
Start altitude:	3710m (12,172ft)
Low point:	Tatopani, 1190m (3904ft)
Descent:	2520m (8268ft)

After the crossing of the Thorong La a rest day would no doubt be welcome. With a short foray into the surrounding countryside there's plenty of interest to fill your time, while for those a little short of energy there are splendid views to enjoy while seated upon a lodge rooftop with a cold drink before you, the life of the village going on below, and distant snow-capped peaks gleaming against a deep blue sky.

The continuing trek through the valley of the Jhong Khola and along the Kali Gandaki is full of beauty, as you are drawn into a landscape of contrasts with something to delight every step along the trail. The medieval fortress-like village of Jharkot, a few minutes below Muktinath, is just the first of several extraordinary villages on the way to Tatopani. There are apple and peach trees to contrast the otherwise barren hillsides, irrigation streams and shallow pools that belie the arid nature of the Jhong Khola, the modest stream that long ago carved a deep ravine whose walls of fluted rock are pitted with numerous small caves that can be seen from the trail.

Hillsides far off are yellow shading into ochre, vegetation-free and appearing for all the world like an extension of the Tibetan plateau, but down at the confluence of the Jhong Khola and Kali Gandaki, Kagbeni commands a fertile oasis.

Known in its upper reaches as the Thak Khola, the Kali Gandaki is a broad and stony valley, the river that snakes through having begun its life north of the border, well inside Tibet. In the valley bed black stones called *shaligrams* may be found. When broken open they reveal ammonites, or fossilised sea creatures that lived around 100 million years or so ago in a sea that was lost when the Indian tectonic plate collided with the main landmass of Asia. Now raised 4 vertical kilometres above sea level, these *shaligrams* are revered by Hindus, but samples are frequently offered for sale by Tibetan traders at the wayside.

Between Kagbeni and the river's sharp curve below Larjung, notoriously strong winds pummel the valley most days from mid-morning on. At its worst, trekking into this wind can be hard work, for it stirs up clouds of dust, lifts small stones, and can take your breath as you battle into it. Locals and trekkers alike often cover both mouth and nose with a scarf during the worst gales.

However, the three or four days needed to trek to Tatopani are comparatively easy stages, since they're mostly downhill at a moderate gradient. Landscape, vegetation and climate change dramatically, but the scenic quality of the route remains ever high, as does the standard of lodging. These are days to enjoy to the full.

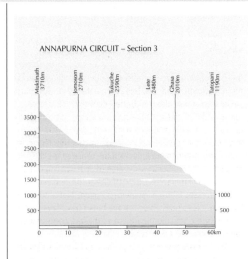

ANNAPURNA CIRCUIT – Section 3

Muktinath to Tukuche (6–7hrs)

A new *kani* has been erected over the trail by the Hotel Dream Home on the western edge of Muktinath (Ranipauwa), and passing through this you descend towards one of the loveliest sights of the whole Circuit, reaching in little more than 20mins the village of

JHARKOT (3550m, 11,647ft). This is an impressive medieval village built around the ruins of a mud-brick fortress on a spur of land extending from a grove of peach trees. At the far end of the village stands a *gompa* of the Sakya sect; there's also a picturesque *kani*, and a *mani* wall within the village, as well as a traditional medical centre, a post office and accommodation for trekkers in several lodges, including: the Hotel Himali, Peace Land, Sonam (which also has a camping ground), New Plaza Hotel and the Prakash Hotel.

Below Jharkot you will come to a major trail junction. Continue straight ahead on the upper path and follow this easily beside streams, drystone walls and trees, and then pass along the edge of

KHINGAR (3200m, 10,499ft, 50mins), a small settlement boasting four lodges: Hotel Sweet Dream, Hotel Yak, the Blue Sheep Valley Lodge and Hotel Nirvana. A few minutes out of Khingar you come to the Romeo & Juliet Lodge.

The trail winds along the hillside below Khingar, where in autumn, when the harvest has been gathered, the countryside appears more arid and barren than ever, except where clumps and lines of trees break the monotony of dusty fields. The trail is as wide as a jeep track and easy underfoot, and for a while it accompanies an irrigation channel. The Jhong Khola's gorge is off to the right, its strangely sculpted cliffs giving evidence of wind and water erosion that over untold millennia have created a landscape of unique proportions. Now the way crosses a broad, open scrub plain, high and gently sloping, while to north and west the hills and valleys are tan, featureless and remarkable for the contrasts they offer to the majestic snowpeaks downvalley.

Across this broad plain, about 1hr 40mins from Muktinath, the trail forks. There are no markers, but the junction comes

123

shortly after passing a stone shelter on the left. The main route to Eklebhatti and Jomosom continues ahead, while the right-hand option descends to Kagbeni – rejoining the main route later at Eklebhatti – and will be described first.

THE KAGBENI OPTION

Take the right-hand path, which soon descends to a small plateau, from which you look down onto Kagbeni, with its red-walled *gompa* and fertile terraced fields where the Jhong valley flows into that of the Thak Khola (Kali Gandaki). You can also see back to the Thorong La before making a final descent to the village. About 2hrs after leaving Muktinath you enter

KAGBENI (2800m, 9186ft), an oasis of a village on the trail leading to the long-forbidden Kingdom of Mustang. Despite the medieval, Tibetan nature of the village, the clash of cultures makes for an incongruous sight as flat rooftops display prayer flags, satellite dishes, solar panels and black plastic water storage tanks. The first building you come to is the aptly named Hotel Nilgiri View, which stands at a junction of walled paths on the southern edge of the village. In total Kagbeni has 15 lodges. Apart from the Nilgiri View, these are the Royal, New Asia Trekkers' Home, Shangrila, Mona Lisa, New Dhaulagiri, the Mustang, Mount Everest, Himalayan, Kali Gandaki Guesthouse, Snow Lion Hotel, the Red House, Annapurna, Muktinath View and Hotel Star. There are a few shops with an assortment of goods for sale. There's a so-called German bakery, a kerosene depot, a **health post**, post office, a police check-post, an ACAP information centre, and a **safe drinking-water station**.

The village itself consists of a maze of narrow alleys and doorways that open to stables and houses. There are three *mani* walls adorned with prayer wheels, the *gompa* known as Thupten Samphel Ling (100Rps entrance fee – excellent view from the rooftop), a *kani* and a large *chorten*. The Jhong Khola runs through the village, while at its northern edge by the police post you can enjoy a splendid view along the stony valley towards Upper Mustang. Unless you have a a special permit to enter the restricted northern part of Mustang District, this is as far as you are allowed to go.

The importance of Kagbeni is easy to understand, for it lies at a crossroads: east is the route to Muktinath, Thorong La and the Marsyangdi; west is a trail that climbs across the mountains to Dolpo; north is the way to Upper Mustang and Tibet (a once-important trade route); and south leads through the Kali Gandaki to lowland Nepal and India.

A permit to trek in Upper Mustang costs $700 for 10 days, plus $70 for each additional day, plus the standard ACAP Rps2000 fee and the services of a liaison

At the northern end of Kagbeni, a mani *wall directs your attention towards Upper Mustang*

officer, but the unique atmosphere, cultural history and landscape contribute to a very special experience

On the west side of the valley a trail can be seen that disappears into a side-valley. This is the route to the 'hidden land' of Inner Dolpo – another magical restricted region that lies beyond the mountains walling the Kali Gandaki's valley.

The same high permit fees and limitations set for trekking in Upper Mustang also apply here.

Leaving Kagbeni, the trail to Jomosom keeps to the eastern side of the valley on a good stony path that starts near Hotel Nilgiri View. Passing above more neat fields it takes just 30mins to join the main path at **EKLEBHATTI**.

Main route to Eklebhatti and Jomosom: Instead of branching off to Kagbeni, the main trail continues ahead and soon over-looks the flat, stony bed of the Thak Khola (Kali Gandaki). Kagbeni can also be spotted from this main trail. Climbing through a rock band suddenly Tilicho Peak, last seen from just above Manang, appears ahead, alongside Nilgiri North, both being outliers of the Annapurna massif, while on the oppo-site side of the valley Dhaulagiri towers over its neighbours, a graceful, chisel-headed peak (from this view) of 8000m – the world's seventh highest mountain. Between these two monstrous massifs the Kali Gandaki pours its waters through the deepest valley on earth.

The broad trail descends easily to the valley bed, and about 2½hrs from Muktinath reaches the lodge buildings of

EKLEBHATTI (2740m, 8990ft), where it is joined by the trail from Kagbeni. Eklebhatti means 'one hotel', but the significance of this name is lost, as it has grown into a small settlement of lodges and shops. As you pass through you'll see the New Hilton Hotel, Munal Guesthouse, Tibet Guesthouse, Old Kagbeni Lodge and the Holiday Inn.

Ten minutes beyond Eklebhatti you come to a long suspension bridge spanning the river. The path forks here. The original trail to Jomosom follows the left-hand side of the valley bed, crossing and recrossing numerous rivulets on the way, while a new route has been created on the right bank which rewards with some tremendous views. Cross the bridge then angle down to the left on a path which drops into the valley bed. Nilgiri North looks stunning from here, as the full majestic sweep of the mountain can be seen from its gleaming 7061m (23,166ft) summit to its roots in the Kali Gandaki 4500m (14,770ft) below.

A path ripples along the right bank of the valley, but most trekkers, locals and pony trains cut across the bed of sand and

THE THAK KHOLA

In the upper reaches of the Kali Gandaki's valley, the river is known as the Thak Khola. Though its source is on the edge of the Tibetan plateau, for millions of years it has managed to keep pace with the cataclysmic forces that built, and continue to build, the Himalaya, forcing its way through the mountains as fast as they have risen. The Indian tectonic plate is estimated to move north at a rate of about 5 centimetres a year, while the mountains are growing annually by about a millimetre. So, while the mountains are still rising (albeit very slowly), the Kali Gandaki steadfastly pursues its southerly course, and where it flows between Dhaulagiri and Annapurna it is now an astonishing 5½ vertical kilometres (3 miles) below their summits, making it the world's deepest valley. Neither Dhaulagiri nor the Annapurna Himal, then, acts as a watershed, for the Kali Gandaki flows undeterred all the way through from north to south. Before the continental collision took place which gave birth to the Himalaya, about 25 million years ago, Tibet had consisted of fertile, well-watered plains. But being deprived of its rainfall by the rising mountain wall, it gradually turned into the high, cold desert it is today.

stones when the river allows. Inevitably there will be the braid-ings of side-streams to cross, either by wading or on stepping stones. If you prefer not to get your feet wet, stick to the path; otherwise join the crowd and enjoy the variety. Eventually you will be forced back onto the path to round a rocky spur before returning to the valley bed for the final approach to Jomosom, by which time Dhaulagiri will have reappeared once more.

After crossing the long suspension bridge over the Thak Khola, the route strays into the bed of the valley

JOMOSOM (2710m, 8891ft), reached in 4hrs from Muktinath and 2hrs from Kagbeni, is the main township of the valley and the administrative centre for Mustang District. Straddling the river, it's a busy place and the largest habitation on the Circuit since leaving Besisahar. It has plenty of lodges on both sides of the river, although most facilities are located on the right bank. There are shops, banks, administration buildings, a military post, police check-post where you should have your details entered in the leger, an ACAP information office, **hospital, safe drinking-water station**, post office, telephone facil-ities, airline offices and an airstrip. Daily scheduled flights link Jomosom with Pokhara, but aircraft land and take off from here only when weather conditions allow. Once the day's wind picks up, no flights are possible. At the far end of town a Mustang Eco Museum has an interesting exhibition with a video show depicting Mustang culture (open 9am–5pm Sunday to Friday – not holidays). The Thakalis who inhabit the Thak

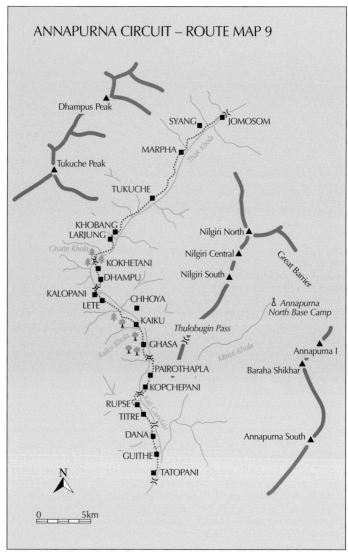

ANNAPURNA CIRCUIT – ROUTE MAP 9

Khola valley are noted hoteliers, and standards of accommodation are high. However, there are almost too many lodges in Jomosom to list them all here; as an example of how the Annapurna region may develop in the future – if demand is proven – the upmarket luxury Jomsom Mountain Resort has been built on a shelf of hillside between Jomosom and Syang. The prospectus boasts heated indoor swimming pool, sauna and jacuzzi, health spa and gymnasium, and a magnificent view of Nilgiri North from every room. (You can check it out on www.south-asia.com/soi.)

A dirt road now leads between Jomosom and Tukuche. Apparently a road has already been built from Tibet to Lo Manthang, the capital of Upper Mustang, and for some years a Chinese-built road has pushed into the lower reaches of the Kali Gandaki as far as Beni. Such piecemeal development is very worrying, even though these sections of road, as yet, do not connect. The unstable geography of the area may suggest they never will, but the mere presence of a bulldozed road threatens to destroy the very nature of the Annapurnas that so many trekkers come to experience.

Leaving Jomosom on the right bank of the river follow the road for about 10mins where it then forks. The right branch

THE NILGIRI PEAKS

Between Kagbeni and Jomosom the dominant mountain on show is Nilgiri North, a huge shapely peak of 7061m (23,166ft) first climbed by way of its North Face and Northwest Ridge in 1962 by Frenchman Lionel Terray, acting as climbing leader with an expedition from Holland. (Terray had been a member of the successful 1950 Annapurna team, and earlier in the year that he climbed Nilgiri North he made the first ascent of Jannu, or Kumbhakarna, in eastern Nepal.) There are three main Nilgiri peaks, the others being Nilgiri Central (6940m, 22,770ft) and Nilgiri South (6839m, 22,438ft), and all three are seen as a great snowy block across the valley from Tukuche, while their unseen east and south-east flanks form part of the amphitheatre wall that encloses the headwaters of the Miristi Khola in which Herzog's team made their base camp for the attack on Annapurna I. From this amphitheatre Herzog described them as 'the proud and inaccessible Nilgiris'. Being closely hemmed in by its neighbours, Nilgiri Central does not have the individual character of the other two, but the impressive South Face of Nilgiri South is clearly seen from the lower Kali Gandaki near Tatopani, and is one of its prime features.

goes to **SYANG** (2700m, 8858ft), a small village with an active *gompa* and a few facilities for trekkers, whose outskirts are fertile with small terraced fields and dotted with trees. The left fork strays down to the valley bed, works a way below the village and passes alongside an agricultural training centre supported by a Japanese aid project. It then rejoins the road on the approach to

MARPHA (2670m, 8760ft). Reached in about 1½hrs from Jomosom, Marpha is one of the most attractive villages in the Kali Gandaki, its narrow streets paved with flagstones which hide the local drainage system, and its handsome whitewashed buildings typical of the regional Thakali architecture. Some of the lodges alongside the main street have inner courtyards and upper sheltered restaurants; these offer additional interest with their views to the Nilgiri peaks opposite and down onto the street, where a constant procession of villagers, trekkers, Tibetan traders and pack animals wander by. Marpha has several shops, including one advertising boot repairs; there's also a recently enlarged *gompa* at the head of a flight of steps, a post office, a library and money changing facilities. At either end of the village you pass through a decorated Buddhist *kani*. The upmarket (and expensive) Hotel Trans Himalaya is the first of the lodges on the northern side of Marpha, but there are several others alongside the main street, among them, the Dhaulagiri Guesthouse, Hotel Shangrila, Baba's Lodge, the Paradise Guesthouse, Neeru Guesthouse, Hotel Sunflower and the Sun Rise Lodge. At the southern end of the village there's the small Hungry Eye Inn.

Leaving Marpha you come onto the dirt road once more and continue downvalley, passing the orchards and buildings of the Marpha Horticultural Research Station which dates from 1966 and was begun by the much-travelled Pasang Khambache Sherpa, David Snellgrove's companion on his journey through Nepal in 1956. It's possible to buy fresh fruit in season and locally made cider.

Beyond the orchards the way leads through more open country, with the Nilgiri peaks walling the east side of the valley. About 45mins out of Marpha the track rounds a bend to be rewarded with yet another wonderful view of Dhaulagiri, and 15mins or so later you enter

TUKUCHE (2590m, 8497ft). This is a large, two-part village divided by a 5min walk across an open flat meadow. The first, and smaller, part of Tukuche is paved, its street lined with a few simple shops, restaurants and lodges, then you cross the meadow to the main village where the majority of accommodation is located. There are at least 10 lodges flanking the stone-paved street, including Sunil Guesthouse, Himalayan Hotel Inn, Laxmi Lodge, the Tukuche, New Nilgiri, Lotus and Sherpa guesthouses, the Thak Khola Lodge and the High Plains Inn. Of the four *gompas* here, just one – the Kyupar Gompa of the Nyingmapa sect – is active with a lama and 12 monks. In October or November a festival is held at the monastery

Tukuche lodge, with the Nilgiri peaks as a backdrop

during which the monks perform a masked dance known as the 'Dhekep'. Tukuche boasts a post office and a **safe drinking-water station**; there's also a library and a well-known distillery which makes apple, peach, and apricot brandy, and a rough cider. Locally dried fruit and nuts are sold at village shops and in some of the lodges.

Tukuche to Tatopani (8–10hrs) ◀

About 45 minutes from Tukuche you come to a stand of willows with close views of Dhaulagiri, now towering almost overhead, and across the valley to the West Face of the Nilgiris, the 'blue mountains'. The few simple houses of **KHANTI** are strung in a line, then, set back in a trim garden on the right, the single-storey building of the Musk Deer Valley Resort. The trail goes through a brief avenue of willows, then alongside a row of prayer wheels to enter

South of Tukuche the usual route crosses the small valley of the Thapa Khola, where there are several rivulets to leap, then you have a choice of either following the main trail against the lower slopes of the right-hand mountains or (conditions willing) walking along the river bed itself. If you choose the latter, follow the trodden path which leads to easy crossings of numerous streams that feed into the Thak Khola. The main trail is a switchback offering good views at every turn.

KHOBANG (2560m, 8399ft), whose houses are located from a partially enclosed central tunnel which passes through the settlement. This tunnel system was apparently created in order to protect the houses from the strong winds that sweep through the valley, but the 'tunnel' is now much more open and consequently less remarkable than it used to be. As you wander through, half-opened doorways give onto the inner courtyards of houses, many of which have finely carved windows, similar to those at Tukuche. If, in the past, Tukuche was the economic centre of the valley, Khobang claims to be its cultural hub; there's a *gompa* set high above Khanti, a pagoda-style monastery in the heart of Khobang, and the Makila Khang Gompa, said to have been established at the end of the 15th century, located below the village near the river. Within the village there's a post office and public telephone, a small **health post** and currently just three places to stay: the Peaceful, Sunrise and Sunflower lodges. Should you choose to stay here or in Larjung (see below), there are a few side-trips worth making. i] **Naurikot**, an old village to the west; ii] **Guru Sangbo Cave** beyond Naurikot, where Guru Rimpoche is said to have meditated – 3½hrs; iii] **Sekung and Bhuthurcho Lakes**, about 1½hrs, on the way to the Dhaulagiri Icefall; and iv] the **Dhaulagiri Icefall** itself, a fairly tough 5hr hike (3hrs back) on the south side of the Gatte Khola valley with a climb of about 1200m (4000ft) to gain some stunning views – but there is potential danger from avalanche, so don't go too near.

Khobang and neighbouring Larjung are separated only by a modest stream and a few walled orchards. On leaving Khobang the trail forks by a row of prayer wheels. Take the left branch and moments later cross the stream to enter

LARJUNG (2550m, 8366ft). The first building houses a **safe drinking-water station**, then you wander through the village, which is very different to Khobang and has much more accommodation for trekkers. Among the hotels there's the Malayan (Himalayan?), Riverside, Mount Ice View, Larjung and Dhaulagiri lodges. Dhaulagiri itself towers overhead.

On the edge of the village ACAP authorities have placed a sign indicating a 'winter route' (ie: when the river level is low) along the bed of the Thak Khola which, apparently, saves about 30mins walking time. The alternative, standard trail is a switchback among pinewoods, with huge snow- and ice-plastered peaks rising ahead and across the valley. The river-bed trail keeps more or less to the right-hand edge of the valley below the pine slope. The valley is very wide at this point, but after about 10mins you rejoin the true path to rise over a bluff, then descend past a simple tea-house into a vast amphitheatre of mountains created by the mass of Dhaulagiri. This is the mouth of the Ghatte Khola tributary valley, which has to be crossed. ▶

As there are no proper bridges it is worth studying the vague trail that leads across. It is not always easy to find, although you may see other trekkers and porters working a route over. If they're not too deep and you don't mind wading the streams, okay. But if you aim to stay dry, you'll need to scout to and fro to find the most convenient places to cross the many meandering rivulets that snake through the stony bed. You'll possibly find that some have stepping stones or temporary log 'bridges' across them. Trekking poles can be a distinct advantage here.

DHAULAGIRI

The world's seventh highest mountain is a huge, graceful peak measuring 8167m (26,795ft). In Sanskrit Dhaulagiri means 'white mountain', and considering the quantity of snow and ice with which it is covered, it's well named. Admired by tens of thousands of trekkers who pass beneath it through the Kali Gandaki, and by even more who view its enormous South Face from Poon Hill above Ghorepani, Dhaulagiri is much more evident than the better-known Annapurna, which remains largely hidden. In 1950 Herzog's French expedition initially hoped to find a route to the summit of Dhaulagiri, but after a lengthy reconnaissance decided it was too dangerous and turned their attention to Annapurna instead. (Good descriptions of this reconnaissance are contained in Herzog's classic book, *Annapurna*.) There were six further attempts on Dhaulagiri in the following decade, all of which concentrated on the West Ridge, but it was not until 1960 that a Swiss expedition finally won through – albeit in controversial style, since they used a light aircraft to ferry food, equipment and even climbers to the Northeast Col at around 5700m (18,700ft)! (The Pilatus Porter eventually crashed on the mountain, without loss of life.) Included in the Swiss expedition was the highly experienced Austrian mountaineer Kurt Diemburger who, on 13 May, reached the summit without supplementary oxygen, in company with Peter Diener, Ernst Forrer, Albin Schelbert and the Sherpas Nyima Dorji and Nawang Dorji. Two other members of the team (Michel Vaucher and Hugo Weber) also reached the top 10 days later. (See Diemburger's *Summits & Secrets* for an account of this expedition.) Since 1960 a number of different routes have been made on the White Mountain, but there have been many lives lost too. In 1969, for example, seven members of a strong expedition from the USA attempting a route on the Southeast Ridge were killed by an avalanche from the notorious Dhaulagiri Icefall. Their memorial can be seen beside the west bank trail north of Kalopani.

Locate the main valley trail on the south side of the Ghatte Khola and climb once more among pines. Shortly after, you come to a large suspension bridge that crosses the Kali Gandaki at a narrowing of the valley where it begins to make a severe leftward curve. It is at this point that the valley becomes the world's deepest, for it cuts between Dhaulagiri and the Annapurnas, whose summits – although 35km apart – are around 5600m (18,400ft) above you. Again there's a choice of routes. That which continues along the west bank takes the broad curve of the river beneath the towering mass of Dhaulagiri, passes a memorial to a group of five Americans and two Sherpas who died when attempting to climb the mountain in 1969 (see Dhaulagiri box), and joins the other trail where it crosses back to the west bank on the outskirts of Kalopani.

The alternative trail, and the one which most trekkers take, crosses the suspension bridge (1½hrs from Tukuche) to the east bank, climbs round the right-hand edge of a pine-covered bluff (do not be tempted to take the narrow short-cut trail which breaks off to the right), and descends to the settlement of

KOKHETANI (2560m, 8399ft). This strip of a village with its wonderful view of Dhaulagiri has four lodges: Dhaulagiri Icefall, Earth Home Hotel, Glacier Fall Lodge and Shikhar Lodge.

Continuing southward the way climbs a slope on broad stone steps, and then slopes down to an ACAP sign (10mins from Kokhetani) showing another winter short-cut route along the stony bed of the valley. The main trail remains on the left bank and soon passes below a line of stone-built houses at **DHAM-PU** (2507m, 8225ft), between which you look across fields to the bulk of Nilgiri South. Behind the village a trail (you'll need local directions to find it) leads to Titi village and a lake, from which there are more wonderful views of Dhaulagiri. On the main trail of the Annapurna Circuit, however, a few minutes' walk from Dhampu brings you to the Friendship Lodge, which has an unobstructed view into Dhaulagiri's amphitheatre. The valley narrows, and on reaching another suspension bridge you cross to the right bank. From here you gain a remarkable view up to Annapurna I and the Nilgiri peaks. Bear left and soon enter

KALOPANI (2530m, 8301ft), where there are several lodges. During a storm in October 1973, a flash flood from a nearby stream buried four houses here, killing 12 people. On the slope leading to the village proper stands Hotel Mountain View, with a small garden restaurant. Over a rise the rest of

Where this bridge crosses the Kali Gandaki, the valley is 5km below the summit of Dhaulagiri

Ngashang, marks both a cultural and a geographical boundary. Alpine-style vegetation is now exchanged for sub-tropical species (the surrounding forests are known for their birdlife), and below Ghasa Tibetan Buddhism gives way to the Hindu faith. Here, though, Buddhism still survives, and there's a large *kani* and *gompa* of the Nyingma sect in upper Ghasa. A paved trail links the three sections of the village. In the first accommodation is to be had at the New Florida Guesthouse, the National Guesthouse (which has a rooftop restaurant) and the Dhaulagiri Lodge. The path then continues between walled fields, past *chortens* and a *mani* wall, with a fine waterfall seen off to the right, and brings you to the second village settlement, which has several typical Thakali houses, a campsite, the Kali Gandaki Guesthouse and a **safe drinking-water station**. After this you come to the third and lowest section, with the simple Mustang Guesthouse and, a few minutes beyond, the Eagle Nest Guesthouse, which stands in a neat garden and is run by the effervescent Sweety Scherchan.

◀ Between Ghasa and Dana the Kali Gandaki flows through its gorge where landslides sometimes force the route to abandon one side of the valley in exchange for the other, so the following description may not always be valid.

A few minutes below Ghasa the trail crosses a suspension bridge to the left bank, and then switchbacks high above the river, where occasionally the path is a little exposed and some care may be needed should pack animals be approaching. About 50mins from lower Ghasa come to

PAIROTHAPLA (1890m, 6201ft), a small two-part settlement with simple tea-houses and two lodges, the Bimala (in the first section) and Hotel Sunflower in the second. The name is a derivation of Pahiro Tabla: 'the landslide place' – an apt name in this geologically turbulent area.

You then make a long, steep and rough descent of a landslide area to

KOPCHEPANI, about 30mins from Pairothapla, where there are some rather basic-looking lodges, albeit with gardens of marigolds and lemon trees. Among the lodges you'll find the

Leaving Ghasa and the high country behind, the continuing descent leads to a more tropical region where the vegetation is somewhat rampant and colourful, and the air much warmer. Village houses are no longer the flat-roofed, Tibetan-style buildings of the upper valley, but dwellings with sloping roofs that signify a rainfall area. Monkeys may be seen in the forests and there's more evidence of birdlife.

THE CONTINUING TRAIL – THE RIGHT BANK OR LEFT?

During research for this edition, the route beyond Kopchepani crossed once more to the right bank, but this may not always be the case. Sometimes a major landslide will put that section of trail out of action, which then forces the route along the left (east) side of the valley. Whichever may be the current route, care is needed where the trail is unstable – on the left bank path there's a memorial to a trekker who tragically fell to her death here in 1994. The last time the right bank route was out of action, a narrow trail climbed steeply out of Kopchepani and, at the top of the initial rise, levelled out to pass a few houses before making the descent towards Dana. From the high point a good balcony view showed the valley ahead and, over to the west bank, to the cascades of Rupse Chhahara with the small village of Rupse below. About an hour from Kopchepani the trail then passed through **GARPUR** before crossing the Kali Gandaki to **DANA**.

Milijuli Hotel, followed by a 10min descent to Hotel Blue Sky, then Annapurna Lodge and the Yak Lodge.

Below Kopchepani cross the long suspension bridge (at 1620m, 5315ft) to the right bank, where a tea-house has been set up, and about 3mins later come to the New World Deep Restaurant & Lodge. The trail then works along the hillside before descending by the splendid cascades of Rupse Chhahara (meaning 'beautiful waterfall') to a wooden bridge and the Waterfall Lodge (1hr 45mins from lower Ghasa). A small water-mill stands beside the stream draining from the waterfall. Over the bridge come to the village of

RUPSE (1560m, 5118ft). The first building is the Lekali Lodge, then there's the Rock Land Guesthouse, Rupse Lodge and several village houses in a lush setting, with lemon trees, oranges, bananas and fields of maize terraced on the steep hillside. Seen in warm, post-monsoon sunshine, Rupse seems a calm and untroubled place, but in the summer monsoon of 2000 a landslide nearby destroyed a bridge and several water-mills, and threatened the buildings below the waterfall.

The valley has begun to open out now; it's less oppressive and with a much broader prospect to enjoy. Ten minutes beyond Rupse you pass through the long and productive settlement of **TITRE**, which has an attractive stream running through it. There are two simple tea-houses, but no accommodation, and as you continue towards Dana the trail edges between rice paddies – the first on this side of the Annapurna Circuit. Then, after passing a suspension bridge on the Kali Gandaki (used by the east bank alternative trail), you enter the first part of

DANA (1400m, 4593ft, 2½hrs from Ghasa). This large, three-section village was clearly once an important centre of trade, for some impressive three-storeyed merchants' houses with ornately carved windows and balconies line the main street. For a time Dana was a customs post charged with collecting taxes from the trans-Himalayan salt trade and, like Tukuche, prospered from its situation. Nowadays it offers trekkers a variety of goods in its few shops. It also has several lodges, the first group of which are the Riverside Lodge, New Annapurna Lodge and Mountain Guesthouse. You then cross the wide bed of the Ghatta Khola and obtain a great view of Annapurna South before coming to the central part of the village. There's the Annapurna Riverside Guesthouse, with a small pharmacy nearby. A few minutes later, in Dana's third settlement, which consists of a few thatched houses as well as others roofed with stone or slate, you come to the Dana Guesthouse and Kabin Guesthouse, with more views of Annapurna South from its garden restaurant.

Nilgiri South, from Tatopani

Out of the village cross the Bhalu Khola on a suspension bridge, negotiate a small landslide and, passing through a small settlement, in about 35mins come to **GUITHE**, which has just two tea-houses. The trail continues along the right bank, rising and falling against the steep mountainside. Once more the valley closes in, but looking back there are splendid views to Nilgiri South and the Annapurna range, and about 1½hrs after leaving Dana you arrive in

TATOPANI (1190m, 3904ft), a busy, popular village with plenty of lodge accommodation and a street lined with an assortment of shops. This makes a good place to rest for a day or two, to soak in the famous hot springs, to refuel with some of the best food of the trail (there are garden restaurants with extensive menus), and generally to take things easy before setting out on the long climb to Ghorepani or the shorter route to Pokhara via Beni. Tatopani has a post office, a telephone facility, a **health post**, bank, official money-changer and a police check-post at the southern end of the main street. Among the lodges, there's the Kamala, Namaste Lodge, Tiptop Hotel, Hotel Himalaya, the Dhaulagiri Lodge (with en-suite bungalow accommodation in a colourful garden), the Pun Hotel, Evergreen Lodge and the Trekker's Lodge with its own garden and access to the hot springs. Tatopani means 'hot water', and that is what you find when you go down to the riverside. There are two pools of steaming water in which to relax, but they're not for bathing or doing your laundry in – keep the water free of soap please.

OPTIONS FOR MOVING ON

Having reached Tatopani, the Annapurna Circuit is nearing completion, and it's necessary to study the options for moving on. Three main alternatives are now available and are described below. You can

- take a 5–6hr walk along the Kali Gandaki to Beni, from where transport will deliver you without effort to Pokhara (Section 4a)

- make the long traditional climb to Ghorepani in order to enjoy sunrise from Poon Hill, then descend steeply to Birethanti, continue to Naya Pul and catch a bus or taxi to Pokhara from there (Section 4b), or

- (for those with sufficient time and energy) climb to Ghorepani and then cut away from the standard Circuit trek to visit the Annapurna Sanctuary (Section 4c).

SECTION 4A:
Tatopani to Pokhara via Beni

Distance:	21km (13 miles) to Beni + 86km (53 miles) Beni to Pokhara
Time:	2 days
Start altitude:	1190m (3904ft)
Low point:	Beni, 830m (2723ft)
Height loss:	360m (1181ft)
Transport:	Bus or taxi (Beni to Pokhara)

Before the Pokhara–Baglung–Beni road was built, it would take at least four days to trek all the way out. The road has changed all that; the trek is contracting, and it's now feasible to reach Pokhara in two easy stages. Although this is the shortest and quickest option, avoiding the long climb over the Ghorepani ridge, it is still a fairly serious trek, for there are numerous landslides to negotiate, as well as one or two quite dramatic and exposed sections of trail. In the spring pre-monsoon season it can be an uncomfortably warm trek, in which case you're advised to make an early start. Thanks to the provision of many lodges, albeit some that are pretty basic, it would make a comfortable 1½ day walk, leaving time for a bus ride to Pokhara on the second day.

Tatopani to Beni (5–6hrs)
The trail out of Tatopani climbs a stone stairway, then descends a little, and in 25mins leads to a long suspension bridge which takes you over to the left bank of the Kali Gandaki. As you cross, pause to enjoy a classic view of the magnificent South Face of Nilgiri South upvalley. Moments later you enter a small village named after the tributary which drains the Ghorepani ridge This is

GHAR KHOLA (1175m, 3855ft, 35mins). The village straddles the tributary, with another bridge linking the two sections. On the south side there's a small shop and the Meet You Hotel.

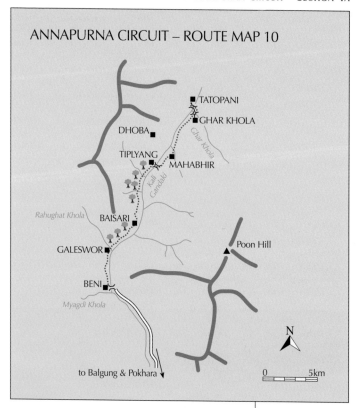

ANNAPURNA CIRCUIT – ROUTE MAP 10

TATOPANI

GHAR KHOLA

DHOBA

Ghar Khola

TIPLYANG

MAHABHIR

Kali Gandaki

Rahughat Khola

BAISARI

GALESWOR

Poon Hill

BENI

Myagdi Khola

to Balgung & Pokhara

N

0   5km

The trail forks by the lodge. The Ghorepani path branches left, but the route to Beni continues ahead, now turning a spur with the Kali Gandaki swirling below, from which there's another fine view back to Nilgiri South. The trail takes you past a school, and a little after this comes to some more lodges exploiting hot springs down by the river: the Hema Hot Spring Lodge and Nilgiri View Hotel.

Heading south the way now climbs to a steep, exposed section of trail high above the river from which you can see the village of Dhoba, once noted for the quality of its tobacco, on the west side of the valley. Then you descend a stone

ANNAPURNA CIRCUIT – Section 4a

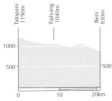

stairway to a solitary tea-house before climbing steeply once more. By now the valley has narrowed to another gorge and there are plenty of signs of landslide. One is crossed by a series of notches cut in a rock slab; there are vertiginous cliffs and a man-made galleried section of path with steps that lead down to **MAHABHIR** and its tea-houses, reached about 2hrs from Tatopani. Mahabhir means 'honey cliff', and according to Harka Gurung, local Magar honey gatherers used to lower themselves by rope down the nearby overhanging cliffs, where they would find honeycombs to rob.

Beyond Mahabhir the way continues between rice paddies until you cross to the right (west) bank of the Kali Gandaki on a suspension bridge at

Out of Tatopani the trail descends to a suspension bridge, with Nilgiri South in the background

TIPLYANG (1040m, 3412ft, 2½hrs). The village has several rather simple lodges on the west bank: Ama Lodge, Hill View, Mustang Restaurant & Lodge, Sherchan Lodge and Star Lodge. There are also two or three tea-houses.

Now between cornfields and forest, the path then works its way across the steep cliffs along another galleried section that brings you to the Beg Khola tributary, which is crossed by a suspension bridge to a group of tea-houses. The next stretch of 1½hrs or so consists of more landslides and forests before arriving at

BAISARI (960m, 3150ft, 4hrs), a small settlement of tea-houses and lodges: the Namaste, Annapurna, Lete and Riverside guesthouses.

Between Baisari and Galeswor the trail crosses more landslide areas, but a little over an hour later you cross the Rahughat Khola on the penultimate suspension bridge of the trek, and on its south side enter

GALESWOR (1170m, 3839ft, 5hrs), also known as Rahughat, an attractive village with good views. The first lodge by the bridge is Hotel Riverside, with the fancy Paradise Guesthouse nearby. Galeswor has a post office, telephone facilities and a Hindu temple dedicated to Shiva, the site of an annual fair which usually takes place in November or early December.

Another hour's walking along the west bank of the river should be sufficient to reach

BENI (830m, 2723ft) at the confluence of the Kali Gandaki and Myagdi Khola, the river that drains the west side of Dhaulagiri through a precipitous gorge. This busy township has plenty of shops and tea-houses as befits a roadhead bazaar. It also has a **hospital**, pharmacies, a bank, telephone facilities and a police station. There are at least three reasonable lodges: the Namaste, where you enter Beni near the Kali Gandaki, then there's Hotel Yeti, which is rather upmarket; and Hotel Dolphin, located near the centre of town by the bank. Buses and taxis bound for Pokhara (in 4–4½hrs) leave from the east side of the Kali Gandaki, which is gained by the trek's final suspension bridge.

SECTION 4B:
Tatopani to Pokhara via Ghorepani

Distance:	28km (17 miles) to Naya Pul + 42km (26 miles) Naya Pul to Pokhara
Time:	2–4 days
Start altitude:	1190m (3904ft)
High point:	Ghorepani Deurali, 2750m (9022ft)
Height gain:	1560m (5118ft)
Low point:	Birethanti, 1025m (3363ft)
Height loss:	1725m (5569ft)
Transport:	Bus or taxi (Naya Pul to Pokhara)

The way from Tatopani to Birethanti follows the traditional, continuing route of the Annapurna Circuit trek. But the route beyond Birethanti has contracted with the building of the Pokhara–Balgung–Beni road. Before that was made, one would continue to Lumle (noted as the wettest place in Nepal), then trek along a ridge to Naudanda and Sarangkot before descending to the lake at Pokhara – a 6–7hr trek. Only the most determined of purists take that way now; by far the majority of trekkers finish their route at Naya Pul, then ride a bus or taxi to Pokhara.

The initial climb to Ghorepani Deurali on the Poon Hill Danda is fairly demanding after having enjoyed several easy downhill stages, but with a number of lodges built along the way, it's possible to break the route into two stages.

Tatopani to Ghorepani (5½–6hrs)
Leaving Tatopani heading south the trail climbs a stairway of stone steps and in about 25mins comes to a long suspension bridge spanning the Kali Gandaki. Cross to the left bank and enter a small village named after the

GHAR KHOLA (1175m, 3855ft). Straddling the Gar Khola tributary, the village has a small shop and the Meet You Hotel where the trail forks.

Over the Ghar Khola bridge break away from the main (Beni) trail (see Section 4a above) and take the path which rises to the left of the lodge. There is a fine view of Nilgiri South from here. Having now deserted the Kali Gandaki, the way climbs a steep hillside lush with terraced fields and exotic trees. The trail soon forks. Take the right-hand option and ascend a formidable stairway of stone slabs that can seem almost endless. Fortunately there are a few tea-houses and *chautaaras* that provide welcome resting places along the trail.

About 1½hrs from Tatopani the trail emerges from forest shade and comes onto the ridge spur of the Durbin Danda at **SANTOSH HILL** (1500m, 4921ft), where a tea-house settled on the ridge crest exploits the views both to the north and the south. The continuing trail leads to a settlement a few minutes'

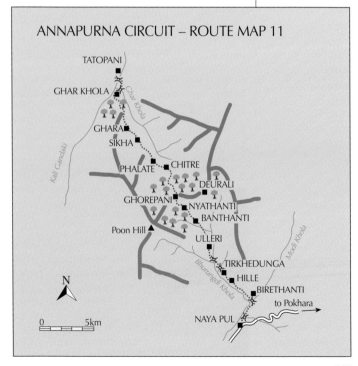

ANNAPURNA CIRCUIT – ROUTE MAP 11

TATOPANI

GHAR KHOLA

Ghar Khola

Kali Gandaki

GHARA

SIKHA

PHALATE

CHITRE

DEURALI

GHOREPANI

NYATHANTI

BANTHANTI

Poon Hill

ULLERI

Bhurungdi Khola

Modi Khola

TIRKHEDUNGA

HILLE

BIRETHANTI

to Pokhara

NAYA PUL

N

0   5km

ANNAPURNA CIRCUIT – Section 4b

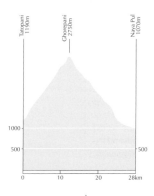

Tatopani 1190m — Ghorepani 2750m — Naya Pul 1070m

1000

500 — 500

0   10   20   28km

walk away. This is **BIRAUTA**, in which there's the Anita Lodge. Paved steps take you through, passing Sangita Lodge. Once again Nilgiri South looks very fine from here, and about 20mins after crossing the Durbin Danda, you arrive in

GHARA (1700m, 5577ft, 1hr 50mins). This village has several tea-houses and shops, and a few simple-looking lodges: the Laxmi, Annapurna View and Mountain Guesthouse. Just above Ghara there's a hint of a view of Dhaulagiri, while Tukuche Peak is clearly defined to its right.

The trail maintains its steadfast climb for another 40mins or so to reach

SIKHA (1935m, 6348ft, 2½hrs), a substantial village built on ascending levels. The lower part has tea-houses and a few lodges: the Shikha Restaurant, Travels Guesthouse, Neha Lodge and the smart-looking Mona Lisa Lodge. After Purnima Guesthouse there's the Moonlight Guesthouse, which boasts a 'European toilet and bathroom'. Sikha's upper, compact settlement (15–20mins walk) lines a ridge, has a few lodges, simple shops and a school – and once more commands a superb panorama, not just to the big mountains but down over a glorious landscape of textured, layered hills, terraced into artistic patterns. Accommodation

The trail between Ghara and Sikha

in this upper section is at the Dhaulagiri View, Shanti View, the large, blue-painted See-You Lodge (with a Nepal Red Cross Society building nearby) and, just above the village, the Hotel Serendipity, a good-looking lodge with a small garden.

The climb to Ghorepani continues through terraces, and about 30mins or so after leaving upper Sikha you pass through another small settlement with a few tea-houses and yet more views of Dhaulagiri. This settlement is known as **GHOPTE KHARKA**. Climbing on, come to the Nilgiri View restaurant and (20mins from Ghopte Kharka) the Nice View Lodge.

PHALATE (2270m, 7448ft, 4hrs 15mins) has a large school, a shop, tea-house and two lodges: the Annapurna View and Mount View.

Just 20 minutes or so beyond Phalate the trail brings you to Mike's Restaurant in

CHITRE (2390m, 7841ft, 4hrs 35mins; accommodation, refreshments). There are several other lodges here and, at the New Dhaulagiri Lodge, a sign gives some rather pessimistic timings – e.g. Ghorepani 2hrs instead of 1hr, and Tatopani 6hrs rather than 4hrs! About 3mins further on, the trail forks by the simple Laligurans Lodge. The left branch goes to Ghandruk and/or the Sanctuary (see box 'The Ghandruk Option'), while the continuing path for Ghorepani passes the Namaste Lodge

---

THE GHANDRUK OPTION

At the trail junction in Chitre, the left fork (heading east) offers a quieter, less travelled way for trekkers to reach either the Annapurna Sanctuary or Ghandruk on the way out to Pokhara, and avoids the 'trade route' to Ghorepani. This alternative trail leads to a saddle in an eastern extension of the Poon Hill Danda (2hrs). The saddle, or pass, is known as **DEURALI** (2990m, 9810ft), where a cluster of lodges provide accommodation – see Section 4c below. From there the way descends through forest, then climbs to **TADAPANI**, where the trail divides. One route goes to **CHHOMRONG** and the **ANNAPURNA SANCTUARY**, the other leads to the important Gurung village of **GHANDRUK**. *Note:* both these options are well supplied with lodges and tea-houses, but because of past muggings neither route is safe enough to be trekked alone. Go in a group and avoid being separated.

Dhaulagiri, from Poon Hill

(with camping ground), the village school and the New Annapurna Lodge.

POON HILL SUNRISE

To capture sunrise from the viewpoint on Poon Hill is one of trekking's not-to-be-missed experiences. That more exciting views may be had elsewhere in the Annapurna range is neither here nor there – a Poon Hill sunrise is unique. Since just about everyone wants to see it, and bedroom walls are thin, there's little chance of over-sleeping. Set out at least an hour before dawn and use a headtorch to follow the path. Several trails climb the slope south-west of Ghorepani and converge long before the viewpoint is reached. One of these begins in the centre of the village and rises past the Annapurna View Lodge. The way climbs among rhododendrons and emerges onto the crown of the hill at 3193m (10,476ft) in about 45mins. A lookout tower stands on the highest point, and below it a tea-house provides welcome mugs of coffee and hot chocolate.

Don't despair if clouds are hiding the distant mountains when you arrive. Be patient, for often the rising sun inspires a change, and the clouds either dissipate or sink into the valleys. The view can be spectacular. Far to the north Dhaulagiri is an enormous block of snow, ice and rock spreading vast ridges to right and left. To the north-east Annapurna South appears to dwarf Annapurna I. Then there's Hiunchuli, with Machhapuchhare on the other side of the hinted slice of the Modi Khola's gorge, and ranges far beyond that catch the morning light, while the low-lying Pokhara valley suggests another world entirely.

From Chitre to the ridge of the Poon Hill Danda involves a steady climb of about an hour through often dank and misty forests of oak and rhododendron. The trail is muddy in places and deeply cut by the strings of pack animals that daily ply this route.

GHOREPANI (2750m, 9022ft), or more specifically Ghorepani Deurali, is a bustling collection of trekkers' lodges, shops and camp grounds crowded together on a saddle in the Poon Hill Danda. Some 20,000 trekkers pass through here each year, making it Nepal's most heavily trekked route. Most of those visitors want to see the sunrise from Poon Hill, so don't expect a solitary experience. The lodge-building boom has had a devastating effect on the rhododendron forests, but ACAP has worked hard in recent years to reduce the impact, with some success. Among the many lodges there's the Nilgiri Guesthouse, then New Mountain View Lodge, Tukuche Peak View, Green View, New Kamala, Dhaulagiri View, Trekkers Lodge, Snow View, Himalaya View, Annapurna View, Pun Hill Guesthouse and Excellent View Lodge. There's also the Fishtail Lodge and the fancy-looking Sunny Hotel, with its bungalow-style rooms in the grounds.

Ghorepani to Naya Pul (5½–6hrs) ▶

Note: For security reasons you should not tackle this section of the trek on your own; the rhododendron forests along the Poon Hill Danda have an unfortunate reputation for muggings.

Descending the broad clear trail south of Ghorepani Deurali, a 5min walk brings you to

GHOREPANI, the original village that has been somewhat overtaken by the crowded development at the pass. Several lodges line the trail, including the Tibetan Mustang, Laligurans, Shikhar and See You. You will notice the horse troughs that give the village its name: Ghorepani means 'horse's water' – or 'horse's watering place'.

An alternative trail breaks off to the right for the climb to Poon Hill, while another forks east to Deurali (a different Deurali to that you've just left) and the route to Ghandruk and Chhomrong. The way to Birethanti continues to descend, leading through oak and rhododendron forests to reach

The southern slopes of the Poon Hill Danda lead to a world very different from that of the Kali Gandaki. Gone are near views of Dhaulagiri and Nilgiri, for the landscape is now dominated by green hills with higher, snow-covered peaks beyond. Gone is the stark regimentation of bare rock and hanging glacier, and the frosty river gorge is no more than a memory as you make the long, knee-jarring descent into a sub-tropical climate where agriculture becomes the dominant theme.

NYATHANTI (2500m, 8202ft, 35mins), which means 'new place'. Also spelt Nangathanti, this settlement comprises a number of lodges in a forest clearing. Among the lodges there's Hotel Sunrise, the Laligurans and the Hungry Eye.

All the way down to Banthanti, the rhododendrons (in Nepali, 'laligurans') are magnificent in springtime, a kaleidoscope of different coloured blooms searing among the dense greenery. It's a place lively with birdsong, but about an hour or so from Nyathanti you reach the settlement of

BANTHANTI (2300m, 7546ft, 1hr 45mins). Banthanti means literally 'the place in the forest', and there's another with the same name farther to the east on the trail which leads from Ghorepani to Tadapani. The village sprawls in a long line beside the trail with a number of lodges and tea-houses: the Poon, Namaste, Mountain View and Fishtail View lodges.

Between Banthanti and Ulleri the trail takes you out of forest and into a region of cultivation. Views replace the forest and, having left regular shade, the temperature rises.

ULLERI (1960m, 6430ft, 2½hrs) is an attractive Magar village of slate-roofed houses on the right flank of the deep valley of the Bhurungdi Khola, with stupendous views down into the valley, where terraced hillsides are reminiscent of those that so dominated the first day or so of the trek out of Besisahar. Other views look towards Annapurna South, Hiunchuli and Machhapuchhare. The landscape is now becoming more settled, an open, smiling countryside with many tea-houses and lodges. Here in Ulleri a group of lodges provide a welcome respite for trekkers ascending the steep staircase from Tirkhedunga. These lodges include: the Kamal, Mountain View, Pratap, the Annapurna Viewpoint, Super View and Excellent View.

Below Ulleri the descent is a seemingly endless stairway of more than 3000 steps leading to the bed of the valley. But if you find this a tiring way to descend, have pity on those who are ascending! On this descent there's just one lodge between Ulleri and Tirkhedunga, the Annapurna View Guesthouse, below which you continue down to reach and cross first the Bhurungdi Khola, then the Tirkhedunga Khola, and then enter

TIRKHEDUNGA (1540m, 5052ft, 3hrs 45mins). The village has a campsite and several lodges: the Laligurans, Laxmi, Kamala, Chandra and Indra – some proudly advertise the fact that they're run by ex-Gurkha soldiers, for these foothills north of Pokhara have in the past been a rich recruitment ground. Within the village an alternative path breaks away to make a cross-country route to Ghandruk.

Now on the east bank of the Bhurungdi Khola, it's only a few minutes after leaving Tirkhedunga before you reach

HILLE (1475m, 4839ft), where there are more lodges and tea-houses: the Laxmi, Susila, Annapurna and See You.

The trail descends more gently now, but with plenty of ups and downs through well-farmed country, passing through **SUDAME** and **MATATHANTI**, both of which have accommodation and refreshment facilities that are especially welcome as you're now in steamy, low-lying country. And about 1½hrs after leaving Hille you come to

BIRETHANTI (1025m, 3363ft). This busy, attractive bazaar village nestles at the confluence of the Bhurungdi Khola and the larger Modi Khola, which drains out of the Annapurna Sanctuary. Birethanti is an obvious place to spend the night. It has plenty of lodges and shops, an ACAP check-post by the bridge which spans the Modi Khola, a post office and a bank. Some of the lodges have dining areas overlooking the river. Vegetation is now sub-tropical, and if you find that the dust of the last few days needs rinsing off, there are tempting pools in both the Bhurungdi river upstream of the village and a short way along the Modi Khola. For accommodation, the Laxmi Lodge is a spruce, expensive hotel with luxurious rooms (for a trekker's lodge, that is) near the Modi Khola bridge, but there are at least 10 other lower-priced lodges to choose from, most of which provide good food and a relaxing atmosphere.

From Birethanti an alternative trail heads up the valley of the Modi Khola, first along the riverside, then climbing a stone stairway to the large Gurung village of Ghandruk, where the ACAP headquarters is housed. From there a choice of routes offers options of either continuing towards the

If you would prefer a taxi, turn left and walk along the road to find a queue of taxis waiting for business. The taxi drivers here rigorously enforce a queueing system, and you will have to take the vehicle at the head of the line. The 42km (26 mile) journey to Pokhara will take about an hour.

Annapurna Sanctuary or crossing the Modi Khola and heading for Pokhara by way of Landruk. (These options are dealt with in more detail under Trek 2: the Annapurna Sanctuary and Trek 4: The Ghandruk Foothill Trek.)

For the route to Pokhara, cross the Modi Khola bridge by the ACAP check-post and turn right to pass the Fishtail Lodge, after which there's a string of tatty tea-houses and shops. About 20mins out of Birethanti come to a further shanty-like collection of tea-houses and shops, cross a suspension bridge over a tributary and take the final short walk of the trek which leads up a dirt road to **NAYA PUL**, a scruffy sprawl of roadside shops and tea-houses where you can catch a bus for Pokhara. ◀

THE POKHARA TREK OPTION

The opening of the Pokhara–Baglung–Beni road has not only shortened the Annapurna Circuit trek, but has had a profound effect on the communities that previously relied on passing trekkers for the majority of their income. Now that tourists mostly bypass these villages, that income has almost completely dried up. But it is still possible to trek out to Pokhara along the old routes, as the following outline suggests. Allow about 6–7hrs for the trek from Birethanti to Pokhara.

Cross the Modi Khola bridge and turn left on a riverside path for about 20mins, then branch uphill for an unrelieved ascent to **CHANDRAKOT** (1580m, 5184ft), a village with tremendous views along the Modi Khola's valley to Annapurna South and its neighbours. Heading east the continuing trail leads through a cultivated landscape with little change in altitude, and in half an hour comes to **LUMLE** (1610m, 5282ft 2hrs). The main street through the village is paved with stone slabs and used to be lined with lodges, but with the coming of the road these all closed down with the exception of the Lumle Guesthouse, which stands near the road. A British-run agricultural project is based nearby.

It's now necessary to walk along the road to the hilltop village of **KHARE** (1770m, 5807ft, 2¾–3hrs) before finding the trail once more, a short-cut descent with distant views of Pokhara's lake. The road winds round **NAUDANDA** (1440m, 4724ft), a long straggling village noted for its views. From here continue along the ridge to **SARANKOT**, then a final hour or so of descent leads to **POKHARA**.

SECTION 4C:
Ghorepani to Chhomrong

Distance:	17km (10½ miles)
Time:	2 days
Start altitude:	2750m (9022ft)
High point:	Deurali, 2990m (9810ft)
Low point:	The Kimrong Khola below Chiuli, 1900m (6234ft)

Trekkers arriving in Ghorepani Deurali having almost completed the Annapurna Circuit have the option of diverting from the main Birethanti–Pokhara route by heading south-east along the ridge with the aim of visiting Chhomrong and the Annapurna Sanctuary (see Trek 2). It's a fairly vigorous helter-skelter route, with about half the trek to Chhomrong taking place in rhododendron forest. There are plenty of lodges and tea-houses along the way, but as with much of the wooded countryside around the Ghorepani–Ghandruk–Birethanti triangle, there have been several cases of lone trekkers being robbed here, so you're strongly advised against trekking on your own. That being said, keep such warnings in perspective, for you're undoubtedly much safer here than you would be wandering after dark in any of a number of cities in the so-called 'civilised' West.

Ghorepani to Chhomrong (6½–7hrs)

The trail leaves the main through-street in Ghorepani Deurali alongside the Fishtail Lodge, and takes you past the Sunny Hotel into rhododendron forest that clothes the eastern ridge. Coming to a *chautaara* the trail forks and you continue ahead. The way becomes paved and, rising in steps, after about 20mins it brings you to the ridge crest with good views of Dhaulagiri in one direction and Machhapuchhare in another. Here the route is joined by a second trail coming from the 'other' Ghorepani, which lies just below the main lodge settlement on the Birethanti side of the pass. Turn left and follow the ridge crest in and out of forest with snatched views to enjoy. On an open patch along the ridge sometimes an enterprising local will be met selling bottled drinks and souvenirs. Then you're back in forest again where the trail twists among exposed tree

ANNAPURNA CIRCUIT – Section 4c

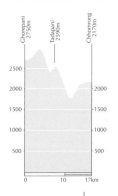

roots and between clumps of bamboo before descending to

DEURALI (2990m, 9810ft, 1¼–1½hrs) at a junction of paths on a saddle in the ridge. The left-hand path is that taken by the short-cut from Chitre on the Tatopani– Ghorepani route. There are two simple lodges here, the Deurali Guesthouse and the Green View Lodge, and plenty of souvenirs for sale.

Turn right and descend past the lodges into what becomes a damp, wooded ravine. In places the path is narrow, steep, heavily eroded and slippery. Later there's a long stepped section that is also greasy when wet. About 5mins below Deurali, pass the solitary Hotel Laligurans.

In the upper part of the ravine the path accompanies a small stream. This grows in volume and width as you descend, with cascades showering over ledges and bordered by green cliffs running with minor rivulets. Primulas add colour to the sometimes gloomy dank recesses.

BANTHANTI (2520m, 8268ft) is reached in a little over 2hrs from Ghorepani. A group of simple lodges has been built near a massive cliff traditionally used as a shelter by porters as they prepared their meals. The first lodge is the Hotel Hungry Eye,

The forested route to Tadapani gives occasional views of Machhapuchhare

156

then Sunrise Lodge, Hotel Sankar and Gurung Lodge. About 5mins beyond these the Tranquility Guesthouse stands at the top of a flight of steps.

The trail turns out of the ravine by the Tranquility Guesthouse and then makes a fine undulating traverse of the steep wooded mountainside, which plunges for hundreds of metres to the tight V-wedge of a valley. About 20mins later come to the Hotel Clean View Top on Banthanti Hill, then descend through forest again into the head of the Bhurungdi Khola's valley. A

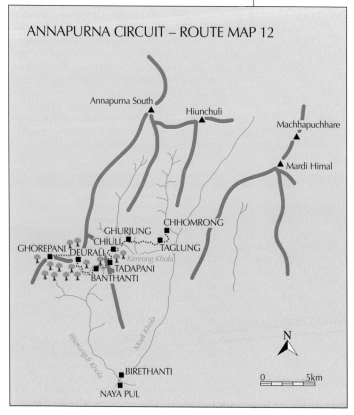

ANNAPURNA CIRCUIT – ROUTE MAP 12

Annapurna South
Hiunchuli
Machhapuchhare
Mardi Himal
CHHOMRONG
GHURJUNG
CHIULI
TAGLUNG
GHOREPANI
DEURALI
Kimrong Khola
TADAPANI
BANTHANTI
Bhurungdi Khola
Modi Khola
BIRETHANTI
NAYA PUL

N

0   5km

bridge takes you across the stream, followed by a steeply winding trail that climbs another wooded hillside and emerges through a saddle to

TADAPANI (2590m, 8497ft, 3–3½hrs). Not to be confused with Tatopani ('hot water') in the Kali Gandaki, Tadapani means 'far water', which gives an indication that until a piped supply came to this remote lodge settlement, locals and porters faced a long haul to bring water here. Seven fairly large lodges enjoy spectacular views across the deep valley of the Kimrong Khola to Annapurna South and Machhapuchhare: Hotel Panorama Point, with its viewing tower, Annapurna View, Fishtail View, Hotel Grand View, Super View, Himalayan Tourist Guesthouse and the Tadapani Guesthouse. Like Ghorepani Deurali, Tadapani can seem a dank and chilly place when afternoon mists blanket the surrounding hills, and the altitude is high enough to make the loss of the sun keenly felt.

You have a choice of onward routes from here: one goes to Chhomrong at the mouth of the Modi Khola's gorge which leads into the Sanctuary; the other is an easy 2½hr trek to Ghandruk. First the Ghandruk option.

THE GHANDRUK OPTION

Take the path which goes alongside, then descends beyond the Himalayan Tourist Guesthouse. Losing height steeply through forest, the way eventually brings you to a clearing in which there's a trail junction and two lodges, the Hillside and Nisha. This is **BAISI KHARKA**. Both trail options lead to Ghandruk. The left fork joins a path linking Ghandruk with the village of Kimrong, and enters the township from the north; the other makes a more direct approach and, after descending to cross a tributary stream, comes into Ghandruk at its top (western) end. (Further trek options from here are described in Trek 4: The Ghandruk Foothill Trek.)

For the continuing route to Chhomrong, leave Tadapani by taking a trail past the Tadapani Guesthouse and Hotel Grand View, then down steps into a charming rhododendron forest replete with hanging banners of moss, lichen and tree orchids. The way descends through the forest, and from brief clearings snatched views of Machhapuchhare tease you on.

After about 40mins you reach a solitary farm which doubles as a tea-house in a lovely open setting. Beyond it the descent continues, and soon comes to the Mountain Discovery Guesthouse, a handsome-looking lodge on a natural hillside terrace, its rooms exploiting an uninterrupted view of Machhapuchhare. Its location is idyllic. This lodge, and the houses passed on the way down to the river, form part of the scattered village of **CHIULI**.

The steep descent from Tadapani to the Kimrong Khola winds through the terraces

Below the Discovery Guesthouse the descending path is even steeper than before, twisting among houses and terraced fields, and past a few more tea-houses and lodges. The first of these is View Top Lodge, then Hillside Lodge, which is located in a farmyard. Beside more fields come to River View Lodge, and about 1¼hrs after leaving Tadapani come to a path junction near the British Ex-Gurkha Lodge. The right-hand path leads to Ghandruk in about 3hrs, but the Chhomrong trail descends past the lodge for another 5mins, and reaches the bank of the Kimrong Khola and a suspension bridge at about 1900m (6234ft).

Cross the bridge and climb steeply for a short way before slanting right to the first buildings of another scattered settlement, **GHURJUNG**. Ten minutes above the river, pass a school with the Buddha Guesthouse next door – note the watermill below. The trail edges narrow terraced fields, then rises to the simple Hotel Denthus, and turns left above the Kamala Lodge.

Cutting across a steep hillside towards a waterfall, cross another suspension bridge and climb a slope to reach Hotel Greenhill and the Ghurjung Lodge. The trail now makes a rising traverse, climbs two or three flights of very steep stone steps, then eases along a more generous contour. Through trees, then across more terraced farmland the way continues, and about 2¼hrs from Tadapani the path is joined by another, which has come from the village of Kimrong, located down by the river on another linking route with Ghandruk. Just beyond this trail junction pass the simple Kaji Lunch Centre, which has a few beds.

In a further 30mins the trail reaches **TAGLUNG**, yet another scattered village whose houses are set on various levels in a steep but highly productive landscape. Then, 10mins later, you turn a spur and come to the Heaven View, first of Chhomrong's lodges, standing near a junction of paths. Ignoring that which descends to the Jhinu hot springs, rise again to the Summit View Lodge, and by way of big stone steps reach Panorama Point Lodge, Fishtail Guesthouse and an ACAP check-post guarding the true entrance to **CHHOMRONG**.

For full details of this village, its numerous lodges, facilities and views, plus descriptions of the route to the Annapurna Sanctuary and the way back to Pokhara, please refer to Trek 2: The Annapurna Sanctuary, below.

POKHARA

After Kathmandu, Pokhara is Nepal's second most popular tourist haunt. But unlike Kathmandu and its neighbouring cities of Patan and Bhaktapur, Pokhara has no ancient, elegant buildings, no historic temples or palaces, no exquisite windows carved by Newari artisans. Instead, it's largely an architectural eyesore, a sprawling town with practically no physical merit, and one that appears to have little planning control to guide its anarchic spread. But it does have two unique features that lift it above the ordinary: the lake of Phewa Tal and a backdrop sufficient to take your breath away. Jimmy Roberts, the 'Father of Trekking', once proclaimed that 'there is no other mountain view in the world to equal Machhapuchhare and Annapurna hanging there in the sky above the green Pokhara plain'. He could be right.

Lying at a modest 820m (2690ft), Pokhara is backed by an amazing wall of mountains that rise, just 40km away, to a cloud-piercing 8000m (26,000ft). This huge panoramic sweep is said to extend for 140km (87 miles) to include Dhaulagiri, the Annapurnas, Machhapuchhare, Lamjung Himal and the Manaslu Himal. Best of all is Machhapuchhare, seen from here as a graceful pyramid with a needle-sharp peak.

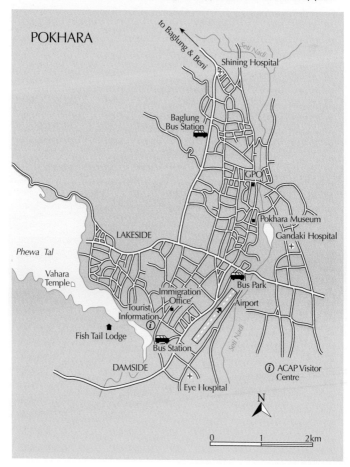

Catch this panorama at daybreak, shimmering its reflection in the still lake waters, or at dusk when the foothills are black and featureless and the mountains above burn with the vanished sun's last gold. Or maybe see it at night, with the valley silent and a big moon sailing high, so that the 'silver snows burn coldly with an overwhelming, undeniable life and spirit of their own', as Dervla Murphy described it in *The Waiting Land*.

Before a trek begins, such a scene can fill you with an urgency to get started. But when the trek is over, Pokhara can hold you there to rest weary limbs, remind you of days gone by, and make you reluctant to leave for home.

Pokhara has two main areas of accommodation: Damside (Pardi Bazaar) and Lakeside (Baidam). The first is located at the southern end of the lake and has the bus park and airport nearby. Lakeside, as its name implies, spills along the eastern shore with countless hotels, restaurants and shops vying for business. To the east of Lakeside the main, modern town is built alongside the Prithvi Rajmarg and the Chinese-built road that leads to Baglung and Beni in the Annapurna foothills. These roads are of comparatively recent construction; that which links Pokhara with Kathmandu was not completed until 1973, while the Baglung–Beni highway dates only from the late 1990s.

Apart from mountain-gazing, eating and browsing the numerous bookshops, there's little to do here except, perhaps, to take a boat out on the lake and maybe visit the small island with its Vahara Temple and cheerful holiday atmosphere. Pokhara, then, is a place in which to relax and let the nearby mountains weave their continuing spell.

The Annapurna Himal at daybreak, seen from Phewa Tal, Pokhara

TREK 2:
THE ANNAPURNA SANCTUARY

*Big mountains heaved to heaven which the
blinding sunsets blazon,
Black canyons where the rapids rip and roar.*

(Robert Service)

TREK SUMMARY

Distance:	84km (50 miles)
Time:	7–12 days
Max. altitude:	4130m (13,550ft)
Start:	Phedi or Naya Pul
Finish:	Phedi or Naya Pul
Trekking style:	Tea-house (lodge accommodation) or camping

Picture moonrise over these mountains. Imagine rising from a high camp among them, or emerging from a lodge or a tent at over 4000m (13,000ft) to be greeted by the sight of their ice-coated flanks lit by the morning sun, their delicate cornices picked out against the deep blue of a Himalayan sky. Imagine hour after hour of scenic perfection that is suddenly snatched from your field of vision by the mid-day clouds that boil up from the hidden gorge as if from a witch's cauldron – there's beauty and drama in that too.

All this, and much much more, awaits the trekker who emerges through the gates of the Sanctuary between Hiunchuli and Machhapuchhare and wanders the trail that rises another 400m (1300ft) or so to gain the panoramic area known as Annapurna Base Camp.

For generations Gurung shepherds had taken their flocks to summer pasture in the Sanctuary, but it was not until 1956 that the first Westerner penetrated the gorge of the Modi Khola and gazed on those scenes of great beauty. Jimmy Roberts, then a Gurkha officer and later Military Attaché at the British Embassy in Kathmandu, was on reconnaissance

The Annapurna Sanctuary is one of the most spectacular mountain amphitheatres imaginable. Picture an almost complete ring of high peaks, seven of which top 7000m (23,000ft), draped with snowfields and glaciers, with great buttresses, rock walls and ice flutings that burst from a rough, undulating basin. There's only one way into this basin, and that entails a trek through a gorge clothed with dense bamboo jungle and rain forest that, combined with the shafting walls of the gorge, effectively captures the mists and denies access to the sun for much of the day. Deep within this gorge thunders the Modi Khola, a river composed of the melt of all glaciers and snowfields trapped within the Sanctuary itself.

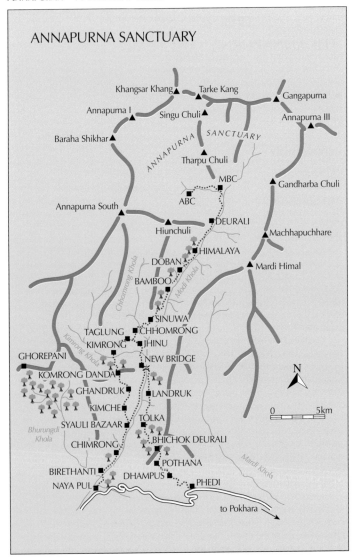

for the only expedition to be sanctioned for an attempt to climb Machhapuchhare (see box 'Jimmy Roberts – the Father of Trekking', below), and it was he who named this great cauldron of peaks the Annapurna Sanctuary; an appropriate name, since it was considered sacred by the Gurungs who lived nearby. As if to reinforce the sanctity of the area he had to abide by certain rules imposed on him by the village elders of Chhomrong, which included 50 eggs being left at a small shrine in the gorge in order to pacify the goddess who dwelt there.

After the Machhapuchhare expedition of 1957 a slow trickle of mountaineers followed the trail through the Modi Khola's gorge. One early group was a Japanese team which climbed Tarke Kang (Glacier Dome 7202m, 23,629ft) in 1964, while a year later a German expedition led by Gunther Hauser made the first ascent of the triangular Gangapurna (7454m, 24,455ft). But without question the most remarkable achievement was by Chris Bonington's team, which in 1970 made the first ascent of the enormous South Face of Annapurna I from a base camp at around 4000m (13,000ft) near the Annapurna glacier – now the site of a group of trekkers' lodges. The Sanctuary has since became a major focus of attention for trekking parties, and since 1978 has also gained in popularity with mountaineers inspired by a number of Trekking Peaks accessible from it.

The Sanctuary makes an undeniably attractive goal. Outstanding high mountain views are to be had during a large part of the approach march, with the contrasts of lowland rice paddies, gloomy jungles of bamboo and dazzling snowpeaks adding much to the broad range of experience. The outlines of the Sanctuary are seen from Pokhara. North of the lake of Phewa Tal the mountains glow in the morning, a perfect snow-bound horizon whose dominant feature is the pinnacle of Machhapuchhare. And along the trail to it this graceful virgin summit appears and reappears with teasing familiarity, soaring beyond the rice paddies, hovering over thatched villages, signalling above the deep, dark gorge.

This trek is a much shorter option than that of the Annapurna Circuit, taking anything from 7 to 12 days for the round-trip from Pokhara, although various options are possible for anyone who wishes to lengthen it. Suggestions are made below. One of these options, which is popular with trekkers nearing completion of the Circuit, is to visit the Sanctuary on the way out to Pokhara by making a diversion from Ghorepani. This approach (Ghorepani to Chhomrong at the gorge entrance) is described in Trek 1: The Annapurna Circuit and is also outlined in the following pages. But although the basic trek is a comparatively short one there are some steep ascents, and the trail, though not unduly difficult, is more demanding than a first glance at the map might suggest.

On this trek there are numerous lodges and tea-houses, so it's perfectly feasible to travel light and rely on food and accommodation at the end of every stage. However, one should remember that for the two days of approach through the Modi Khola's gorge lodges are liable to be very busy during the high season of October–November, with space being at a premium, since the route from Chhomrong to the Sanctuary is used by traffic in both directions.

Another point to bear in mind is the potential danger of avalanche near the overhanging Hinko Cave. This danger is particularly acute in winter and early spring following heavy snowfall when avalanches pour from the unseen Hiunchuli to obliterate the trail. If there is any conceivable possibility of avalanche, do not proceed along the gorge – either up or down – until it has passed. This is Nepal's only major trekking route to have significant avalanche danger, and several trekkers have lost their lives here. Others have found themselves trapped for a few days within the Sanctuary itself, unable to escape until all danger had gone. Remember this when planning your trek and allow enough leeway to accommodate such a time-absorbing delay. It would be prudent to enquire about avalanche risk and trail conditions within the gorge when you register at the ACAP check-post at the entrance to Chhomrong. ◀

The Sanctuary is protected as a special conservation area (ACAP's Annapurna Sanctuary Special Management Zone), where mineral water bottles are banned, and wood fires forbidden beyond Chhomrong. All lodges, and trekkers using tents, are required to use either kerosene or gas for cooking. There's a kerosene depot in the village.

SECTION 1:
Pokhara to Chhomrong

Distance:	38km (23½ miles)
Time:	2–3 days
Start altitude:	820m (2690ft)
High point:	Chhomrong, 2170m (7119ft)
Height difference:	1350m (4429ft)
Transport options:	Bus or taxi (Pokhara to Phedi or Naya Pul)

All routes of approach to the Sanctuary converge on Chhomrong, the large Gurung village standing guard over the entrance to the Modi Khola's gorge. Until the mid-1980s, when a bridge was built across the river at New Bridge (formerly Himalkyo), between Chhomrong and Birethanti, the trail from Pokhara went by way of Ghandruk, but nowadays there are three main options to consider. Each of these begins with a bus or taxi ride from Pokhara. The first, and most direct route (see Section 1a, below), starts at Phedi near the head of the Yamdi Khola's valley, from where the Baglung–Beni road twists up to Naudanda. Leaving the road at Phedi, you then trek up a slope to Dhampus, and from there cross a wooded pass to Landruk, overlooking the Modi Khola. Crossing the river at New Bridge, the way then tackles a final steep climb to Chhomrong.

The other two approach routes both begin in Naya Pul near Birethanti, some 42km from Pokhara. A valley route (see Section 1b) follows the Modi Khola upstream, passes through Syauli Bazaar and continues as far as New Bridge before making the steep climb to Chhomrong on the trail taken in Section 1a.

The third option (Section 1c) is based on the traditional route of approach. This also follows the Modi Khola upstream to Syauli Bazaar, but then leaves the river and makes a long climb to Ghandruk, where the first night is usually spent. Next day you traverse a ridge north of the village, descend to (and cross) the Kimrong Khola, then climb the north flank of the valley to a crossing trail which more or less contours round to Chhomrong.

Each of these routes is scenically and culturally interesting, beginning in low-lying country with rice paddies and fields of millet, with enticing views of Annapurna South, Hiunchuli and Machhapuchhare.

Section 1a:
Phedi to Chhomrong via Dhampus and Landruk

Distance:	18km (11 miles)
Time:	10–12hrs
Start altitude:	1130m (3707ft)
High points:	Bhichok Deurali, 2100m (6890ft), Chhomrong, 2170m (7119ft)
Low point:	New Bridge, 1340m (4396ft)
Total height gain:	1800m (5906ft)
Height loss:	300m (984ft)

Take a taxi or bus for the 15–20min drive along the Baglung–Beni road to the few buildings at Phedi (meaning 'foot of the hill'). The trailhead is found near the Dhampus Mailee Hotel, and the way begins by climbing steps through sal forest, and continues steeply to reach the little Mina Lodge in 40–45mins. The gradient eases as the paved trail leads around rice terraces – or on footpath short-cuts across the fields when the harvest has been taken – passing several houses on the way. There are various alternative paths, so if in doubt as to the correct one, ask a local for the trail to Dhampus. After about 1½hrs from the road you enter the strung-out village of

ANNAPURNA SANCTUARY – Section 1a

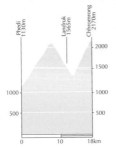

DHAMPUS (1650m, 5413ft). On the way to Dhampus, views had begun to expand ahead, while from the village these views show the high peaks for which you are aiming. There are many lodges here, as well as a campsite and an ACAP check-post. Among the lodges there's the upmarket Ker & Downey-owned Basanta Lodge and the large Dhaulagiri View Hotel.

Wandering through the upper part of Dhampus the way continues to climb heading west, then becomes a paved route through rhododendron forest. There is a major trail junction where you continue ahead, ignoring the (not very clear) left branch which leads to a campsite and, eventually, to Khare on the Baglung–Beni road. Shortly after this you come to the village of

POTHANA (1900m, 6234ft), another hour or so above Dhampus. There are plenty of lodges here and a super view of Machhapuchhare. Among the lodges are the Annapurna, Gurung, See You and the Fishtail Hotel.

North of Pothana wander up to the wooded ridge above the village, follow it for a short distance and then come to a clearing with views that include Dhaulagiri far up the Kali Gandaki's valley, as well as the nearer Annapurna South and Machhapuchhare. This ridge is crossed at

BHICHOK DEURALI (2100m, 6890ft, 3¼–3½hrs), where there are just two lodges, the Trekker's Inn and the Nice View.

The path now descends the north slope, still in rhododendron forest, passing several tea-houses and simple lodges before it reaches **BERI KHARKA** and yet more tea-houses. Crossing a tributary stream before long you emerge from the cover of trees to a broad hillside that has been cultivated in numerous terraces, with the valley of the Modi Khola far below.

TOLKA (1700m, 5577ft) is a small village with a school and a string of lodges alongside the trail, reached in about 5hrs from Phedi. The list of lodges includes the Evergreen, Namaste, Butterfly and the grandly named International Guesthouse.

Crossing the Tigu Khola on a suspension bridge below Tolka, you then rise over a wooded ridge, with the larger village of Landruk seen ahead, and the views expand once more. ▶

LANDRUK (1565m, 5135ft, 6¼hrs) is also known as Landrung. This is an attractive Gurung village with a paved street and a number of circular thatched houses. There are several good lodges, and the views to Annapurna South and Hiunchuli are magnificent. The village is set on the steeply sloping hillside, with a great deal of height difference between the upper

On the far (western) side of the Modi Khola's valley you can see Ghandruk, the main Gurung village hereabouts, visited on the Naya Pul to Chhomrong approach described below as Section 1c.

buildings and those at its lower end. Among the lodges at the top of the village, there's the Hungry Eye and Laligurans. Further down there's the Landruk, Mount View and the Moonlight Hotel.

Descend through the village to a trail junction near the Himalaya Hotel. The left-hand path immediately descends to the Modi Khola and is the one to take if you plan to visit Ghandruk. It also gives access to a riverside trail linking Naya Pul with New Bridge (see Section 1b). The direct route to Chhomrong via New Bridge, however, heads to the right and slopes down through terraces, eventually reaching the heavily vegetated valley bed, which is broken here and there with large boulders. This is the path to take. Once in the valley continue upstream on an easy trail with the Modi Khola to your left, and before long you will come to the Himalpani Lodge and a suspension bridge over the river. Above it, on the opposite bank, is the cluster of buildings of

The steep climb from New Bridge to Chhomrong passes through Jhinu

NEW BRIDGE (1340m, 4396ft). The settlement is reached in a little under 1½hrs from Landruk. It was the construction of the Modi Khola suspension bridge in the mid-1980s which not

only inspired the name change from Himalkyo but has made this more direct route to the Sanctuary possible. In Nepali, New Bridge is 'Naya Pul', and it is this name by which the settlement is also known. Confusion can so easily arise if you use this name, though, since there's another Naya Pul further downstream on the road near Birethanti. New Bridge has a group of lodges, among them the Himchali, Kalapani and Modi Khola.

You now climb steeply to the few houses of **SAMRUNG**, and just beyond these the trail crosses the Kimrong Khola tributary, makes a rising traverse of steep hillside, then climbs more determinedly to

JHINU DANDA (1780m, 5840ft). This has access to hot springs about 15mins walk away – downhill. At least half a dozen lodges suggest this could be a good place to spend the night before tackling the final steep haul up the hillside to Chhomrong. There's the Hot Spring Hotel, Hot Spring Garden Lodge, the Tibet and Namaste lodges, and a few others.

From Jhinu Danda the 400m (1300ft) climb seems relentless, but views to Gangapurna near the headwaters of the Modi Khola provide a good enough excuse for frequent rests. The trail works a way very steeply up a long spur of hillside and at last emerges onto a broad path (the route from Ghandruk and Tadapani) near the Heaven View at **TAGLUNG**, formerly known as Daalu. Bear right, and round a curve of hillside ascend a slope to the Summit View Lodge, then up stone steps to Panorama Point Lodge, the Fishtail Guesthouse and an ACAP checkpost at the entrance to

CHHOMRONG (2170m, 7119ft). This prosperous Gurung village is built in two sections on a steep hillside, with a long paved stairway consisting of more than 2000 steps linking upper Chhomrong, by the ACAP post, with the lower village overlooking terraced fields, just above the bridge which spans the Chhomrong Khola at the foot of the slope. There's a dispensary, a few shops and a kerosene depot in the lower village. Beyond the ACAP post Chhomrong currently has 13 lodges, some of which are among the largest and best kept of the whole Annapurna region, with solar-heated showers and dining rooms with picture windows that gaze out at the

The terrace at Chhomrong Mountain View Hotel

fish-tail peak of Machhapuchhare beckoning above the Modi Khola's gorge and at the dominating block of Annapurna South looming above the village.

Starting at the top of the slope, these lodges are: the Himalaya View Guesthouse, Excellent View Top Lodge, the Kalpana Guesthouse (just below the trail) and the imposing International Guesthouse, then down steps to the Chhomrong Mountain View Lodge, with well-kept flower borders and a good level campsite. Continue down the slope to the Lucky Guesthouse, Moonlight Lodge, Hiunchuli Guesthouse and the Chhomrong Guesthouse. Below the village school there's the Garden Villa Lodge, a trekker's shop, then the Annapurna Guesthouse and, finally, Chhomrong's original trekkers' hotel, Captain's Lodge, where you can rent camping equipment and down clothing for use in the Sanctuary.

Before leaving Chhomrong it's worth enquiring of trekkers who have just come from the Sanctuary about conditions on the trail in – with special attention to any avalanche danger that might exist in the gorge near Hinko Cave. If there's evidence of recent heavy snowfall, or you've experienced much rain on the approach (which would no doubt have fallen as snow higher up), either abandon your plan to go to the Sanctuary or wait in Chhomrong until all danger of avalanche has passed before proceeding.

Section 1b:
Naya Pul to Chhomrong
via Syauli Bazaar and New Bridge

Distance:	16km (10 miles)
Time:	8–9hrs
Start altitude:	1070m (3510ft)
High point:	Chhomrong 2170m (7119ft)
Height gain:	1100m (3609ft)

A little over 42km (26 miles) from Pokhara on the Chinese-built Baglung–Beni road you come to the scruffy, shanty-like row of tea-houses and shops that is **NAYA PUL**. A taxi takes about an hour for this journey; a bus takes nearly twice as long. (Up to 24 buses a day run between Pokhara and Baglung, passing through Naya Pul.) Leave the bus or taxi here and walk down the slope to a suspension bridge over a tributary of the Modi Khola, and on the other side follow a track past more tea-houses and shops. With the river for company on your left, the track soon brings you to the Fishtail Lodge and a suspension bridge that takes you across the Modi Khola and into

BIRETHANTI (1025m, 3363ft, 20mins). This large and attractive bazaar village standing at the confluence of the Modi Khola and Bhurungdi Khola rivers is a busy gathering place for trekkers. Several major routes converge here, including the Annapurna Circuit (Trek 1), the Pilgrim's Trail to Muktinath (Trek 3) and the Ghandruk Foothill Trek (Trek 4). There's an ACAP check-post by the bridge, where you should register your details before moving on. Birethanti has a variety of lodges, shops, a post office and a bank.

ANNAPURNA SANCTUARY – Section 1b

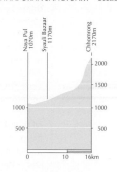

Walk up the main street to a junction near the post office, then turn right. (Alternatively there's a footpath short-cut immediately to the right of the bridge by the expensive Laxmi Lodge, which brings you to a crossing path where you turn right again along the main route out of town.) Passing the Nice View Lodge and Himalayan Lodge, about 10mins later leave the outskirts of Birethanti by crossing a wooden bridge among trees. In another 20mins you pass the entrance to the fancy-looking Sanctuary Lodge, owned by Ker & Downey and set back in extensive gardens spilling down to the river.

The continuing path pushes further along the Modi Khola's valley with Machhapuchhare teasing ahead. Numerous simple tea-houses line the trail in groups, interspersed with open fields of rice or millet. The first group is in the settlement of **CHIMRONG** (1140m, 3740ft). There's another group shortly after, then you cross a stream in a woodland, and not long after this come onto a trail of flagstones between more fields of rice and millet. This paved trail leads directly to

SYAULI BAZAAR (1170m, 3839ft). Reached in about 1½hrs from Naya Pul, the village lies at the foot of the long climb to Ghandruk and has several lodges, including the Machhapuchhare Guesthouse and the Green Valley Lodge.

The continuing path to New Bridge, Jhinu Danda and Chhomrong is not well used, so you should check before leaving Syauli Bazaar for the correct route. The trail leaves Syauli Bazaar by the school and follows the river upstream for about 2hrs before coming to the Beehive Lodge, located near a bridge over the Modi Khola which carries the trail between Landruk and Ghandruk. ◀

Between the Beehive Lodge and New Bridge, a trek of a little over 1½hrs takes you largely through sub-tropical forest, still on the west bank of the Modi Khola. Between the trees teasing views show aspects of Annapurna South, Hiunchuli and Machhapuchhare.

A steep climb left leads to Ghandruk and an alternative route to Chhomrong; the right-hand trail visits Landruk, then goes on to Dhampus and Pokhara.

NEW BRIDGE (1340m, 4396ft, 5–5½hrs) is where you join the main route to Chhomrong from Dhampus and Landruk, described above as Section 1a. There's a group of lodges just above the bridge: the Himchali, Kalapani and the Modi Khola.

From New Bridge to Chhomrong involves a long 830m (2723ft) climb which will take about 3½–4hrs of effort to achieve. Accommodation is available above New Bridge at Jhinu Danda, which has access to hot springs. For a full description of the final stage of the route from New Bridge to Chhomrong, please refer to Section 1a above.

Section 1c:
Naya Pul to Chhomrong via Ghandruk

Distance:	20km (12 miles)
Time:	7–8hrs
Start altitude:	1070m (3510ft)
High points:	Komrong Danda, 2250m (7382ft), Chhomrong, 2170m (7119ft)
Low point:	Kimrong, 1780m (5840ft)
Total height gain:	1570m (5151ft)
Height loss:	470m (1542ft)

Leaving the Baglung–Beni road at the Naya Pul shanty, walk down the slope, cross a suspension bridge over a tributary of the Modi Khola, then follow the riverside track to the Fishtail Lodge and a second suspension bridge, this one spanning the Modi Khola, across which lies **BIRETH-ANTI**. The continuing route through **CHIM-RONG** to **SYAULI BAZAAR** (1170m, 3839ft) is described under Section 1b above.

It takes about 1½hrs to reach Syauli Bazaar from Naya Pul. Thus far the route has remained in the low-lying bed of the Modi Khola's valley, but now the long 770m (2526ft) climb to Ghandruk begins in earnest. After passing the attractive Syauli Bazaar Guesthouse cross another suspension bridge over a minor tributary, then go up a paved stairway between terraced fields – this part of the valley is one vast sweep of terraces, immensely appealing, with Machhapuchhare as a backdrop. There's no shortage of either

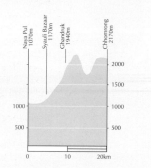

ANNAPURNA SANCTUARY – Section 1c

lodge accommodation or tea-houses along the way, and because the gradient is rather severe for a first day's trek, you will no doubt make the most of the refreshment facilities provided. The next settlement above Syauli Bazaar is

KIMCHE (1638m, 5374ft). The lodges, houses and farms of this village cascade down the steep hillside on either side of the trail, with about 250m (820ft) altitude difference between the upper village and the lower. The village is broken into several settlements with confusingly different names, while locals may even tell you that their village is also known as Syauli. Some of the lodges are rather simple affairs, but one of the first, the Shining River Guesthouse, looks especially welcoming with its colourful garden.

The steep climb continues, with paved steps for much of the way and Machhapuchhare nearly always in view. There's little shade, and on bright days the sun's heat can be debilitating. In the upper part of Kimche you pass the Bikash Guesthouse and the Kimche Guesthouse, both simple places. As you gain height so the mountain panorama ahead grows in extent to take your mind off the gradient. This eventually eases and you reach a few tea-houses beside the trail at **CHANE**. Another path breaks away to the left, cutting across the hillside to Tirkhedunga, which lies on the Birethanti to Ghorepani route.

Machhapuchhare is on show for most of the climb to Ghandruk

The Ghandruk trail is broad and obvious, and continues roughly northward, crossing a stream and a landslide, and going up more steps before passing through a simple entrance *kani*. Shortly before coming to the archway, the trail is joined by another coming from the right – the linking route with Landruk and Dhampus. Having passed through the *kani* you come into

GHANDRUK (1940m, 6365ft, 3½–4hrs). This large and important Gurung village has an impressive location, being set high upon an open terraced hillside with uninterrupted views of Annapurna South, Hiunchuli and Machhapuchhare. Many of the slate-roofed houses have flagstone courtyards, and paved alleys twist through the village with enough side-trails to help you become disoriented. Ghandruk (or Ghandrung, as it's also spelt) has a *gompa*, a Gurung museum and a telephone office. There's a **health post**, a post office, police post and an ACAP Visitor Centre in which a promotional video is shown three times daily: at 9.30am, 11.30am and 3.30pm. The village has several shops and tea-houses, a few camping grounds and more than 20 lodges, among them, the Trekker's Lodge (three-times winner of ACAP's 'Lodge of the Year' award) and the nearby Milan and Manisha hotels. There's the new Hotel Buddha near the ACAP building and, at the upper end of the village, the up-market (and more expensive) Ker & Downey-owned Himalaya Lodge.

Leaving Ghandruk for Chhomrong make your way to the upper, northern, part of the village, where the Shangri La Guesthouse is the last of the lodges. About 10mins later cross a short suspension bridge over a tributary stream and continue on a broad clear path, veering left at a trail junction, and rising gradually above fields and passing several houses and tea-houses to eventually gain a saddle on a wooded ridge at

KOMRONG DANDA (2250m, 7382ft). Also spelt Khomrong, or Khumrong, a small group of tea-houses and basic lodges are tucked in the saddle about an hour's walk from Ghandruk. The Annapurna View, Machhapuchhare Lodge and the Komrong Guesthouse stand together at the pass, but a 20min walk along the ridge to the right leads to a fourth hotel, the Hill Town Lodge, set in splendid isolation. From there a very steep path

The makeshift bridge over the Kimrong Khola

plunges down the hillside to New Bridge on the west bank of the Modi Khola.

Bear left at the saddle, then fork right and descend through forest on an eroded path that makes countless zigzags and, near the lower edge of the forest, passes the Namaste Teashop (more fine views of Machhapuchhare). Shortly after follow a minor stream down to the Kimrong Khola where a log bridge crosses the river to

KIMRONG (1780m, 5840ft), a small village on the north bank of the river, reached in about 45mins from Komrong Danda. The first building here is the simple Kimrong Riverside Hotel, and from it a short walk brings you into the village, where there's the Kimrong Guesthouse and Hotel Navina.

The path now cuts uphill, passing the Kimrong View Teashop and then climbing on a fairly steep winding trail up a wooded hillside to gain a high crossing path near the Kaji Lunch Centre. Turn right and, passing the tea-house/lodge, continue on the lightly undulating path which is used by the Tadapani–Chhomrong route. About 30mins later you come to the scattered village of **TAGLUNG**, and 10mins later turn a spur to find the Heaven View near the junction with the path from New Bridge. Go up the slope to the Summit View Lodge, and continue on stone steps to reach the Panorama Point Lodge, Fishtail Guesthouse and an ACAP check-post at the entrance to

CHHOMRONG (2170m, 7110ft). For full details of the village, its lodges and facilities, please refer to Section 1a.

JIMMY ROBERTS – THE FATHER OF TREKKING

The name of Jimmy Roberts is legendary in mountaineering circles, and is synonymous with trekking in Nepal. And the history of climbing and exploration in the Annapurna region especially is punctuated with his deeds, so it comes as no surprise to learn that as soon as he could, he made his home in Pokhara and died there at the age of 81 in 1997.

Born and brought up in India, Jimmy Roberts joined the old British Indian Army at the end of 1936, mainly, he confessed, because he wanted to climb in the Himalaya – not just one expedition, but to spend a lifetime exploring and mountaineering there. It was an ambition that became reality, thanks initially to his joining a Gurkha Regiment with headquarters in what is now Himachal Pradesh, which gave him regular opportunities to climb in the granite Dhaula Dhar range above Dharmsala. At the age of 20, he took part in his first expedition, to Masherbrum in the Karakoram, but the following year virtually all mountaineering activity came to an end as war broke out. Roberts fought with the Gurkhas and won the Military Cross, and resumed his climbing career in 1946.

Nepal tentatively opened its doors to the outside world in 1949, and a year later Roberts joined Bill Tilman on an ill-organised expedition to the Annapurnas. The climbers reached Manang the day the monsoon began and (in Roberts' words) 'failed to reach even the summit of lowly Annapurna IV'. With the excuse of mild frostbite ending his climbing for the time being, Roberts spent the rest of the monsoon exploring the Manang and Dudh Khola valleys, then walked with a Sherpa to Pokhara, where he claimed to have 'entered my private Mecca.'

The 1950s were busy Himalayan years. In 1953 Roberts organised the transportation of oxygen for the successful British attempt on Everest, and while that climb was taking place he went off to explore the Lumding, Inuku and Hongu valleys, and made the first ascent of Mera and a south–north crossing of the icy Amphu Lapcha pass in basketball boots. In 1954 with Sherpa Ang Nyima, he climbed Dhaulagiri VII (Putha Hiunchuli) during a reconnaissance of the Dhaulagiri massif; he was the first foreigner to enter the Annapurna Sanctuary in 1956, and led the Machhapuchhare expedition of 1957. In 1958 Roberts began a three-year posting as Military Attaché in Kathmandu, led the successful British/Indian/Nepalese expedition to Annapurna II in 1960, then retired from the army in 1961, but managed to stay on in Nepal. Two years later he played a part in the American Mount Everest Expedition that saw Unsoeld and Hornbein climb the West Ridge and then make the first traverse of the mountain.

By then, Roberts had realised that while high-altitude mountaineering was often an uncomfortable, masochistic pursuit, the walk-in to the mountains was by contrast both relaxing and highly enjoyable, and prophesied that it would appeal to adventurous holiday-makers. Remembering how in Kashmir agents used to help organise the hunting trips of his friends, providing camping gear, staff, porters and food, he developed the theme in terms of journeying to and around the high mountains. Trekking was born, and by the end of 1964 'Mountain Travel' had registered with the Nepalese Government as the country's first trekking agency. The first clients arrived a year later when Roberts accompanied three American ladies on a springtime trek to the Khumbu. And the rest, as they say, is history.

SECTION 2:
Chhomrong to Annapurna Base Camp

Distance:	21km (13 miles)
Time:	3 days (12hrs)
Start altitude:	2170m (7110ft)
High point:	Annapurna Base Camp, 4130m (13,550ft)
Height difference:	1960m (6430ft)

The two-day trek through the gorge of the Modi Khola is something of a switchback, with a number of steep ascents and descents on a trail that in places can be very slippery. The gorge is notoriously damp and misty, and for much of the time views are severely restricted as the route progresses through forests of rhododendron and bamboo thickets. But when views are clear Machhapuchhare dominates, now revealing the fish-tail summit ridge that gives the mountain its name. Since the gorge route is used in both directions by every visitor to the Sanctuary – trekkers, mountaineering expeditions and their porters – at times bottle-necks occur. Lodges also become heavily used, and you're advised not to push on too late in the day before booking a bed for the night.

In the introductory paragraphs to the Sanctuary Trek, a warning was given with regard to avalanche danger near Hinko Cave. This warning is repeated: if there's been recent heavy snowfall, do not risk crossing the exposed area until it is safe to do so. If in doubt, ask lodge keepers for advice.

Once you enter the Sanctuary proper near Machhapuchhare Base Camp, you're too close to the mountains to gain a proper perspective, but another 400m (1300ft) of ascent to Annapurna Base Camp will enable you to appreciate the full impact of this magical arena. For this you'll need to be acclimatised, so on the way through the Modi Khola's gorge, you're advised to drink copious amounts of liquid and to ascend slowly to give your body time to adjust to the altitude. (See notes on Mountain Sickness under the 'On-Trek Healthcare' section in the Introduction.)

In recent years ACAP authorities have been pro-active in managing the Sanctuary Trek by closing those lodges located in possible danger areas and regrouping them in designated sites, limiting the size of individual hotels, and outlawing the cutting and burning of timber. Sections of trail are being upgraded and paved, and litter drums have been provided. These measures should help control the environmental impact of large numbers of visitors being funnelled into a relatively small area, and at the same time improve the experience for those visitors.

Below Chhomrong, at 1860m (6102ft), cross a suspension bridge over the Chhomrong Khola, with Annapurna South towering at the head of its gorge to your left. The trail now begins a long twisting climb up and round the hillside spur that divides the valleys of the Chhomrong and Modi Kholas. An interminable flight of steps takes you past a few simple tea-houses, and in 30mins from the bridge you reach the Hotel Himal, which commands a fine view of Chhomrong across the valley. Continue a little higher to Sherpa Guesthouse, built on the spur where the trail turns into the Modi Khola's gorge. Machhapuchhare looks magnificent from here. Continue along the trail for a few more minutes to gain

SINUWA (2340m, 7677ft), about 1hr from the bridge. There's a group of three lodges and stunning views of Machhapuchhare,

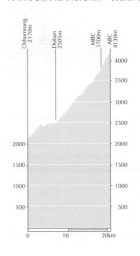

ANNAPURNA SANCTUARY – Section 2

On leaving Chhomrong a view through the valley of the Chhomrong Khola looks directly at Annapurna South and Hiunchuli

Annapurna III and Gangapurna from Sinuwa Lodge, Hilltop Lodge and the Sinuwa Guesthouse.

The trail leads on, somewhat rougher than before, and enters rainforest whose rhododendrons are wonderful in the springtime. About 55mins from Sinuwa the trail forks. There's little to indicate that this is close to the site of **KULDE** (Khuldigar; 2540m, 8333ft), a former British sheep-breeding station whose buildings were taken over by ACAP as a check-post and visitor centre. These too have now been closed. Take the lower branch and pass an abandoned building, then begin the steep descent that leads through dense bamboo and rhododendron jungle to the appropriately named lodge complex of

BAMBOO (2335m, 7661ft, 2½hrs). There are five stone-built hotels here: the Buddha, Bamboo and Trekking guesthouses, the Bamboo Lodge and Green View Lodge.

The 1¼hr climb from Bamboo to Doban is less severe than the earlier part of the walk, and you make a steady ascent, albeit with a few short steep sections. On the way there are several side-streams to cross. These are usually aided by large stepping stones or with bamboo poles lashed together to form a bridge. The route continues to be slippery when wet. Moments after passing a small hydro-plant you arrive at

DOBAN (2505m, 8219ft, 3¾–4hrs). Also spelt Dovan, the three lodges and camping grounds spread in a line within a brief forest clearing are: the Dovan Guesthouse, Annapurna Approach Lodge and Hotel Tip-Top. Machhapuchhare can once again be seen soaring overhead to the north-east.

Continuing in forest, more switchbacks and narrow sections of trail lead deeper into the gorge. About 45mins after leaving Doban you come to a small Hindu shrine opposite a string of waterfalls. ▶

    About 1hr 10mins beyond Doban you cross a stream and come to another clearing with the two lodges and camping area of

HIMALAYA (2875m, 9432ft, 5¼hrs). Himalaya Guesthouse and Himalaya Hotel stand close together below Mardi Himal, the southern outlier of Machhapuchhare. An ACAP sign warns of avalanche danger between here and Machhapuchhare Base Camp, proposing that you cross the area of risk before 10am and follow the advice of local lodge owners. Should conditions suggest that you take the alternative trail beyond Hinko Cave, please do so even though it will probably take longer than the standard route.

Leaving Himalaya Hotel the trail winds up among bamboo thickets and forest, narrow in places and still slippery after rain or snow, then steepens to gain **HINKO CAVE** (3150m, 10,335ft). For a few years a simple lodge that could sleep about a dozen people was tucked against the huge overhanging boulder formerly used as a bivouac site by the shepherds and hunters who forced this trail, but this has been closed by the ACAP authorities and resited a little futher upvalley.

    Beyond Hinko descend to cross a ravine and climb out on the other side. This is a classic avalanche trap. On occasion the gorge is virtually blocked here, and it is often necessary to climb over the debris brought down from the slopes of Hiunchuli, unseen above to the left. The way continues across several streams and between boulders, and about half an hour from Hinko brings you to the four lodges of

This is the shrine of Panchenin Baraha, the local deity, beyond which, according to custom, no person of menial caste should proceed, nor may any flesh of chicken, cow or pig be taken. In *Climbing the Fish's Tail*, Jimmy Roberts reported that 'The Goddess must be propitiated at the shrine … by the offering of small gifts and dhaja, streamers of coloured cloth.' On his first visit in 1956 Roberts himself had found it necessary to leave 50 eggs at a nearby grazing area, and a few coins and some cigarettes at the shrine, as a peace offering.

DEURALI (3230m, 10,597ft, 6½hrs): the Deurali, Shangrila, Panorama Guesthouse and Dream Hotel. In the event of avalanche danger, check with the lodge owners here for the safest route above Bagar.

The valley broadens and there's a change in vegetation as the trail meanders across a fairly level section where Gangapurna shows itself ahead, framed by the steep walls that form the gateway to the Sanctuary. More avalanche chutes are crossed, and the path once more climbs against the left-hand mountainside, then drops to the river, which it follows to a meadow where there used to be two small lodges. This area was known as **BAGAR**.

When the standard, west side, route is blocked or threatened by avalanche, you should use an alternative trail on the eastern side of the Modi Khola above Bagar. Apparently there's usually a sign to indicate the way. The standard path, however, continues along the western flank and eventually enters the Sanctuary. A stream pours down from the left and is crossed by a bridge, and over this the trail forks. Immediately in front a stone stairway climbs a vegetated bluff to the Machhapuchare Cosy Lodge, with a German weather station nearby. The left fork skirts below the bluff and brings you to the other buildings of

MACHHAPUCHHARE BASE CAMP (MBC) (3700m, 12,139ft, 7½–8hrs). There are five lodges in all, including the Cosy Lodge; the others are: the Gurung Co-op, Annapurna View, the Sankar and the Fish Tail Lodge. Machhapuchhare (6993m, 22,943ft) rises abruptly to your right: a great shaft of rock, snow and ice seriously foreshortened and failing to provide the beautiful fish-tail profile for which it is known (see box 'The Fish-Tail Peak', p234)). Above to the left can be seen the north-eastern aspect of Annapurna South, while more extensive views are reserved for the belvedere of Annapurna Base Camp.

It was around here that Jimmy Roberts and his small team made their base while attempting to climb Machhapuchhare in 1957, the story of which is told by Wilfrid Noyce in Climbing the Fish's Tail. Then in 1970, during his reconnaissance in advance of the successful ascent of the South Face of Annapurna I, Don Whillans made a temporary camp here and saw, first, a moving shape then tracks that his Sherpas swore belonged

Annapurna III (left) and Gandharba Chuli from Annapurna Base Camp

to a Yeti. Whillans describes this experience in Chris Bonington's book Annapurna South Face.

The altitude here at MBC is sufficient to produce symptoms of Acute Mountain Sickness in unacclimatised trekkers, so if you are being affected, under no circumstances should you attempt to go any higher until the symptoms disappear.

The final 400m climb to Annapurna Base Camp ascends at a steady gradient, never very steeply, yet the altitude is likely to have a tiring effect. Don't be tempted to hurry, even if you are fit and untroubled by the altitude; instead it's best to ascend slowly and enjoy the expanding panorama. The route is on a clear, well-defined trail that angles along a trough below the vegetated moraine of the unseen South Annapurna glacier, and as you gain height so the lodge buildings are revealed ahead. The final rise to gain these lodges is the steepest part of the approach.

Beginning this last stage of the route from the Fish Tail Lodge area, simply follow the path which heads west to join the main trail rising through the centre of the valley. This rises easily through the undulating ablation valley, below the glacial moraine, and with the slopes of Hiunchuli rising above to your left. Cross a minor ridge to a flat area with rivulets flowing through and continue upvalley with views to Annapurna

South and its northern ridge leading towards Annapurna I, which remains frustratingly obscure until almost the last minute. Pause now and then to enjoy the growing views behind, and you will realise just how much altitude is being gained.

ANNAPURNA BASE CAMP (ABC) (4130m, 13,550ft) is gained about 1½–2hrs from MBC, and is where Chris Bonington's successful 1970 expedition to the South Face of Annapurna was sited. (The 1950 French expedition, of course, attacked the mountain from the north, with its base camp located at the head of the Miristi Khola.) It's a cold, often windy and snowbound place rimmed by glacial moraines – but with the most amazing high mountain panorama to make it all worthwhile. But note that clouds often fill the Sanctuary around midday and remain there to deny all views until early evening.

Perhaps the very best views to be had by non-mountaineers are from the crest of the moraine wall just beyond the lodges – a magical place that looks out at soaring buttresses of rock and ice, hanging glaciers, snowfields, shapely peaks and ridges whose pristine cornices are etched against the deep blue of a Himalayan sky. You'll find a memorial up here to Russian mountaineer Anatoli Boukreev, who was killed by an avalanche on the Southwest Face of Annapurna I on Christmas Day 1997 – one of many climbers to have lost their lives within this arc of visual splendour.

There are four lodges here: the Annapurna, Annapurna Sanctuary, Snowland and the Paradise Garden. They all serve reasonable meals, offer private rooms and have surprisingly good toilet facilities for such a remote location. But be warned: if you are suffering any effects of the altitude, you should not consider spending a night here, but descend at least as far as MBC.

THE SANCTUARY

This extravagantly beautiful amphitheatre forms an almost complete circle, with only the narrow cleft of the Modi Khola's gorge breaking the ring of high mountains. Beginning in the south and working clockwise, those peaks on display are: Hiunchuli, Annapurna South, Baraha Shikhar (otherwise known as Fang) and Annapurna I; then Singu Chuli (Fluted Peak) and Tharpu Chuli (Tent Peak) effectively block the continuing rim of the Sanctuary until you gaze on Gangapurna,

Annapurna III, the delicate peak of Gandharba Chuli (Gabelhorn) and Machhapuchhare, whose face appears to plunge into a bottomless well.

Four mountains within, and on the edge of, the amphitheatre are on the official list of Trekking Peaks. (This title is something of a misnomer, since high-mountaineering experience and equipment will be required in order to tackle them.) These are: Hiunchuli (6441m, 21,132ft), Singu Chuli (6501m, 21,329ft), Tharpu Chuli (5663m, 18,580ft) and Mardi Himal (5588m, 18,333ft), this last-named being an extension of Machhapuchhare and the most southerly of the Annapurna group.

Of these Hiunchuli was first climbed by an American Peace Corps expedition in 1971; Singu Chuli by Wilfrid Noyce and David Cox following their failed attempt on Machhapuchhare (1957); Tharpu Chuli by a Japanese expedition bound for Annapurna South in 1964; while Mardi Himal fell to Jimmy Roberts and two Sherpas in 1961.

In time, all the higher mountains of the Sanctuary have naturally drawn the attention of full-scale expeditions. The Japanese were among the very first, climbing both Tarke Kang (Glacier Dome, 7202m, 23,629ft) and the superb Annapurna South, referred to as Ganesh by Roberts in the 1950s, but also known as Annapurna Dakshin. This 7219m (23,684ft) peak which so dominates the village of Chhomrong received its first ascent, via the North Ridge, from an expedition mounted by Kyoto University in 1964.

Annapurna I (8091m, 26,545ft), as has already been mentioned, was the first 8000m mountain to be climbed when Herzog and Lachenal reached the summit from the north in 1950. Both summiteers suffered severe frostbite, were forced to bivouac in a crevasse on the way down, and only narrowly escaped with their lives (see box, p209). The awesome South Face was climbed by Bonington's British expedition in 1970, with Don Whillans and Dougal Haston reaching the summit just seven days after the original North Face route had received its second ascent from a British Army expedition.

Gangapurna (7454m, 24,455ft) was won by a German team led by Gunther Hauser in 1965. The original aim of this expedition was to climb Annapurna I from the Sanctuary, but on appraisal they altered course and decided instead to tackle this fine, hitherto unclimbed peak to the west of Annapurna III.

Annapurna III (7555m, 24,787ft) and its extensive south-projecting ridge, which forms one of the embracing arms of the Sanctuary, effectively blocks the eastern part of the massif from view. (Beyond it rise Annapurnas IV and II, and Lamjung Himal.) Annapurna III was climbed in 1961 by an Indian expedition and, as has already been stated, a small British team led by Jimmy Roberts climbed to about 50m below the summit of Machhapuchhare (6993m, 22,943ft) in 1957, since when all further applications to attempt the mountain have been refused by the Nepalese authorities. It is rumoured, however, that Machhapuchhare has received at least one illegal ascent by a solo climber.

RETURN ROUTES TO POKHARA

All routes out of the Annapurna Sanctuary retrace the inward trek as far as CHHOMRONG (1–2 days), but from there a choice of trails becomes feasible. These are outlined below. Each alternative route is well supplied with lodge accommodation and tea-houses

To POKHARA via LANDRUK and DHAMPUS (2 days). This retraces the main trek described above as Section 1a, and is a little less strenuous than the way in. From CHHOMRONG descend to the Modi Khola at NEW BRIDGE, and over the river take the path which climbs to LANDRUK and continues over the ridge at DEURALI to DHAMPUS and, eventually, down to PHEDI near the head of the Yamdi Khola, from where it's possible to take a short bus or taxi ride to POKHARA.

To POKHARA via GHANDRUK and NAYA PUL (2 days). Reversing Section 1c, this makes a very pleasant two-day trek. Leave CHHOMRONG walking along the high trail through TAGLUNG to a junction near the Kaji Lunch Centre. Descend to KIMRONG, cross the Kimrong Khola and climb through forest for a little over an hour to the few simple lodges of KOMRONG DANDA. GHAN-DRUK is less than an hour's walk away. Next day descend to SYAULI BAZAAR on the Modi Khola, then follow the river downstream to BIRETHANTI and NAYA PUL for the bus or taxi ride out to POKHARA.

To POKHARA via GHANDRUK and LANDRUK (2–3 days). This combines the two previous options to give a longer and more strenuous trek which retains fine views throughout. After reaching GHANDRUK by way of the previous route, descend directly to the Modi Khola at Beehive Lodge, then cross the river and climb to LANDRUK, where you join the first option to DHAMPUS, PHEDI and POKHARA.

To POKHARA via NEW BRIDGE and BIRETHANTI (1–2 days). This, the shortest route, was described in reverse as Section 1b. It begins by descending to NEW BRIDGE, as in the first option above, but instead of crossing the river here, it fol-lows the right bank of the Modi Khola all the way to SYAULI BAZAAR and BIRETHANTI. There you cross the river and wander along a track to NAYA PUL for the bus or taxi ride out to POKHARA.

TREK 3:
THE PILGRIM'S
TRAIL TO MUKTINATH

This world is but a thoroughfare full of woe,
And we being pilgrims passing to and fro.

(Geoffrey Chaucer)

TREK SUMMARY

Distance:	88km (54 miles) to Muktinath
Time:	7–9 days (plus time to return)
Max. altitude:	3710m (12,172ft)
Start:	Beni or Naya Pul
Finish:	Muktinath or Jomosom
Trekking style:	Tea-house (lodge accommodation) or camping

Unlike that of Chaucer's knight, the thoroughfare of the Pilgrim's Trail, which leads from Pokhara to Muktinath, though steep at times, is far from being one of woe. Instead it is a constant evolution of delights, and pilgrims of both the Hindu and Buddhist faiths who tread it do so in a spirit of calm expectation – as might we trekkers.

This trail has been known for centuries, for it is thought that pilgrims were drawn through the valley of the Kali Gandaki to Muktinath as early as 300 BC, and the greater part of the route was used by generations of traders on journeys to and from Mustang and Tibet. This trade, which came to an end in the late 1950s with the Chinese occupation of Tibet, largely consisted of rice and barley from the lowlands of Nepal being carried north, with Tibetan salt and wool being brought back downvalley.

The Pilgrim's Trail follows the Kali Gandaki upstream through the world's deepest valley, passing from the lush fertility of the foothills to the stark and arid hillsides on the northern side of the Annapurna Himal – in the rain-shadow of the mountains.

It is the busiest of all trails in Nepal. In addition to Western trekkers and their entourage of guides and porters embarked upon this and the Annapurna Circuit, which shares it, there are the long strings of pack animals that continue to carry goods from one end of the valley to the other – though no longer crossing into Tibet. There are the heavily laden porters who keep the lodges and tea-houses stocked with goods, local Nepalis about their everyday business and, of course, the pilgrims for whom Muktinath is a holy site, one of the most important in Nepal for Hindus.

The trek from the roadhead out of Pokhara to Muktinath and back will take about two weeks, but for those with limited time there is a possibility of shortening the return by flying out of Jomosom – weather conditions permitting.

Features of the journey, which reverses the second half of the Annapurna Circuit (Trek 1), are the stupendous mountain views, of course – with close views of some of the world's highest mountains that form an avenue through which you walk day after day. In addition there are the dramatic contrasts of vegetation from one end of the valley to the other; climatic, architectural and cultural variations; and a sense of shrugging off one world in exchange for a very different one on the northern side of the Himalayan Divide – 'beyond the last blue mountain'. The barrier of this Himalayan Divide is breached by the Kali Gandaki, and by following the river upstream you enter a high and seemingly barren land that has more in common with Tibet than the colourful Nepal of the trek's early stages. ◀

The Pilgrim's Trail is one of Nepal's classic tea-house treks. The Thakalis who inhabit much of the region through which it passes are noted hoteliers, and their mountain lodges are among the finest in the country. Lodges and tea-houses are liberally scattered along the route, so you can rely on frequent refreshment stops and accommodation all the way, and are therefore able to travel light.

It's possible to trek the Pilgrim's Trail throughout the year, although the summer monsoon period makes the early stages somewhat unpleasant with mud, landslide danger and leeches. In March, April and early May the rhododendron forests of the Poon Hill Danda can be spectacular, while the clearest weather and sharpest views can be enjoyed in the post-monsoon period of October to mid-December.

This is not a difficult or demanding trek by Himalayan standards. Mostly the trails are clear and well made, except where landslides may have swept the route and temporary path sections have been created. Route-finding is easy, and the maximum altitude reached is comparatively modest for Nepal, for Muktinath stands at only 3800m (12,467ft). As this height is gained steadily over a number of days, altitude sickness should not be a problem. But as Pokhara lies at only 820m (2690ft), the difference in altitude from start to finish should add sufficient spice.

The trek is shrinking in length. Since construction of the Pokhara–Baglung–Beni road, hardly anyone treks all the way from Pokhara now. Instead there are two main starting points, both of which are accessible by bus or taxi. The first is Beni, a roadhead township at the confluence of the Kali Gandaki and Myagdi Khola rivers; the other at Naya Pul, a roadside shanty 20mins walk from Birethanti on the Modi Khola.

From Beni two easy riverside days lead to Tatopani, the village known for its hot springs and gastronomic delights; while to reach Tatopani from Naya Pul and Birethanti entails a 3–4 day crossing of the Poon Hill Danda, a substantial crest of rhododendron forest at over 2700m (8858ft), from which exciting views reveal the way ahead.

Beyond Tatopani the Pilgrim's Trail heads upvalley all the way: sometimes on the left bank, sometimes on the right, the big mountains soaring to unguessable heights above the river. Two or three days after leaving Tatopani you pass between Annapurna and Dhaulagiri. The trail then curves north-east-ward and visits attractive villages such as Khobang, Tukuche and Marpha before reaching Jomosom, the valley's administrative centre. From this busy little town you face a choice of routes to Muktinath. One visits medieval Kagbeni before climbing through the valley of the Jhong Khola; the other is a direct route which turns a mountain spur and makes a gradual ascent to handsome Jharkot and, finally, to Muktinath itself.

SECTION 1:
Pokhara to Tatopani

Distance:	70km (43 miles)
Time:	2–4 days
Start altitude:	820m (2690ft)
High point:	Ghorepani Deurali, 2750m (9022ft)
Height difference:	1930m (6332ft)
Transport options:	Bus or taxi (Pokhara to Beni or Naya Pul)

This first section of the route assumes you will take advantage of the Baglung–Beni road from Pokhara. Up to 24 public buses a day serve this road, leaving the bus terminal in the north-west of town near Bhairab Tole. Alternatively, hire a taxi for greater comfort and speed.

As mentioned above, there are two main options for the Pilgrim's Trail as far as Tatopani. The shortest and easiest route follows the Kali Gandaki upstream from Beni, and is the route taken by Herzog's 1950 expedition to Annapurna I, but by taking this you miss the spectacle of sunrise from Poon Hill, which is a highlight of any trek in the Annapurna region. On the other hand, the climb from Birethanti to Ghorepani on the Poon Hill Danda is something of a baptism of fire for trekkers newly arrived in the country, with thousands of stone steps to labour up before finding the relief of forest shade. Scenic rewards, however, make it all worthwhile.

The Beni–Tatopani option reduces the overall length of the trek by about two days, and is growing in popularity. Lodges and tea-houses are not only increasing in number, but improving in the quality of service they provide, and it's quite possible that this will soon become accepted as the main route.

Section 1a:
Beni to Tatopani

Distance:	21km (13 miles)
Time:	7hrs
Start altitude:	830m (2723ft)
High point:	Tatopani, 1190m (3904ft)
Height gain:	360m (1181ft)

The Chinese-built road that currently ends at Beni heads out of Pokhara along the valley of the Yamdi Khola, twists over the Kaski Danda ridge at Naudanda, then descends to the lower reaches of the Modi Khola at Naya Pul. Now heading south-west the road remains with the Modi Khola as far as Kusma, before turning north-west into the Kali Gandaki's valley. It forks near Pang, with one branch crossing the river to Baglung, the district administrative headquarters, some 74km from Pokhara, while the other continues upstream for another 12km or so to reach Beni.

BENI (830m, 2723ft) stands at the confluence of the Myagdi Khola and Kali Gandaki rivers. It's a busy little township with a variety of shops and tea-houses, as well as a **hospital,** police station, bank, telephone facilities, a cinema and a pharmacy. There are at least three lodges: Hotel Yeti, Namaste and the Dolphin.

The trek from here to Tatopani follows the Kali Gandaki all the way – and will continue to do so as far as Jomosom. This initial section crosses a number of landslide areas, and in places the trail is rather exposed, but it's an interesting route and one to enjoy at a relaxed pace as you settle into your stride. In the pre-monsoon months temperatures are high, and during these early stages you'll no doubt be eager for any shade available.

Leaving Beni remain on the west bank of the Kali Gandaki heading north, and crossing a few landslides reach the attractive village of

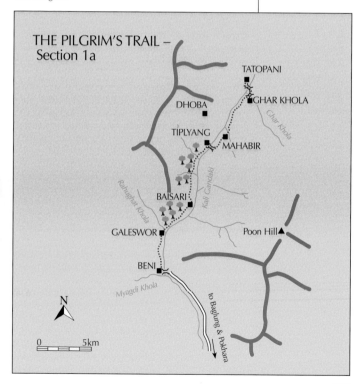

THE PILGRIM'S TRAIL – Section 1a

PILGRIM'S TRAIL – Section 1a

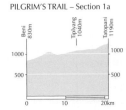

GALESWOR (1170m, 3839ft) in a little over an hour. Also known as Rahughat after the tributary on whose bank it sits, the village is the site of an annual fair which takes place in November or December. Facilities here include a post office and two or three lodges. Hotel Riverside is located near a suspension bridge over the Rahughat Khola.

Cross the Rahughat Khola to **RANIPAUWA**, and soon after the valley narrows. As it does, there are more landslides to negotiate during the hour or so it takes to reach

BAISARI (960m, 3150ft), a small settlement of tea-houses and simple lodges: the Namaste, Annapurna, Lete and Riverside guesthouses. Just beyond, there are a few more tea-houses and the Super View Lodge.

Between Baisari and Tiplyang where you cross the Kali Gandaki, the trail is largely contained by forest. It's something of a switchback, with several more landslides to tackle, but after crossing the Beg Khola tributary the route has been created along a rock gallery, then among fields of corn and hemp (marijuana) before reaching

TIPLYANG (1040m, 3412ft, 4–4½hrs). This small village consists of several tea-houses and simple lodges: the Star, Sherchan, Mustang, Hill View and Ama Lodge.

The trail now crosses the Kali Gandaki by suspension bridge, passes through another settlement and continues upvalley along the east bank among rice paddies to reach **MAHABHIR** and its tea-houses. After this a stone stairway and gallery works a route across abrupt cliffs, then descends steeply to river level and another small tea-house. More stone steps take you up and along an exposed section of trail, and finally down once more to some lodges built near the hot springs of **RATO PANI**. Twenty minutes or so beyond these lodges you come to

GHAR KHOLA (1175m, 3855ft, 6½hrs). As you reach the Meet You Hotel and a shop, there's a path junction. The right branch is the trail to or from Ghorepani used by the alternative route (see Section 1b).

Continue ahead, cross the Ghar Khola tributary, and shortly after recross the Kali Gandaki to its west bank by a long suspension bridge. The path now rises a little and enters

TATOPANI (1190m, 3904ft). The fame of this popular village rests on its hot springs and a reputation among trekkers for good food. Down by the river, reached through charming sub-tropical gardens, two rectangular pools of steaming water attract locals and trekkers alike – in the morning locals are usually there before most Westerners arrive. Please do not pollute the water with soap – the pools are for relaxing in, not for laundry or bathing. Facilities in the village are the best you'll get until reaching Jomosom, even though the architecture of some of its buildings leaves a lot to be desired. There's a variety of shops, a post office, **health post**, bank, official money-changer, telephone facility and several lodges and restaurants. Among the hotels there's the Trekker's Lodge and Dhaulagiri Lodge, both of which have gardens and access to the hot springs. There's also the Evergreen Lodge, Pun Hotel, Hotel Himalaya, Tiptop Hotel, Namaste Lodge and the Kamala.

Note: For the continuing route to Jomosom and Muktinath, please turn to p203.

Section 1b:
Naya Pul to Tatopani

Distance:	28km (17 miles)
Time:	11–12hrs
Start altitude:	1070m (3510ft)
High point:	Ghorepani Deurali, 2750m (9022ft)
Height gain:	1680m (5512ft)
Low point:	Ghar Khola, 1175m (3855ft)
Height loss:	1575m (5167ft)

The shanty of Naya Pul lies about 42km (26 miles) from Pokhara on the road to Baglung and Beni, a journey of about an hour by taxi. From there it's a 20min walk to Birethanti, the real start of the Pilgrim's Trail as far as we are concerned. After leaving Birethanti the climb to Ghorepani Deurali on the Poon Hill Danda is remorseless, with plenty of height gain, and much of that on the ascent to Ulleri is by way of thousands of stone steps. But on the northern side of the ridge the descent to Tatopani is rewarding for the colourful terraced hillsides and distant mountain views. On both sides of the Poon Hill Danda there's no shortage of either teahouses or lodges.

From the road at Naya Pul wander down the slope, cross a tributary by suspension bridge, and follow a broad track

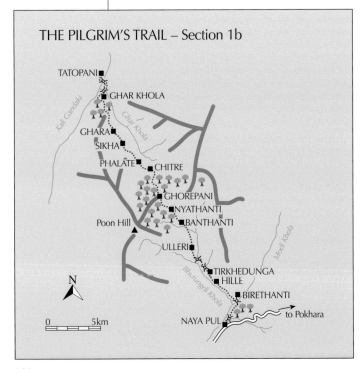

THE PILGRIM'S TRAIL – Section 1b

TATOPANI

GHAR KHOLA

Kali Gandaki

Ghar Khola

GHARA

SIKHA

PHALATE

CHITRE

GHOREPANI

NYATHANTI

Poon Hill

BANTHANTI

ULLERI

Modi Khola

TIRKHEDUNGA

HILLE

BIRETHANTI

Bhurungdi Khola

N

0   5km

NAYA PUL

to Pokhara

at first between basic shops and tea-houses, then alongside the Modi Khola, and in 20mins come to the Fishtail Lodge and another suspension bridge. Cross the Modi Khola to enter

BIRETHANTI (1025m, 3363ft), a busy, attractive and important bazaar built at the confluence of the Modi Khola (the river that drains the Annapurna Sanctuary) and Bhurungdi Khola. An ACAP check-post is located by the bridge, and you should show your entry permit and, for safety purposes, register details there. Birethanti has a number of shops, a post office, bank, hotels and tea-houses. The street is paved with flagstones, and from it two major trekking routes set out: the trail to Ghandruk and the Annapurna Sanctuary follows the Modi Khola to the right; while the path to Ghorepani and Tatopani passes through the village heading left.

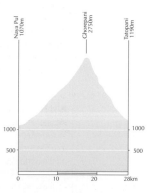

THE PILGRIM'S TRAIL – Section 1b

Out of Birethanti the trail keeps to the north bank of the Bhurungdi Khola, so ignore the temptation to cross by either of two bridges. The way goes through bamboo forest, passes a large waterfall and a landslide, continues through **MATATHANTI** and **SUDAME**, both of which have lodges and tea-houses, then rises steadily through cultivated farmland to reach

HILLE (1475m, 4839ft, 2hrs). This settlement has several tea-houses and lodges, including the Laxmi, Annapurna, Susila and See You.

Ten minutes or so further along the trail lies

TIRKHEDUNGA (1540m, 5052ft), some of whose lodges are advertised as being run by ex-Gurkha soldiers, among them, the Indra, Chandra, Kamala, Laxmi and Laligurans. There's also a campsite near the river.

The village is near the confluence of the Tirkhedunga and Bhurungdi Khola rivers, and the continuing trail crosses both before tackling the long staircase of stone steps (over 3000 of them) that lead to Ulleri. Tea-houses offer welcome refreshment along the way, and there's just one lodge before Ulleri (the Annapurna View Guesthouse), but as you gain height so views to Annapurna South and Hiunchuli help take your mind off the ascent. Two hours or so from Tirkhedunga brings you to

ULLERI (1960m, 6430ft, 4½hrs). This attractive, slate-roofed Magar village makes a pleasant overnight resting place. From it you gaze deeply into the valley of the Bhurungdi Khola and out towards Pokhara, the way you have come, as well as off to the north-east where the big mountains look very fine. There are plenty of lodges, both in the village itself and a little above it, that make the most of the panorama reflected in their names: the Excellent View, Super View, Annapurna Viewpoint, the Pratap, Kamal and Mountain View.

Above the village the trail climbs steadily through farmland, and about an hour after leaving Ulleri you arrive in the settlement of

BANTHANTI (2300m, 7546ft, 5½hrs), which means 'the place in the forest'. This marks the beginning of the oak and rhododendron forest that straddles the ridge. The village consists of tea-houses and lodges spread in a line alongside the trail: the Fishtail View, Mountain View, Namaste, Poon and Green Hill View.

◀ Keen bird watchers should enjoy this stage. Nepal boasts an impressive bird count, and more than 440 species have been recorded within the Annapurna region alone. The grey langur also inhabits the forests either side of Ghorepani's ridge and may be seen swinging through the trees above the trail.

Crossing one or two streams the way climbs on and reaches

NYATHANTI (2500m, 8202ft), a collection of lodges in a forest clearing: Hotel Sunrise, the Hungry Eye and Laligurans.

From here to Ghorepani Deurali you're advised not to trek alone. There have been several instances of solo trekkers being robbed in these forests, and although the risk is probably not high, it would be sensible to heed the warning and find a companion for the trek to Ghorepani.

The majority of the climb is over by now, for there are only another 250m (820ft) or so to ascend before coming onto the ridge at Ghorepani Deurali. First, though, you come to

GHOREPANI, the original settlement, built before the demand for trekkers' accommodation turned the pass into a resort of lodges and tea-houses. Ghorepani is a rather haphazard collection of lodges and houses in a much denuded patch of forest. It gained its name, which means 'horse's water', because this is the last point to rest and water pack animals before crossing the pass.

Another ten minutes or so uphill on the stone-slab trail will bring you to the unattractive and crowded gathering of trekkers' lodges filling the pass on the Poon Hill Danda known here as

GHOREPANI DEURALI (2750m, 9022ft, 7–7½hrs). Before there were any trekkers' lodges here, the Deurali (meaning 'pass') had only a *chautaara* (porters' resting place) built around a tree, whose branches were garlanded with prayer flags. Now there's an ACAP information office, as well as a few shops and numerous blue-painted tin-roofed hotels. Accommodation

Birethanti marks the start of the long climb to Ghorepani (Photo: Alan Payne)

The magic of Poon Hill

Poon Hill (3193m, 10,476ft), the hill to the left (west) of Ghorepani Deurali, whose viewing tower can be seen from the village, can be reached in about 45 minutes. The hill was apparently named after Major Poon, a retired soldier who created the path to it. From the summit there are magnificent views of Annapurna South, Hiunchuli and Machhapuchhare to the north-east, and to the great mass of Dhaulagiri hovering above the Kali Gandaki to the north. Both sunset and sunrise from this belvedere can be outstanding. A simple tea-house provides mugs of coffee and hot chocolate.

is in the following: the Fishtail Lodge, Sunny Hotel, Excellent View, Pun Hill Guesthouse, Annapurna View, Himalaya View, Snow View, Trekkers Lodge, Dhaulagiri View, New Kamala, Green View, Tukuche Peak View, New Mountain View Lodge and the Nilgiri Guesthouse.

The descent from Ghorepani to Tatopani, much of it among terraced hillsides with intricately patterned fields, is a beautiful walk. After the visual restrictions imposed by forest on the southern side of the Poon Hill Danda it's a delight to be wandering downhill with open views ahead. Dhaulagiri dominates the northern horizon – a great block of mountain draped with snow and ice. Below it the shadowed defile of the Kali Gandaki's valley is vaguely hinted, but as you descend to it, so the well-crafted profile of Nilgiri South rises from the valley to add a new dimension.

Descend initially through rhododendron forest beyond the last of Ghorepani's lodges. The trail is likely to be muddy here, churned as it is by the hooves of countless pack animals, but as you emerge below the forest so the way improves.

CHITRE (2390m, 7841ft) is the first village met on the descent, a little under an hour from Ghorepani. It's a scattered settlement with a few lodges and tea-houses. An alternative trail cuts back to the right by the simple Laligurans Lodge, making for the ridge east of Ghorepani at another pass named Deurali.

From the ridge below Poon Hill, Annapurna South appears taller than Annapurna I

From there a continuing trail goes to either Ghandruk or Chhomrong and the Sanctuary (see Trek 1: Section 4b).

Ignore this option and continue to descend the main trail, soon coming to

PHALATE (2270m, 7448ft), a village with a shop, tea-house, Annapurna View and Mount View lodges, and a school.

Below Phalate there's the Nice View Lodge, then the Nilgiri Restaurant and the small settlement of **GHOPTE KHARKA** enjoying views of Dhaulagiri. Terraced fields and a few scattered houses lead down to the large Hotel Serendipity, which stands in its own garden. A few minutes beyond this you enter the first part of a subtantial village.

SIKHA (1935m, 6348ft, 2hrs from Ghorepani Deurali) is the largest village between Ghorepani and Tatopani. Built on descending levels it has a number of lodges, tea-houses and shops, and exploits a wonderful vista dominated by Dhaulagiri – an arctic world lodged in the sky high above a foreground of cultivated terraces. The upper part of Sikha lines a secondary ridge, below which the rest of its houses straddle the stone-paved trail. The See-You Lodge, Shanti View and Dhaulagiri View are the first hotels. Then you pass the Moonlight Guesthouse (with a 'European toilet and bathroom'), Purnima Guesthouse, Mona Lisa Lodge, Neha Lodge, Travels Guesthouse and the Shikha Restaurant.

The path winds on, steadily losing height, skirting the terraces and crossing a landslide, and about 30mins from Sikha comes to another village.

GHARA (1700m, 5577ft) has one or two shops and several tea-houses, while its lodges look rather more simple than those of Sikha: Mountain Guesthouse, Annapurna View and the Laxmi. Again, views of Dhaulagiri are magical from here, with its long and icy north-east ridge extending to Tukuche Peak clearly visible.

The ridge of the Durbin Danda has to be crossed for the final descent to the Ghar Khola's confluence with the Kali Gandaki.

The trail below Ghorepani, near Ghara

On the way to it you go through the small settlement of **BIRAUTA**, but on the ridge itself, in a dip through which the trail passes, a tea-house stands at a point known as **SANTOSH HILL** (1500m, 4921ft). From here you gaze down onto the forests that clothe the lower slopes, then descend into them. Far below can be seen the first glimmer of the Kali Gandaki.

More stone-paved steps lead down past several tea-houses. At the foot of the stairway join another trail and bear left, and soon after come to a group of buildings at

GHAR KHOLA (1175m, 3855ft), about 3hrs 45mins from Ghorepani Deurali. The Meet You Hotel and a small shop stand at a trail junction above the east bank of the Kali Gandaki. The left branch is the route taken by the Beni option (see Section 1a).

For Tatopani bear right, cross a bridge over the Ghar Khola tributary, pass through the rest of the village, and shortly after cross a long suspension bridge to the west bank of the Kali Gandaki, with a superb view upvalley towards Nilgiri South. The trail then heads upstream on a modest switchback and soon reaches

TATOPANI (1190m, 3904ft). For details of the village and its facilities, please refer to the end of Section 1a.

SECTION 2:
Tatopani to Muktinath

Distance:	60km (37 miles)
Time:	4–5 days
Start altitude:	1190m (3904ft)
High point:	Muktinath, 3710m (12,172ft)
Height gain:	2520m (8268ft)

On the next few stages of the trek the landscape grows wilder and more alpine. Heading north towards the Himalayan Divide you turn your back on the sub-tropical vegetation of the Middle Hills and wander into a rugged countryside where terraced fields are rare, deciduous trees mostly give way to conifers, and the architecture of village houses reflects a changing climate. It's

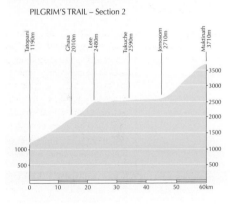

PILGRIM'S TRAIL – Section 2

very much a helter-skelter trail, shared with dozens of colourful and exotic caravans of laden horses and mules. Because the Himalayan range is still rising, this is a geologically volatile land whose instability is made worse by the heavy monsoon rains that affect the lower valley. Between Dana and Ghasa landslides sometimes force the route onto the opposite side of the river, while from Kalopani to Larjung the valley is arguably the world's deepest where the river flows between Dhaulagiri and Annapurna I. The valley of the Thak Khola, as the river is known in its upper reaches, is something of a wind tunnel. Gales usually begin to surge along the valley in mid-morning and last until late afternoon or early evening.

The continuing route out of Tatopani is in full view of the soaring face of Nilgiri South (6839m, 22,438ft), one of the western outliers of the Annapurna massif. It lures you on for some way, but later Dhaulagiri takes command of the valley. Across the river a short distance from Tatopani the Miristi Khola tributary valley provides an enticing view of the upper ice walls of the Annapurna massif, a promise of things to come.

Tatopani to Tukuche (10–12hrs) ◀

Follow the trail upvalley, passing groves of orange trees and keeping to the west side of the river. The settlement of **GUITHE** has two tea-houses and is located opposite the entrance to the Miristi Khola's valley. It was at the head of that valley that the first successful expedition to climb Annapurna established its base camp in the pre-monsoon season of 1950 (see box, p209). A bridge over the Kali Gandaki below Guithe takes a trail to a hydro-electric scheme, but you remain on the west bank and eventually come to a suspension bridge spanning the Bhalu Khola tributary. Shortly after this you arrive in the first part of

DANA (1400m, 4593ft, 1½–2hrs), a large and prosperous village built in three distinct sections, each of which has lodge accommodation. There are also a few shops, including a pharmacy. The first of Dana's lodges, the Kabin and Dana guesthouses, have fine views of Annapurna South across the valley to the east. The middle part of the village has the Annapurna Riverside Guesthouse, but before coming to the third and final section you have to cross the Ghatta Khola, a tributary stream draining through a broad and stony bed. On its north side you have the Mountain Guesthouse, New Annapurna Lodge and Riverside Lodge. Large three-storey merchants' houses with intricately carved windows give evidence of Dana's former importance. Sadly some of these buildings look rather neglected today.

THE ONWARD TRAIL – WEST BANK OR EAST?

As mentioned earlier, the continuing route upvalley is subject to landslides, and although the trail remained on the west bank beyond Dana during research for this edition, that has not always been the case, and it's possible that more landslides in future will determine that the trail crosses the river here to the east bank. Check for up-to-date information before leaving Dana. The west bank route is described in the main text, but should it be necessary to take the east bank trail, use the bridge just outside Dana to cross the Kali Gandaki. Once across you head upvalley, go through a small settlement and follow the trail as it climbs over a high shoulder of hillside with fine views across to Rupse Chhaharo and its waterfalls. There's a memorial here to a trekker who tragically fell from the trail in 1994. From the high point you descend steeply to the edge of **KOPCHEPANI** to rejoin the main route.

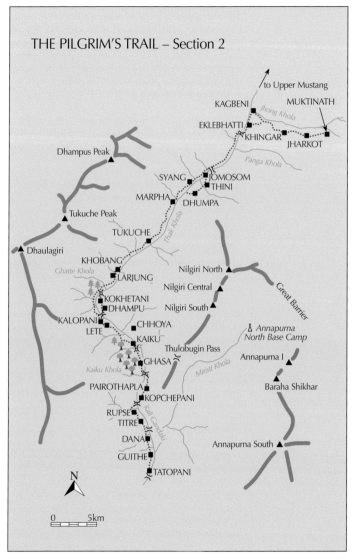

THE PILGRIM'S TRAIL – Section 2

to Upper Mustang

KAGBENI MUKTINATH

Jhong Khola

EKLEBHATTI

KHINGAR JHARKOT

Panga Khola

Dhampus Peak ▲

SYANG JOMOSOM
THINI

MARPHA DHUMPA

Tukuche Peak ▲

TUKUCHE

Thak Khola

▲ Dhaulagiri

KHOBANG

Ghatte Khola LARJUNG

Nilgiri North ▲

Nilgiri Central ▲

KOKHETANI
DHAMPU Nilgiri South ▲

KALOPANI CHHOYA

LETE KAIKU

△ *Annapurna
North Base Camp*

Kaiku Khola GHASA Thulobugin Pass

Miristi Khola Annapurna I ▲

PAIROTHAPLA Baraha Shikhar ▲

KOPCHEPANI

RUPSE

TITRE

Kali Gandaki

DANA Annapurna South ▲

GUITHE

TATOPANI

Great Barrier

N

0   5km

Out of Dana remain on the west bank trail, ignoring the suspension bridge across the Kali Gandaki, and take the path which soon leads alongside rice paddies on the way to **TITRE**, a productive little settlement with two tea-houses and lush vegetation growing right up to the buildings. Bananas, lemons and oranges grow among fields of millet and rice as the trail rises to the small village of

RUPSE (1560m, 5118ft). Reached in about 1¼hrs from Dana, among the few houses of Rupse there are two lodges, the Rock Land Guesthouse and Rupse Lodge.

Moments later you have a fine view of the cascades of Rupse Chhahara, then cross a bridge below them and climb past the aptly named Waterfall Lodge. Nearby you can see a small water-mill beside the stream. Crossing the steep mountainside beyond the waterfall, the trail angles down towards the river, and shortly before reaching a long suspension bridge passes the New World Deep Restaurant & Lodge. Cross the bridge to the east bank of the Kali Gandaki where the valley is squeezed into a rocky gorge – the narrowest part of the whole trek, and come to

KOPCHEPANI (1640m, 5381ft). This inauspicious village has a few simple-looking lodges, some of which have gardens of marigolds and orange or lemon trees. The first group of lodges consists of the Yak, Annapurna and Hotel Blue Sky. You then climb an eroded trail to the Milijuli Lodge.

The trail climbs on, steeply in places, over a rough and rocky section disturbed by landslides, and reaches

PAIROTHAPLA (1890m, 6201ft), a small settlement whose name means 'the landslide place'. This two-part settlement has a few tea-houses and just two lodges: Hotel Sunflower and the Bimala.

With a few switchbacks high above the river the trail is exposed in places as it works a way through the gorge, then you recross to the west bank by another suspension bridge, and about 15 minutes later reach the Thakali village of

GHASA (2010m, 6594ft, 5–5½hrs from Tatopani). Like Dana, Ghasa is a three-part village, each section of which has accommodation. The street is paved and has a stream running through; there's a nearby waterfall and teasing views upvalley. Some of Ghasa's flat-roofed buildings stand on stilts, while others are of a more solid stone construction. The first of its hotels is the Eagle Nest Guesthouse, run by Sweetie Scherchan, an energetic woman with an infectious smile and efficient kitchen. A short stroll beyond the Eagle Nest stands the Mustang Guesthouse. The middle section of Ghasa has a **safe drinking-water station** provided by ACAP to encourage trekkers to do without bottled mineral water. There are several of these recommended safe drinking-water stations between Ghasa and Muktinath operated by local villagers. Nearby is the Kali Gandaki Guesthouse and a campsite, as well as some traditional Thakali houses. The third, and upper part, of Ghasa has a large kani (an archway marking the entrance to a Buddhist village), a gompa (Buddhist monastery) and three lodges: the Dhaulagiri, National and New Florida guesthouses.

MUSTANG DISTRICT

Ghasa marks the southern boundary of Mustang District, which stretches as far north as Lo-Manthang, capital of the desert-like hidden Kingdom of Mustang near the Tibetan border (see box p. 216). Inhabited mainly by Bhotias in the north, and Thakalis (the people of the Thak Khola, which is their name for the Kali Gandaki) below Jomosom, the District's many villages are grouped into four historical divisions, the first of which is Thak Satsae. This name refers to the original 700 (satsae) houses of the region, and includes all the villages between Ghasa and Tukuche. North of Tukuche, the Panch Gaon ('five villages' – there are now eight) reaches up to Jomosom. Then come the 12 villages (now 19) of Bara Gaon, whose boundary contains Muktinath and Kagbeni. Finally, there is the restricted area of Upper Mustang north of Kagbeni, formerly known as Lo Tsho Dyun, 'the Land of Lo'.

The population of Mustang District is primarily Buddhist in culture, and numbered in 2002 a little under 14,000, with a per capita income of less than Rps7000 ($90). Despite the huge influx of trekkers, the main occupation centres on agriculture and animal husbandry (largely subsistence farming), but living alongside a major trade route the Thakalis have become noted hoteliers, whose hospitality and efficient lodge management is a positive feature of the trek to Muktinath.

On leaving Ghasa there will be no more sub-tropical vegetation. Instead forests are coniferous, and the scenery more alpine. The trail winds uphill, makes an undulating course along the steep hillsides that form the western wall of the valley, then descends a little to cross the Kaiku Khola on a wooden bridge. Up steps on the other side, you then pass through the tiny settlement of **KAIKU** (2085m, 6841ft), with the rather basic Bimala Hotel being the only available source of accommodation. After this continue to the solitary Green Forest Guesthouse, cross a major landslip, then descend stone steps to a suspension bridge over the Lete Khola. Across the bridge stands the Namaste Guesthouse (about 1½hrs from Ghasa). A steep ascent then tackles a dusty, eroded trail up a hillside spur jutting between the Lete Khola and the Kali Gandaki. At the top of the climb pass through a stand of pines and enter

LETE (2480m, 8136ft, 7–7½hrs). This is another long, straggling village, and it's difficult to know where it ends and Kalopani begins. Towards the northern, Kalopani, end there's a police check-post and a number of hotels. Dhaulagiri is seen almost directly ahead, while Annapurna I and the Nilgiri peaks stand in a line off to the east. From Lete the alpenglow on Annapurna

Tukuche Peak, from Lete

can be outstanding. The lodges here include: the Eco Guesthouse, Lete Guesthouse, Paradise Lodge, Hotel Mountain Top, Hotel New Horizon (which houses a **safe drinking-water station**), the Annapurna Guesthouse, Kasturi Cottage, Everest, See You, Black Horse, Alpine Lodge, Angel Guesthouse and the Pine Forest Lodge, which is run by hotel management trainees from the nearby Dhaulagiri Technical School. There's also a government **health post**, kerosene depot and a telephone facility.

KALOPANI (2530m, 8301ft) is next to Lete, and as you descend across a small tributary you come to the pleasant Hotel Mountain View with its small garden restaurant. Across the Kali Gandaki, a trail (unseen from here) leads to Chhoya and the Thulobugin ridge, a ridge that was crossed in 1950 by members of the French expedition on their way to making the first ascent of Annapurna I.

ANNAPURNA – TRIUMPH AND BITTER AFTERMATH

The story of Annapurna's first ascent is one of bewilderment, frustrated exploration, and an ill-prepared dash for the summit as the monsoon was about to break. It's a story of triumph, heroism, tragedy and an aftermath of suppressed bitterness. Maurice Herzog's classic account of the expedition, *Annapurna* (Jonathan Cape, 1952), is one of mountaineering's most gripping and enduring horror stories which has sold more than 11 million copies in 40 languages worldwide. But does it tell the full story?

The French expedition to the Himalaya in the spring of 1950 included some of the world's finest mountaineers – among their number the Chamonix guides Lionel Terray, Louis Lachenal and Gaston Rébuffat. Having failed to find an acceptable route up Dhaulagiri, their primary objective, the team turned to the lower but more distant Annapurna (8091m, 26,545ft). But where was Annapurna? First they had to find it. Unfortunately their map contained enough errors to send them on one wild goose chase after another, and by the time they did find the mountain and established a base camp at the head of the Miristi Khola, it was 18 May and the monsoon was due in about a fortnight.

There followed five wasted days as they tried in vain to force a route up the Northwest Spur, and it was only by Rébuffat's canny route-finding through a maze of crevasses and seracs that a way was eventually discovered that made the North Face a viable option – if they could climb it before the weather broke.

Wearing themselves out with the effort, five successive camps were established on the dangerous face, the topmost camp being placed at about 7500m

(24,600ft). From there, at 6am on 3 June, Herzog, the expedition leader, and Lachenal set out unroped for the summit about 600 vertical metres (1970ft) above them. The cold was intense, and the effort of climbing at that altitude exhausting. Lachenal began to fear frostbite in his feet; Herzog could not feel his own either, but when Lachenal pleaded for them to turn back, Herzog insisted he would continue alone. Lachenal, a professional guide, would not leave his partner on the mountain, so the two continued and the summit was reached some time after midday as a storm was closing in.

The descent turned to disaster. Herzog dropped his gloves. Lachenal fell and slid past the tent, losing his axe, mittens and a crampon before crawling to shelter, where Terray and Rébuffat spent the night trying vainly to restore life to their companions' frozen toes and fingers. Next day, as the storm increased, the four men staggered down, lost their way and made an emergency bivouac in a crevasse. Rébuffat and Terray became snow-blind, but they were eventually rescued by Schatz who, in waist-deep snow, led them to safety.

Neither Herzog nor Lachenal could walk, and the return through the monsoon-lashed foothills became a nightmare of monumental proportions. Lachenal lost all his toes, and Herzog all his toes and his fingers – the telling of which is a ghoulish piece of journalese by Herzog and his brother Gerard, who edited the book.

On the return to France Herzog became a national hero who built a career in politics, becoming Minister for Sport and Youth under de Gaulle and, later, Mayor of Chamonix. As for Lachenal, he died in a skiing accident in the Vallée Blanche in 1955.

A year after his death, Lachenal's autobiography was published. *Carnets du Vertige* included the first account of the ascent of Annapurna not to carry Herzog's by-line (all team members had been prevented from publishing anything about the expedition for five years). However, *Carnets* was edited by Herzog's brother, who had skilfully omitted all critical comments, and it was only in 1996 that Lachenal's original text was restored in an unexpurgated version (published by Editions Guérin). The same year came Yves Ballu's biography of Rébuffat (who died of cancer in 1985) – *Gaston Rébuffat: Une Vie pour la Montagne* (Editions Hoëbeke). Both books tell another side of the expedition. They do not dispute the basic facts of the ascent, but recount a story that differs in many ways from the official line. Even Herzog himself contradicts crucial aspects of his earlier account in his memoir *L'Autre Annapurna* (Editions Robert Laffont, 1998), while American climber and writer David Roberts pulls all the threads together in his book *True Summit* (Simon & Schuster, 2000/Constable, 2001). One man to stand by Herzog through these late controversies, however, is Reinhold Messner, who dismisses the revisionist accounts in his monograph *Annapurna* (The Mountaineers, 2000): 'Maurice Herzog rightly bears the title Monsieur Annapurna', he says.

Descending the slope beyond Kalopani come to a suspension bridge where you have a choice of onward routes. The west bank trail is slightly longer, but much less travelled than the standard east bank route, and the two regroup again upstream by a second suspension bridge in a little under 1½hrs.

Following the normal route cross the bridge over the Thak Khola (as the Kali Gandaki is now called) and continue upstream, now on the east bank with an unobstructed view of Dhaulagiri's amphitheatre. Overlooking the broad river bed with its exposed gravel bars, the Friendship Lodge exploits that view, and minutes later, along an easy, gentle trail, you pass below a line of stone-built houses at **DHAMPU** (2507m, 8225ft). *Note:* A short-cut winter trail avoids Dhampu by taking to the stony bed of the valley, and this rejoins the main trail midway between Dhampu and

KOKHETANI (2560m, 8399ft), which is reached about 3–3½hrs from Ghasa. There are four lodges in this small village: Shikhar, Glacier Fall, Earth Home and the Dhaulagiri Icefall.

Ahead, the valley makes a determined sweep to the right (north-east), backed by the high white wall connecting Dhaulagiri and Tukuche Peak. It's an awesome sight, and as you continue along the trail it's not unusual to hear and see avalanches pouring from Dhaulagiri's icefall. Beyond Kokhetani climb over a pine-covered bluff and descend to a long suspension bridge that returns you to the true right bank of the river, now on its northern side, to be rejoined by the alternative trail from Kalopani. At this point the river is 5½ vertical kilometres (3 miles) below the summits of Annapurna and Dhaulagiri, making this the world's deepest valley. Bear right, and a few moments later descend into the wide bed of the Ghatte Khola.

Continuing on the Pilgrim's Trail, cross the bed of the Ghatte Khola to the far side. ▶

Having crossed the Ghatte Khola follow the continuing trail past a simple tea-house, climb over a bluff then undulate along the left-hand hillside among pinewoods. Views through the trees and across the valley show the three Nilgiri peaks (North, Central and South) effectively blocking the way to Annapurna. In a little over an hour from Kokhetani you reach

There is no major trail, but you will no doubt be able to see vague paths made by porters and previous trekkers. The tributary consists of a series of streams and rivulets, and as there is no permanent bridge you must either wade these streams or use whatever aids have been put there (stepping stones or temporary log 'bridges').

THE GHATTE KHOLA

This major tributary emerges from a vast amphitheatre blocked by the east-facing walls of Dhaulagiri. In a dry season the valley's confluence with the Thak Khola is a broad gravel bar cut by rivulets, but this is very different in the monsoon. Though seriously foreshortened, Dhaulagiri I is the peak high above to the left. The Northeast Col, on which the Swiss expedition of 1960 landed their single-engined Pilatus Porter aircraft, is the dip in the centre, and to the right of that the ridge climbs to Tukuche Peak (6920m, 22,703ft). Thakali herdsmen used to take their animals to pasture in the high meadows upstream, and their steeply climbing trails may be used to approach the notorious Dhaulagiri Icefall – falling seracs constitute a permanent source of danger. It's a long, steep walk, the route is not always easy to find, and you'll need to be equipped for an overnight camp on the upper meadows which make, apparently, a fine site from which to view the alpenglow on Annapurna. With a climb of something like 1200m (4000ft), you should allow about 5hrs from Khobang and another 3hrs for the return.

LARJUNG (2550m, 8366ft), which almost merges with Khobang. The lodges here are grouped near the entrance to the village: the Dhaulagiri, Larjung, Mount Ice View, Riverside and the Malayan (Himalayan?) Lodge. The trail leaves Larjung by crossing a stream which separates the village from Khobang. The last building before the stream houses a **safe drinking-water station**. Walled orchards arc around the village boundary.

KHOBANG (2560m, 8399ft) lies about 10mins beyond Larjung. It's an architecturally interesting village whose houses are accessed from a partially enclosed central tunnel designed to give protection from the strong winds that gust through the valley on most days. This 'tunnel' is less enclosed than it used to be, but as you pass through, you have a glimpse of inner courtyards above which houses are graced with elaborately carved windows. Khobang was once the cultural hub of the Thak Khola; it has a pagoda-style monastery in the heart of the village, and a 15th-century *gompa* below it. Guru Rimpoche is said to have meditated in a cave 3½hrs walk from here. Khobang has a post office, public telephone, a small **health post** and three hotels: the Sunflower, Sunrise and Peaceful lodges.

Out of Khobang there's a charming avenue of willows, and on the left, set back in a neat garden, the single-storey lodge

The broad expanse of the Thak Khola, backed by the Nilgiri peaks, from near Larjung

known as the Musk Deer Valley Resort, followed by a row of simple house at **KHANTI**. From here you can either choose to continue upvalley along the trail which hugs the left-hand slope, or walk in the stony bed of the valley itself. If you choose the latter course there will be a few modest streams to leap, but during the main trekking seasons these should create no real problems.

TUKUCHE (2590m, 8497ft) is reached in about an hour from Khobang. This large and important village consists of two sections divided by an open flat meadow where Nepali traders used to meet their counterparts from Tibet in order to conduct business. Accommodation is found in both sections of the village. Most lodges, however, are located in the southern part. There are at least 10 hotels flanking the paved street, including

The Thak Khola valley below Tukuche

213

the High Plains Inn, the Thak Khola Lodge, the Sherpa, Lotus, New Nilgiri and Tukuche guesthouses, Laxmi Lodge, Himalayana Hotel Inn and the Sunil Guesthouse. Tukuche also has four *gompas*, a few shops, a post office, **safe drinking-water station**, a library and a distillery producing apple, peach, and apricot brandy, and a rough cider.

Upvalley from Tukuche you pass into the rain-shadow of the mountains and gain a veiled hint of the mysterious, once-forbidden Kingdom of Mustang. It's mostly an easy, undemanding stage, for there's little height to be gained until you climb out of the valley for the final approach to Muktinath.

Tukuche to Muktinath (8–9hrs) ◀

Sadly, a dirt road has been made between Tukuche and Jomosom, and its presence devalues this particular stretch of the valley. Not only is a road out of context here (there's no vehicular traffic since it has no link with the 'outside world'), but when the winds blow it becomes a source of billowing dust clouds. Where feasible, it's better to walk in the gravel bed.

It takes a little under 1½hrs to walk from Tukuche to Marpha, with continuing fine views of mountains on the opposite side of the valley, and with Tilicho Peak beginning to show itself beyond Nilgiri North. Shortly before reaching the village you pass the Marpha Horticultural Research Station, whose orchards provide fruit for the local cider.

MARPHA (2670m, 8760ft) is one of the valley's most attractive villages, whose narrow paved street is flanked by many well-run Thakali lodges. Some have inner courtyards where you can sit protected from the winds; others have partially sheltered rooftop restaurants with magnificent views of the mountains rising in the east. With an entrance *kani* at both ends, Marpha has a recently enlarged gompa, a post office, money-changing facilities and a library. Of its several shops one advertises boot repairs – a point worth noting if you've trouble with your footwear or the stitching on your rucksack. The first of its lodges is the Hungry Eye Inn. Others include the Sun Rise Lodge, Hotel Sunflower and Neeru Guesthouse. There's the Paradise Guesthouse, Baba's Lodge, Hotel Shangrila and the Dhaulagiri Guesthouse.

Leave Marpha through the *kani* on its northern side, and follow the clear trail which soon takes you past the upmarket Hotel Trans Himalaya. Just beyond this you can either walk along the dirt road or use the valley-bed trail. On the approach to the next village, Syang, note the small terraced fields created along the edge of the valley bed – a picture of ingenuity

TUKUCHE

A number of buildings in this large Thakali village proclaim its former importance as the economic centre of the valley. Constructed round an inner courtyard, many of the whitewashed two-storey houses have ornately carved windows, doors and balconies, and attractive latticework screens. In its heyday these courtyards were used for assembling pack animals or goods for transit to and from Tibet, while the living quarters were accessed from the upper balcony. The original village stood a short distance to the north, at a place called Jhongo, but its present location better suited its dual role as customs post and caravanserai for the trans-Himalayan salt and grain trade – its name is a derivation of the Tibetan *dhuche*, meaning 'the flat land of grain'. In the meadow behind the village, salt and wool from Tibet was transferred from yaks to pack-ponies for the long journey south, while grain and other goods from the south would pass to yak trains for shipment upvalley.

But this trade was suddenly halted as a result of the Chinese invasion of Tibet and the Lhasa uprising of 1959, which had a devastating effect on the prosperity of Tukuche's merchant families – as on many other regions of Nepal. However, the Thakalis are a robust and enterprising people, and many moved out to Pokhara or the Terai where they became involved in a variety of business ventures, including the development of hotels. While some houses in Tukuche were abandoned, others were retained and, with the onset of tourism, converted to lodges. Some of the best hotel facilities, not just in Tukuche, but throughout Nepal, are now provided by Thakali entrepeneurs.

It was in Tukuche that Herzog's 1950 Annapurna expedition had its first base, but it is hard to reconcile the description of the village given in advance by Lucien Devies, expedition promoter, when he called it 'the Chamonix of Nepal'. Herzog himself described it as a 'maze of alleys' whose houses were 'regular little fortresses'.

Six years later, David Snellgrove arrived in Tukuche during his epic journey studying Buddhist *gompas* throughout western and central Nepal, and was sadly disillusioned by what he found. In one monastery he saw 'a great refuse-heap…of what were once well printed books and laboriously copied manuscripts'. Another of the monasteries he described as being 'in a lamentable condition' with many of the frescoes having been defaced, while the young lama in charge of the 'new' Gompa Samba was in despair, saying: 'How can I act as a lama if no one believes in me?' Yet Herzog had written of the piety of the people during his visit. And today? The Kyupar Gompa of the Nyingmapa sect, which was moved here in the 1980s, is now thriving with a lama and 12 monks in residence.

and determination to wrest a harvest from a harsh and uncompromising land. **SYANG** (2700m, 8858ft) is a small village with a *gompa* perched on the hill above. The trail winds below it and heads across the tributary of the Syang Khola, where a

Valley bed fields near Syang

wooden bridge spans the stream. Rising round a spur you rejoin the road and come in view of Jomosom.

A foretaste of tourism's future?
Between Syang and Jomosom the luxury Jomsom Mountain Resort has been built on a hillside shelf with tremendous views across the valley to Nilgiri North. The prospectus boasts heated indoor swimming pool, sauna, jacuzzi, health spa and gymnasium. (You can check it out on www.south-asia.com /soi.) Is this a foretaste of tourism for the Annapurna region in years to come?

JOMOSOM (2710m, 8891ft) is reached in 3hrs from Tukuche, a large, sprawling township that straddles the river. As the administrative centre for Mustang District, it's an important place, and by far the largest habitation since leaving Pokhara. There are many lodges on both sides of the river. There are also plenty of shops, banks, administration buildings, a military post, **hospital, safe drinking-water station**, an ACAP information office, post office, airline offices and a STOL airstrip with scheduled flights to and from Pokhara – weather conditions permitting. There's a Mustang Eco Museum with an interesting exhibition and a video show depicting Mustang culture (open 9am–5pm Sunday to Friday – not holidays), and a police check-post on the right of the main street where you should show your ACAP entry permit and register details.

There are two options for the continuing route to Kagbeni. The original route crossed the Thak Khola at the northern end of Jomosom and, after going through the old town, worked its way along the south-eastern side of the valley – sometimes along the hillside, elsewhere on the gravel bed. But a new route was created in 1999 on the north-west side of the river. In the dry season it begins by heading along the valley on a stony, sometimes sandy trail, where you can stride along with the wind at your back and make good progress. In places the trail undulates along the lower hillside, but mostly it takes you through the bed itself, crossing several minor streams, and with each pace you tread deeper into a strange, seemingly barren, but utterly magical land. Most of the minor streams can be crossed without getting wet feet, but if wading through is unavoidable, do not neglect to remove boots and socks, or you may suffer blisters as a result of walking in wet boots. ▶

Turning a spur you will see a long suspension bridge ahead high above the river. The path twists up to it, and as you use it to cross to the eastern side Nilgiri North looks hugely impressive, for you can see its full height, from valley bed to ice-glistening summit, some 4500m (14,770ft) above. Over the bridge turn left, and soon after – about 2hrs from Jomosom – come to a group of buildings at the foot of the slope. This is

EKLEBHATTI (2740m, 8990ft, 5hrs). The name means 'one hotel', although there are now at least five lodges here. Apparently the original name was Chyancha Lhrenba, but that has long fallen into disuse. As well as the Holiday Inn, Old Kagbeni Lodge, Tibet Guesthouse, Munal Guesthouse and the New Hilton Hotel, Eklebhatti has one or two small shops.

It is along the valley bed that *shaligrams* are found. These mostly oval-shaped, black stones contain ammonites that were formed more than 100 million years ago, but are now prized by Hindus, for whom they represent the god Vishnu. In various places along the valley you will no doubt have seen Tibetan traders offering these *shaligrams* for sale.

A long suspension bridge carries the trail across the Thak Khola between Jomosom and Eklebhatti

DIRECT ROUTE TO MUKTINATH

The trail forks at Eklebhatti. The main route to Kagbeni continues ahead along the east side of the valley, and is described below. But there is a direct route to Muktinath that avoids Kagbeni altogether and takes 3–3½hrs. It is this trail which is followed by most pilgrims and also by many trekkers. Kagbeni, however, is such a delightful place that, should you decide to take the direct trail to Muktinath, you ought to consider diverting to it on your return. (That part of the route is described in Section 3 of the Annapurna Circuit trek.)

For Muktinath take the right-hand trail, climb the initial slope, then angle along the hillside on a broad, easy path that leads to a spur, where you turn east into the arid valley of the Jhong Khola. This is a very different landscape to that through which you have been trekking for the past few days, and is reminiscent of Tibet, with dun-coloured, wind-eroded rocks and distant groups of low trees providing the only hint of vegetation. Looking back, views of Nilgiri North and Dhaulagiri are stunning. A little over an hour from Eklebhatti you join the trail from Kagbeni, which comes from the left. For the continuing route to Muktinath, please see below.

To Muktinath via Kagbeni

Leaving Eklebhatti, continue ahead along the right-hand edge of the valley on a good trail, and in about 30mins you will reach the willow-girt oasis of

KAGBENI (2800m, 9186ft). Standing at the confluence of the Jhong Khola and Thak Khola rivers, Kagbeni is an atmospheric, medieval village of narrow alleys, *chortens, mani* walls and a large red-walled *gompa* overlooking all. Currently there are no less than 15 lodges within the village, plus a few shops, a kerosene depot, a **health post**, post office, an ACAP information centre and a **safe drinking-water station.** Accommodation will be found at the following: Hotel Nilgiri View, the Royal, New Asia Trekkers' Home, Shangrila, Mona Lisa, New Dhaulagiri, the Mustang, Mount Everest, Himalayan, Kali Gandaki Guesthouse, Snow Lion Hotel, the Red House, Annapurna, Muktinath View and Hotel Star. Kagbeni also has a police check-post on the northern edge of town, as befits the gateway to an ancient trading route leading to Mustang and Tibet. This is the northernmost limit for trekkers in the valley, other than those with special permits for Upper Mustang (see box). From the police post you can gaze upvalley towards that forbidden land, while all around rise dun-coloured hills, barely vegetated, arid and barren in the dry atmosphere that is

UPPER MUSTANG

North of Kagbeni, the trans-Himalayan kingdom of Upper Mustang is geologically, ethnically and linguistically Tibetan, and it is said that a visit there provides a more authentically Tibetan experience than can nowadays be found in Chinese-dominated Tibet. Once an autonomous region, now an enclave of Nepal projecting thumblike into the high, wild spaces of Tibet, Mustang has long held a fascination for adventurous dreamers. Until recently untouched by the outside world – both that of the Chinese Cultural Revolution and the West – an original culture survives among the villages and in the walled capital, Lo Manthang, with its four extraordinary monasteries, a large prayer wheel, *chortens* and scores of flat-roofed, fortress-like houses. In the centre of Lo Manthang stands the impressive four-storey palace of the present king – or Raja – Jigmi Palbar Bista, who proudly traces his ancestry back 24 generations to the founding King of Lo, Ame Pal, who founded his dynasty here in 1380. Now that a road has been built from the Tibetan border to Lo Manthang, bringing supplies by Chinese trucks, Upper Mustang's isolation has been compromised.

In this high, desert-like land, agriculture depends heavily on irrigation to produce crops of barley, buckwheat, peas and potatoes. Yak crossbreeds (*dzo*) plough the fields, while large herds of sheep and goats graze the scant pasturelands. When the harvest has been taken, many villagers move south and spend the winter months in Pokhara, Kathmandu or even working in India.

The landscape is rich with remarkable features: pillars of sandstone, medieval castles and caves, ancient dusty moraines and stony terraces. For many years Upper Mustang was out of bounds to foreign visitors, but since 1992 it has become a highly prized, if expensive, destination for a limited number of trekkers. See 'Other Annapurna Treks', below, for further information.

The view towards Upper Mustang from Kagbeni

more akin to that of the Tibetan plateau than of the rest of Nepal to the south.

For the final stage of the trek to Muktinath, leave Kagbeni by the path which rises behind Hotel Nilgiri View, and continue climbing up the side of the Jhong Khola's valley above oasis-like fields and orchards. The gradient is persistent, and after about 40mins you join the direct trail from Eklebhatti approaching from the right. By now you should have escaped the worst of the Thak Khola's winds as you wander along the broad, dusty trail into an increasingly attractive landscape. For a while the trail is accompanied by an irrigation channel, while off to the left a deep cleft hides the Jhong Khola, its upper cliffs piped and pitted by wind erosion. Shortly after passing the Romeo & Juliet Lodge you come to

KHINGAR (3200m, 10,499ft). About 1½hrs above Kagbeni, this is a small settlement with four lodges: Hotel Nirvana, Blue Sheep Valley Lodge, Hotel Yak and Hotel Sweet Dream.

The trail actually bypasses Khingar, but a series of streams, drystone walls and trees guide the onward route to the next charming, fortress-like village of

JHARKOT (3550m, 11,647ft). Jharkot was once fortified and, like Kagbeni, is also a medieval village, but built on a spur of hillside with a few small willow-fringed ponds lying below, and poplars and peach trees nearby. A *gompa* of the Sakya sect stands at one end of the village; there's also a very fine *kani*, a *mani* wall and a number of lodges, including: Hotel Himali, the Peace Land, Sonam, New Plaza and the Prakash Hotels.

Jharkot, a wonderful village in a magnificent setting

The trail edges through Jharkot and resumes on a clear rise above it, now climbing a little more steeply, and in another 35 minutes reaches the village of Muktinath, more properly known as Ranipauwa. Muktinath is the name of the religious site a few minutes' walk above the village, the focus of so many pilgrims.

MUKTINATH/RANIPAWA (3710m, 12,172ft) has grown around a large rest house for pilgrims. It has many lodges, tea-houses, a few shops and campsites. A police check-post is located towards the upper end of the main thoroughfare, with an ACAP information centre nearby. This is where you'll find the **safe drinking-water station**. Lodge accommodation is in: the Dream Home, Hotel Nightingale, Royal Mustang, North Pole, Hotel Caravan, Mount Kailash, the Laligurans, Hotel Bob Marley, Hotel Nilgiri, the Mona Lisa and Hotel Moonlight. Tibetan traders squat in the street, where they spread out their wares beneath the feet of pilgrims, trekkers, ponies and yaks. Across the valley, on the northern side of the arid Jhong Khola, can be seen the ruins of Dzong, at one time the most important village in this corner of the mountains and seat of the local ruler. (Another name for the tributary stream below is Dzong Khola.) Above Muktinath, village and shrine, the route to the Thorong La, which is crossed on the Annapurna Circuit, bears right into the nearby obvious valley, but the pass itself cannot be seen from here. Downvalley a wonderful view shows Dhaulagiri hovering pristine white on a far horizon. Catch it at sunset if you can.

MUKTINATH

Muktinath's complex of sacred shrines is located a short distance above Ranipauwa in a walled poplar grove. To Buddhists as to Hindus this is very much a place of salvation, and for centuries it has attracted pilgrims of both faiths. In deference to these pilgrims, please dress modestly when visiting Muktinath, remove footwear before entering any of the temples, and be sure to leave a donation.

The pagoda-style temple of **Vishnu Mandir** contains images of both Vishnu and Laxmi, and in its courtyard springs have been diverted to feed 108 cow-head water spouts that hold mysteries of life and death, and which grant salvation to believers who bathe in the pools beneath them. Pilgrims who are not hardy enough to bathe in the near-freezing water should at least drink a few drops from each spout.

Snellgrove wrote of six Tibetan Buddhist temples here, the most famous of which is the **Jwala Mai**, with its small jets of natural gas that produce a constant

221

flame beside a trickling spring of water – a sacred combination of earth, fire and water venerated with equal fervour by Hindu and Buddhist.

Gompa Sarwa contains terracotta images of Avalokitesvara, Sakyamuni and Padamsambhava, the eighth-century Buddhist saint Guru Rimpoche, whose footprints are said to be imprinted in a stone outside.

RETURN ROUTES TO POKHARA

Unless you plan to fly back to Pokhara from Jomosom, or cross the Thorong La above Muktinath and descend through the valley of the Marsyangdi (in effect reversing the Annapurna Circuit trek described as Trek 1), the return to Pokhara will naturally be a reversal of most of the upward route through the Kali Gandaki. For a description of this route, please refer to Trek 1: Sections 3 and 4. However, there are some variations that could be made and these are briefly outlined below.

MUKTINATH to MARPHA along the east bank of the Thak Khola (1½ days). Instead of descending to Kagbeni, take the direct route to EKLEBHATTI and remain on the east bank (old route) to JOMOSOM. Do not cross the valley here, but continue on the east bank to THINI, a village on the Lungpughyum Khola. Cross this tributary to DHUMPA, where a bridge takes you over the Thak Khola to join the standard route a short distance from MARPHA.

LARJUNG to KALOPANI via the west bank route (2–2½hrs). While the standard trail crosses to the left (east) bank of the Thak Khola below LARJUNG on a long suspension bridge, an alternative trail continues on the west bank. After crossing two tributaries immediately below Dhaulagiri, it rejoins the main route at KALOPANI.

TATOPANI to POKHARA via BENI (2 days). If you began the Pilgrim's Trail at Naya Pul and Birethanti, and crossed the Poon Hill Danda at Ghorepani, the trek out to Beni makes a sensible alternative. Following the Kali Gandaki all the way, the trail goes through TIPLYANG, BAISARI and GALESWOR before reaching BENI. A bus or taxi ride completes the journey out to POKHARA. (This route is described as Section 4a of Trek 1: Annapurna Circuit.)

TATOPANI to POKHARA via GHOREPANI (2–4 days). This option reverses Section 1b of the Pilgrim's Trail, and is the alternative way out for those who began their trek at Beni. South of Tatopani this route makes the long climb to GHOREPANI DEURALI on the Poon Hill Danda, and gives an opportunity to watch the sunrise from the summit of Poon Hill. You then descend the southern side of the ridge to ULLERI, and on to BIRETHANTI and NAYA PUL for road transport out to POKHARA. (This option is described under Trek 1: Annapurna Circuit, Section 4b.)

TREK 4:
THE GHANDRUK FOOTHILL TREK

*In the early morning light it was easy to sympathise with
the belief that these mountains are sacred.*

(Wilfred Noyce)

TREK SUMMARY

Distance:	38km (23 miles)
Time:	4–5 days
Max. altitude:	2250m (7382ft)
Start:	Naya Pul
Finish:	Phedi
Trekking style:	Tea-house (lodge accommodation) or camping

The foothills north of Pokhara are so wound about with trails
that a host of different circuits could be created. This is just
one option (other outline suggestions are made below). Not
only does it exploit some of the finest Himalayan views available to the non-climber, but it visits charming villages whose
lodges are mostly comfortable and welcoming, and at the
same time serve some of Nepal's best trekkers' meals. Access
to and from the trailhead is uncomplicated, and paths are
almost everywhere clear and well made.

Although there are plenty of fairly steep uphill and downhill sections, numerous tea-houses provide frequent opportunities to stop for refreshment. The maximum altitude gained
is a modest 2170m (7119ft), so unless one tackles it in the
winter, the temperature should be very pleasant.

This horseshoe-shaped route begins at Naya Pul near
Birethanti, and ends below Dhampus at Phedi, both places
being located along the Pokhara–Baglung–Beni road, so transport is straightforward. As for the trek itself, it starts by following the Modi Khola upstream, then climbs to the idylli-
cally placed Gurung village of Ghandruk 'with a superb dress-
circle view of Machhapuchhare and Modi Peak' (Chris

While the three
previously described
routes are, to varying
degrees, fairly commit-
ting experiences, this
short four- or five-day
foothill trek can be
both relaxing and
highly rewarding.
Many visitors to Nepal
have neither the time
nor the desire to spend
more than a week
trekking, yet wish for a
more intimate relation-
ship with some of the
world's most spectacu-
lar mountains than can
be had from either
Kathmandu or
Pokhara. The
Ghandruk Foothill Trek
answers that dream.

Bonington). From there the route crosses an easy ridge and descends steeply to the Kimrong Khola, then up the other side to a contouring path which leads to Chhomrong, gateway to the Modi Khola's gorge that reaches into the Annapurna Sanctuary. Chhomrong shares Ghandruk's 'dress-circle view',

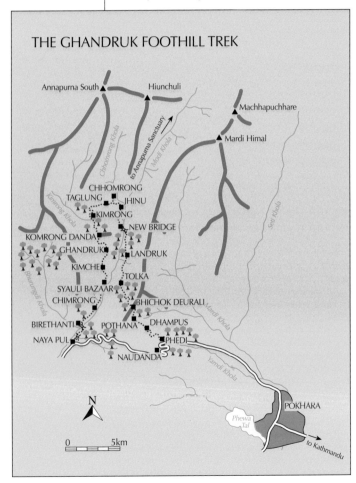

THE GHANDRUK FOOTHILL TREK

Annapurna South ▲
Hiunchuli ▲
Machhapuchhare ▲
Mardi Himal ▲

Chhomrong Khola
to Annapurna Sanctuary
Modi Khola
Seti Khola

CHHOMRONG
TAGLUNG
JHINU
KIMRONG
Kimrong Khola
NEW BRIDGE
KOMRONG DANDA
GHANDRUK
LANDRUK
KIMCHE
TOLKA
SYAULI BAZAAR
CHIMRONG
BHICHOK DEURALI
Bhurungdi Khola
BIRETHANTI
POTHANA
DHAMPUS
NAYA PUL
PHEDI
NAUDANDA
Mardi Khola
Yamdi Khola

POKHARA
Phewa Tal
to Kathmandu

N

0   5km

but since the village is much closer to the mountains it almost feels possible to reach out and touch them – Annapurna South especially.

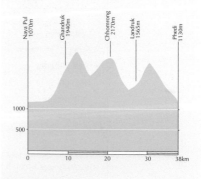

THE GHANDRUK FOOTHILL TREK

On leaving Chhomrong a steep descent leads to New Bridge on the Modi Khola. The river is crossed, and ascent made of the eastern hillside to Ghandruk's 'twin' village, Landruk. The continuing trail sneaks up to and over a rhododendron-clad ridge, on the other side of which you come to Dhampus, a popular place from which to enjoy sunrise over the mountains. Phedi, and the road back to Pokhara, lies a short walk below.

While this trek could be tackled at any time of the year, be warned that the summer monsoon months in this heavily vegetated region are notorious for leeches. The pre-monsoon period of March and April rewards with spectacular displays of rhododendrons, but heat haze often obscures views except at dawn and dusk. The optimum period is unquestionably from October to mid-December, when the atmosphere is at its clearest, the weather mostly settled, and the views their sharpest. But this is also the busiest time, when it's quite possible to find that some of the lodges are full night after night. From December to February trails and lodges are much less frequented, but the weather is also less settled. However, when it is fine, this can be a magical time to go trekking in the foothills.

Despite being short, the Ghandruk Foothill Trek is still quite energetic, and to gain most from the experience you need to be reasonably fit. The first day's climb to Ghandruk will illustrate this – but since the fish-tail peak is on show almost every step of the way, you'll have plenty of excuses to pause along the trail to catch your breath and absorb the scenic wonders all around you.

SECTION 1:
Naya Pul to Ghandruk

Distance:	12km (7½ miles)
Time:	4hrs
Start altitude:	1070m (3510ft)
High point:	Ghandruk, 1940m (6365ft)
Height gain:	870m (2856ft)
Transport:	Bus or taxi (Pokhara to Naya Pul)

In Pokhara the bus terminal for the 2hr journey to Naya Pul is located near Bhairab Tole in the north-west part of town. Leaving at roughly 30min intervals, some 24 buses a day travel via Naya Pul to Baglung across the Kaski Danda. Some of the drivers are reckless, in which case you'll probably have a rough ride and an 'ethnic experience'. It may be preferable to hire a taxi for the 42km (26 miles) trip. The road takes you along the broad, flat valley of the Yamdi Khola between rice fields and groups of houses, then twists up to the Kaski Danda at Naudanda for wonderful views of the Annapurna range. (Before the road was built, this village was on the main trekking route into the mountains.) Over the ridge, the road then snakes down to Naya Pul and the wooded valley of the Modi Khola.

Naya Pul is a grim roadside shanty of tin-roofed huts, shops and tea-houses. With Indian music screeching, it has practically no redeeming features, and you may ask yourself what you're doing there. But don't despair, for it will only take a few minutes to escape to the sanity of the foothills. To do this go down the slope to a river (a tributary of the Modi Khola) and cross on a suspension bridge. There are more shanty-like shops and tea-houses on the other side. Bear left and follow a broad track for about 20mins, and you'll come to the Fishtail Lodge and a second suspension bridge, this one spanning the Modi Khola. Across the bridge an ACAP check-post stands at the entrance to

BIRETHANTI (1025m, 3363ft). This large and important bazaar is an attractive place built at the confluence of the

Modi Khola and Bhurungdi Khola rivers. Before the Baglung–Beni road was opened numerous caravans of pack animals would pass through the village to begin the long climb over the Poon Hill Danda to access the Kali Gandaki trade route. Birethanti has not only lost some of the caravans but also some of its trekking business to the road, but it still remains busy. The Ghandruk Foothill Trek is not the only one to begin here, for the first two days of this route are shared with trekkers bound for the Annapurna Sanctuary, while one of the Pilgrim's Trail options also sets out from Birethanti for Ghorepani. Before embarking on the trek, you should show your ACAP entry permit at the check-post. Although you'll probably have no intention of spending a night here, preferring to go as far as Ghandruk, it's worth noting that Birethanti has many lodges, including the upmarket Laxmi Lodge near the bridge. This smart and well-run hotel is sometimes reserved for clients of the Foreign Window agency which specialises in luxury treks. Birethanti has a number of shops, a post office, bank and tea-houses.

From the check-post walk up the paved street to a junction by the post office and turn right. (The alternative route climbs to Ghorepani, and is the one taken by trekkers following the Pilgrim's Trail to Muktinath.) The trail to Ghandruk passes the village school, the Nice View Lodge and Himalayan Lodge, and soon after leaves the outskirts of Birethanti by crossing a wooden bridge among trees with a small Hindu shrine nearby. Heading upstream, with the Modi Khola flowing off to the right, about 20mins later pass the entrance to one of a group of upmarket lodges owned by Ker & Downey, the Sanctuary Lodge, which is set in an extensive tropical garden.

Along this stretch of trail you will pass numerous simple tea-houses and lodges, wooded areas and open fields of rice, millet or barley. In places the trail may be muddy, with little streams spilling across it. The way takes you through the settlement of **CHIMRONG** (1140m, 3740ft), and soon after crosses a stream in a woodland glade, then on a flagstone-paved trail between more fields. Machhapuchhare teases ahead, a distant, seductive mountain that marks the entrance to Annapurna's Sanctuary. Hiunchuli is its near neighbour to the left, forming the Sanctuary's other gatepost.

About 1½hrs from Naya Pul (a little over 1hr from Birethanti) you come to the first village of any size, and that a fairly modest one. Set among a splay of rice fields, this is

SYAULI BAZAAR (1170m, 3839ft). Lying at the foot of a vast terraced slope, the village has several nice-looking lodges, including the Machhapuchhare Guesthouse, Shikhar Guesthouse and the Green Valley Lodge.

There now begins a long 770m (2526ft) climb to Ghandruk. In places the gradient is steep, and for a first day on the trail it can be tiring – especially in the warm springtime months – but mostly the path makes a steady ascent, often on paved steps that lead from one small settlement to the next, through

LANDSCAPE WITH FIGURES

As you gaze across these terraces, remember that every plant you see growing there has been individually pressed into the soil by someone's thumb, and each terrace has been hand-carved without mechanical aid. The amount of physical effort involved in creating and maintaining this wonderland of agriculture is impressive. In the springtime you will see fields being ploughed by buffalo. There'll be men and women bending calf-deep in muddy paddies planting the rice; in late October and November these same fields will be busy with the harvest. Brightly clad villagers lay low the yellowing rice with short-handled sickles whose blades flash in the sunlight, spreading fan-like swathes to be carried away for threshing. Grain is tossed from large circular trays, the chaff blowing as dust in the breeze. Conical hay stacks speckle the hillsides, buffalo traipse round and round in circles as part of the winnowing process or stand tethered on bare terraces to fertilise the

soil in readiness for the next sowing. In the millet harvest, women wade slowly through the fields, pluck the brown seed heads and toss them over their shoulder into the waiting *doko*. At all times these foothills are lively with activity, and the trek experience is enriched by it.

Rice paddies in the foothill country

the most amazing terraced landscape, backed by high mountains.

After passing the Syauli Bazaar Guesthouse, cross a short suspension bridge over the Sadhu Khola and continue up a paved stairway to

KIMCHE. This long, strung-out village of lodges, farms and small houses cascades down the hillside with about 250m (820ft) difference in altitude between the lower and upper settlements, of which there are several with confusingly different names. To add to the confusion some locals even refer to this village as Syauli. Several lodges alongside the trail appear to be rather simple affairs, while others – notably the Shining River Guesthouse with its colourful garden – look more welcoming. ▶

The paved stairway continues, winding up the slope with little shade, but with Machhapuchhare nearly always in view. The upper part of Kimche has the Bikash Guesthouse and the Kimche Guesthouse, both simple-looking lodges, above which the mountain panorama grows in extent.

Eventually the gradient eases, and you come to a few teahouses at **CHANE** (1690m, 5545ft), where there's a trail junction. The left-hand path cuts across the hillside heading west to Tirkhedunga, a village 4hrs walk from here, set high above Birethanti on the way to Ghorepani. Your way, the way to Ghandruk, continues ahead, crosses a stream and a landslide, contours along the hillside, then resumes the ascent on more paved steps. Shortly before coming to a *kani* (an entrance archway) another path breaks away to the right on a steep descent to the Modi Khola. On the far side of the valley you can make out the clustered houses of Landruk, which is on the outward route to Pokhara.

Go through the *kani* and soon after enter

GHANDRUK (1940m, 6365ft), about 3½–4hrs after leaving Birethanti. Also known as Ghandrung, this is the second largest Gurung town in Nepal (after Siklis), an important, prosperous township, many of whose residents are retired Gurkha soldiers. Ghandruk has an impressive location and is built in two parts. The upper village is perhaps the most attractive, with a number of its slate-roofed houses built around paved courtyards, with attached stables and granaries, and tall drying racks filled

As the climb progresses you will no doubt be sharing the trail with caravans of laden pack-ponies carrying supplies to the more remote villages and lodges. These pony trains are often decorated with colourful plumes and headbands, some with deep-clonking bells, others with harnesses jingling with smaller bells. Such exotic caravans make a good subject for a photograph, but you should take care when you see one descending, for sometimes the animals come cantering down the slope towards you, and you'll need to stand aside to avoid being knocked over.

Ghandruk, a classic village in a classic landscape

with maize. Flagstone paths wind through the town, with many side-streets cutting between houses to make a rough grid-like layout, the paths either coming to a dead-end in someone's courtyard or spilling into fields that step the surrounding hills.

Ghandruk has a Gurung museum, a *gompa* (Buddhist monastery), a police post, telephone office, post office, **health post** and several small shops. ACAP has a Visitor Centre (next to the health post) in which a promotional video is shown three times daily: at 9.30am, 11.30am, and 3.30pm. The village has tea-houses and camping grounds, and more than 20 lodges, among them, the Trekker's Lodge (three-times winner of ACAP's 'Lodge of the Year' award); the nearby Milan and Manisha hotels; the new Hotel Buddha, which stands just above the ACAP building and has a particularly fine view; and the upmarket (and more expensive) Himalaya Lodge, owned by Ker & Downey.

Not surprisingly, when you consider its location, Ghandruk appears on countless photographs that depict the essential Nepal – on calendars, posters, postcards and in trekking brochures. There's a serenity in the composition of a cluster of houses, terraced fields tumbling into a hint of valley, and the stunning backdrop dominated by Annapurna South, Hiunchuli and Machhapuchhare. Through the Modi Khola's gorge Annapurna III and Gandharba Chuli are also visible from certain points around the village. Such a scene makes all the effort of the trek worthwhile, and (to paraphrase alpine connoisseur R.L.G. Irving) if you're not hooked after gazing at that, you're better away from mountains.

SECTION 2:
Ghandruk to Chhomrong

Distance:	8km (5 miles)
Time:	3½–4hrs
Start altitude:	1940m (6365ft)
High points:	Komrong Danda, 2250m (7382ft), Chhomrong, 2170m (7110ft)
Low point:	Kimrong, 1780m (5840ft)
Height gain:	700m (2297ft)
Height loss:	470m (1542ft)

Find your way to the Shangri La Guesthouse in the upper part of Ghandruk, where the trail to Chhomrong leaves the village and, 10mins later, crosses a short suspension bridge over the Kyunri Khola tributary where another path breaks left to Ghorepani. Your path is broad and easy, and at a major junction you veer left to angle round the hillside above fields, passing several houses and tea-houses and rising towards an obvious ridge. This is gained about an hour's walk from Ghandruk, at the saddle of

KOMRONG DANDA (2250m, 7382ft). Also spelt Khomrong, or even Khumrong, this saddle holds a group of simple lodges and tea-houses: the Annapurna View, Machhapuchhare Lodge and the Komrong Guesthouse. Another is found about 20mins to the right along the ridge, where Hill Town Lodge stands in splendid isolation.

Over the ridge the trail forks and you descend into forest on a path that becomes heavily eroded as you lose height. Near the lower edge of the forest the Namaste Teashop overlooks the valley into which you are descending, and has a direct view of Machhapuchhare to the north-east. Out of the forest follow a tributary stream down to the Kimrong Khola, where you cross a log bridge to the north bank.

KIMRONG (1780m, 5840ft), also spelt Kyumnu, Kymnu, Kimnu and Khumnu, is gained about 45mins from the saddle. The first building of this small village is the rather basic Kimrong Riverside Hotel, run by a very friendly woman. The rest of the village is a short distance away, where there are three more lodges, the Kimrong Guesthouse, Peaceful Lodge and Hotel Navina.

Out of the village the path slants uphill towards the Kimrong View Teashop and, passing this the way, then twists steeply into forest to regain most of the height you've just lost on the descent from Komrong Danda. Eventually, at the top of the climb, you gain a crossing path and turn right. Moments later reach the Kaji Lunch Centre, a tea-house/lodge standing beside the trail at about 2180m (7152ft). The path contours along the steep hillside with a few fairly insignificant ascents and descents, heading east above more wonderful terraces that turn the slopes into vast agricultural stairways.

About 30mins from Kaji you come to the scattered village of **TAGLUNG**, whose houses seem to hang from the steep hillside on terraces at different levels. Turning a spur 10mins later you reach the Heaven View Lodge near the junction with a path that descends steeply to New Bridge – this path will be taken on the way back to Pokhara. Ascend the slope to the Summit View Lodge, and continue on stone steps to the well-named Panorama Point Lodge, Fishtail Guesthouse and an ACAP check-post at the entrance to

CHHOMRONG (2170m, 7110ft). Like Ghandruk, the village has been developed as two settlements, but unlike Ghandruk, Chhomrong does not have a compact togetherness or a maze of alleys in which to get lost. Instead, it tumbles down the hillside astride a magnificent stairway of more than 2000 paved steps, with an altitude difference of more than 300m (984ft) between the ACAP check-post and the lower houses. In the 1950s, when Jimmy Roberts came here on his Machhapuchhare reconnaissance, he described a little village of well-watered lawns, golden barley and painted Gurung houses nestling into a scene whose views were perfectly balanced. Like Ghandruk, Chhomrong is dominated by Annapurna South, Hiunchuli and Machhapuchhare, but here, of course, those mountains are much closer, and they positively glow at sunrise and sunset.

Chhomrong's Mountain View Hotel has a colourful garden of marigolds

Chhomrong is the perfect place from which to study them, and there's no shortage of accommodation in which to base yourself for a day – or two – to do just that. Some of the lodges have dining rooms with picture windows, or garden terraces with marigold borders that make a colourful foreground to the scene. Practically every building faces the view.

Beginning at the head of the slope, accommodation may be had at: the Himalaya View Guesthouse, Excellent View Top Lodge, the Kalpana Guesthouse, the imposing International Guesthouse and the Chhomrong Mountain View Lodge with its friendly staff, immaculate flower borders and campsite. Then there's the Lucky Guesthouse, Moonlight Lodge, Hiunchuli Guesthouse and the Chhomrong Guesthouse. Below the village school you come to the Garden Villa Lodge, a trekkers' shop, then the Annapurna Guesthouse and, finally, Captain's Lodge, the first to be opened here.

The lower village consists of more than trekkers' lodges, for several traditional houses spill out into the fields above the confluence of the Chhomrong Khola and Modi Khola rivers. The first of these drains the south side of Annapurna South; the second thunders out of the gorge that leads to the Annapurna Sanctuary. If you have the time and energy while staying here, it could be worth crossing the suspension bridge over the Chhomrong Khola and labouring up the opposite slope for an hour or so as far as Sinuwa, a group of lodges on a spur at 2340m (7677ft), from which you can see into the Modi Khola's gorge, and from where Machhapuchhare shows its magnificent fish-tail peak.

THE FISH-TAIL PEAK

The fish-tail peak of Machhapuchhare is one of the most elegant, distinctive and awesomely beautiful mountains in all the Himalaya. Seen from Pokhara it has a tapering, pinnacle-like gracefulness. From the north-east it consists of two enormous ice pillars fused together. From Annapurna Base Camp it reveals a vast, angular Northwest Face; but from Ghandruk, Chhomrong and the southern approaches through the Modi Khola's gorge it displays the upper twin-topped ridge that gives the mountain its descriptive name. *Machha* in Nepali means 'fish', while *puchar* is 'tail'.

In any other mountain range Machhapuchhare's 6993m (22,943ft) would make it a giant, but standing among giants of the Annapurna Himal, it's only in the second rank – in terms of altitude, that is. When it comes to architectural symmetry, the fish-tail peak is in a league of its own. Wilfred Noyce called it 'the steepest, most exciting and alluring mountain that I know'. No wonder it's considered to be sacred, a holy mountain where, according to local Hindus, Shiva resides above the clouds.

In the spring of 1957 Jimmy Roberts (see box 'Jimmy Roberts, the Father of Trekking', above) led a small expedition in an attempt to climb Machhapuchhare. There were just five British climbers and four Sherpas in the team, plus an army of 50 porters to carry food and equipment from Pokhara. On 24 April Base Camp was set just inside the Sanctuary, and from there they chose a route that would take them onto the North Ridge by way of ice flutings that from a distance looked like a pleated curtain. Before gaining the ridge, however, one of the team members, Roger Chorley, was struck down with polio and had to be carried out to Pokhara in the care of Roberts, leaving just Noyce, Cox and Wylie to continue the attempt with support from their Sherpas.

Machhapuchhare holds the evning light while the Modi Khola's gorge fills with shadow – a view from Chhomrong

Three camps above base, the trio came onto the ridge and then settled Camp IV under the rock buttress which carries the ridge south to the upper pyramid. From there they could make out the summit obelisk, but the intervening ground was obscured by a short knife-edged ridge which fell steeply to the Seti Khola. But a glacial projection offered a possible way onto a snowy shelf, from which, it was conjectured, the upward route could be carried. Reaching the shelf was an epic in itself, and once there it was found to be 'a mountain freak', as Noyce described it. 'It is supported by nothing and one day will go crashing down into the Seti'. Fortunately it held, and Camp V was pitched above a large crevasse at about 6400m (21,000ft) on 1 June.

At 4.20am next morning Noyce and David Cox made their bid for the summit, which rose nearly 600m (2000ft) above them, 'a fluted, furrowed series of ribs sweeping straight up to a jagged crest'. Soft, knee-deep snow led to easy step-cutting, then they continued round and above a bulbous 'onion' of ice, the size of a cottage, which took an age to pass. Out of a clear sky long rolls of cloud gathered and engulfed the neighbouring peaks. Snow began to fall at 9.00am, and in worsening conditions they spent the next 2hrs climbing two ice chimneys, then rounded a rib to discover four or five columns of beautifully polished ice, each one of which ended in a skyline pinnacle. Snow fell more thickly now, and after labouring to cut steps up one of the columns Noyce and Cox called it a day and turned back. They were less than 50m (160ft) from the top. 'The Goddess had drawn her firm line here,' wrote Noyce, 'with that we must be content.'

The story of this, the only authorised attempt to climb Machhapuchhare, is told in *Climbing the Fish's Tail* by Wilfred Noyce (Heinemann, 1958/Book Faith India edition, 1998). See also the *Alpine Journal Vol LXII*, November 1957.

SECTION 3:
Chhomrung to Landruk

Distance:	8km (5 miles)
Time:	3hrs
Start altitude:	2170m (7110ft)
Low point:	New Bridge, 1340m (4396ft)
Height loss:	830m (2723ft)
High point:	Landruk, 1565m (5135ft)
Height gain:	225m (738ft)

Starting the return trek to Pokhara, make your way to the ACAP check-post at the head of the Chhomrong slope and register your departure before going down the steps to the trail junction near Heaven View Lodge. Turn left and take the steeply descending path that twists between fields, with the river seen as a ribbon far below. After about 40mins of this descent you come to

JHINU DANDA (1780m, 5840ft), with several lodges, including the Hot Spring Hotel, Hot Spring Garden Lodge, the Tibet and Namaste Lodges. The hot springs referred to are found another 15mins from here along a branching path. If you're tempted to try them, be warned that it'll take you another 30mins or so to get back to Jhinu and the outward trail.

The path continues down for another 350m, steeply at first, then on a descending traverse, to cross the lower reaches of the Kimrong Khola on a concrete bridge at about 1430m (4692ft). Passing the few houses of **SAMRUNG** the descent resumes and eventually comes to

NEW BRIDGE (1340m, 4396ft), just above the Modi Khola. Formerly known as Himalkyo, the name was changed when a suspension bridge was built across the river in the mid-1980s. 'New Bridge' in Nepali is 'Naya Pul', and the settlement is sometimes also known by this name – which can cause confusion thanks to the existence of the other Naya Pul near Birethanti, where the trek began. A few lodges have been built here, among them the Modi Khola, Himchali and Kalapani. There are fine views of Annapurna South and Hiunchuli.

Cross the bridge over the Modi Khola to the Himalpani Lodge, and follow the easy trail downstream along the left bank of the river among rhododendrons. Before long it begins to climb the hillside among terraced fields, then goes over a small suspension bridge and by a flight of steps leading to the first lodges of

LANDRUK (1565m, 5135ft). Also known as Landrung, this attractive Gurung village stretches for several hundred metres up the hillside. With terraces above and below, Landruk has a paved street, a number of circular ochre-walled thatched houses, and views across the valley to Ghandruk and, once more, up to the Annapurnas. There's no shortage of accommodation, and the village makes a very pleasant place in which to spend a night. The Himalaya and Annapurna lodges are located at the bottom of the village by a trail junction (one path descends steeply to the river downstream from New Bridge and is the direct access route to Ghandruk). Other lodges include the Moonlight Hotel, Mount View and the Landruk Lodge. At the top end of the village there's the Hungry Eye and Laligurans.

SECTION 4:
Landruk to Dhampus and Pokhara

Distance:	10km (6 miles) + 18km (11 miles) by road
Time:	4–5hrs trekking + 30mins by transport
Start altitude:	1565m (5135ft)
High point:	Bhichok Deurali, 2100m (6890ft)
Height gain:	535m (1755ft)
Low point:	Phedi, 1130m (3707ft)
Height loss:	970m (3182ft)
Transport:	Bus or taxi (Phedi to Pokhara)

This last stage of the Ghandruk Foothill Trek finally leaves the Modi Khola's valley to cross a wooded ridge, and on the eastern side gains a distant view of the low-lying Pokhara valley and glistening Phewa Tal. Sadly, sections of this route have a history of lone trekkers being robbed, so you are advised not to walk alone here, but to ensure you always have company you can trust.

Climb up through Landruk, then wind round to cross the Ghora Khola by suspension bridge, followed by an easy contour that takes you past more circular houses overlooking neat-textured farmland. The trail then crosses a spur and descends among trees to another tributary, this one the Tigu Khola, which is also crossed by suspension bridge with a stairway leading in a little under an hour to

TOLKA (1700m, 5577ft). Previously known as Medigara, or Medigala, this small settlement has a village school and a string of trailside lodges: the International Guesthouse, Butterfly, Namaste and Evergreen among them.

Beyond Tolka the path meanders on without any appreciable height gain until it has crossed another stream at **BERI**

KHARKA, where there are several tea-houses and a lodge. Now the way rises past more simple lodges as the gradient steepens through rhododendron forest, the pink-barked trees hung in places with orchids and sprouting ferns. About 2½hrs after leaving Landruk you come onto the ridge at the saddle of

BHICKOK DEURALI (2100m, 6890ft). There are just two lodges here, the Trekker's Inn and the Nice View.

It's virtually all downhill from here, on an easy paved trail through yet more rhododendron forest, and after about 30mins you come to

POTHANA (1900m, 6234ft), a somewhat untidy collection of lodges, of which there are plenty, as well as a good view of Machhapuchhare. The Fishtail Lodge exploits the view, although the mountain from this angle has lost its distinctive twin summit and looks more individually pointed. Other lodges include Annapurna, Gurung and See You.

The paved trail continues down, leaving the forest and gaining views ahead of the Pokhara valley and its lake, while backward views of the mountains entice you to pause again and again. It takes about an hour to reach the last village of the trek.

DHAMPUS (1650m, 5413ft, 4hrs) has an ACAP check-post, one or two shops, several reasonable lodges, a few simple ones and the de-luxe Basanta Lodge owned by Ker & Downey.

Out of Dhampus the trail takes you alongside rice paddies, then steeply down to the road at **PHEDI**, where there are usually taxis waiting to ferry weary trekkers through the valley of the Yamdi Khola to Pokhara.

OTHER ANNAPURNA TREKS

Do you see the mountain ranges there, far away?
One behind another. They rise up. They tower. That is my
deep, unending, inexhaustible kingdom.

(Henrik Ibsen – *The Master Builder*)

Three major routes and one short foothill trek still leave many other trekking possibilities in the Annapurna region. The following outline routes are suggestions that can be followed up by consultation with local maps or discussion with agents on the ground. Some are simply variations or combinations of trails already described, but which make splendid alternative circuits. A few are feasible without resorting to a fully-equipped camping outfit, as there are plenty of lodges and tea-houses along the way; but those that hint at off-the-beaten track tours will need tents, porters and a local guide as a bare minimum. Despite the huge popularity of the Annapurna region, it is still possible to wander a few hundred metres from a busy trail and there experience the unchanged Nepal. There are side-valleys and accessible ridges where you can travel for days at a time, see no other Westerners, and receive a genuinely warm welcome from local villagers. Some of these less-trodden places are mentioned below. But first, a trek to the borders of Tibet.

Upper Mustang

Distance:	130km (80 miles)
Time:	10–14 days
Max. altitude:	4325m (14,190ft)
Start:	Jomosom
Finish:	Jomosom
Trekking style:	Camping, with registered agent only

Upper Mustang was opened as a trekking destination only in 1992, and the number of visitors is strictly limited and subject to certain regulations that include: the use of a registered trekking agency; employment of a government-appointed liaison officer; and purchase of a special trekking permit which costs at present $700 for 10 days, plus $70 for every additional

At the head of the Kali Gandaki/Thak Khola valley north of Kagbeni (a village visited on Section 3 of the Annapurna Circuit Trek and Section 2 of the Pilgrim's Trail), the restricted, long-forbidden kingdom of Upper Mustang is one of the most culturally interesting and scenically remarkable districts in the Annapurna region – see box, Trek 3 Section 2.

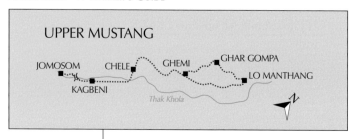

day – in addition to the standard Rps2000 ACAP entry fee. Trek groups must be self-contained with regard to food and fuel supplies, and all non-biodegradable packaging must be carried out. Although by nature a there-and-back route, a variation is possible on the final approach to, and return from, the capital, Lo Manthang.

The majority of treks to Upper Mustang begin by flying from Pokhara to Jomosom. It then takes about five days of trekking via **KAGBENI** and **CHELE**, passing old forts and wind-eroded cliffs, before reaching **LO MANTHANG**, which lies at an altitude of about 3840m (12,598ft). At least two full days should be spent exploring the old walled town and its immediate neighbourhood before returning on a south-westerly loop that crosses the **CHOGO LA** to **GHAR GOMPA**, and rejoins the main route at **GHEMI**, a large village of whitewashed houses, a restored *gompa* and a red-walled nunnery.

A number of commercial trekking companies in the West offer trips to Upper Mustang – consult available brochures for details. The trek also features in the following publications: *Trekking in the Nepal Himalaya* by Stan Armington (Lonely Planet, 8th edition 2001), *Trekking & Climbing in Nepal* by Steve Razzetti (New Holland, 2000), *Mustang: A Trekking Guide* by Bob Gibbons & Sîan Pritchard-Jones (Tiwari's Pilgrims Book House, Kathmandu, 1993). See also *A Nepalese Journey* by Andrew Stevenson (Constable, 2002).

The foothill country above Pokhara is scored with numerous trails to entice the inquisitive trekker, some of which form part of previously described routes. Trek 4: The Ghandruk Foothill Trek was just one of many possible circuits or loop-treks. Other ideas are outlined below.

Annapurna Panorama

Distance:	60km (37 miles)
Time:	5–6 days
Max. altitude:	3193m (10,476ft)
Start:	Naya Pul
Finish:	Phedi
Trekking style:	Tea-house (lodge accommodation)

This loop trek makes a fine introduction to trekking in Nepal, for it gives lots of cultural interest and exciting high mountain views. It's a little longer and more strenuous than the Ghandruk Foothill Trek, but visual rewards are excellent.

Beginning with a bus or taxi ride from Pokhara to the shanty of Naya Pul, the trek proper starts in **BIRETHANTI**, visited by each of the main treks described in this guide. It takes two days to climb the Poon Hill Danda by way of **ULLERI** to gain the ridge at **GHOREPANI DEURALI**, from where Dhaulagiri is revealed far to the north. Next morning make the 40min trek to **POON HILL** in order to capture the magic of sunrise lighting Dhaulagiri and the Annapurnas.

Leaving Ghorepani trek east via **BANTHANTI** to **TADA-PANI**, then work south-eastward to **BAISI KHARKA** and **GHAN-DRUK**. Both Tadapani and Ghandruk are superb viewpoints, while Ghandruk is one of the most attractive villages in the Annapurna region.

The final two stages take the route steeply down to the Modi Khola, then up the eastern side to **LANDRUK**, another fine Gurung village, then over a rhododendron-clad ridge to **DHAMPUS** and **PHEDI** for the short road journey to Pokhara.

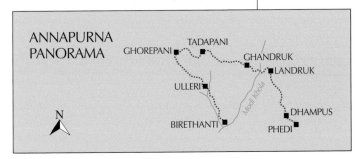

ANNAPURNA PANORAMA

N

GHOREPANI TADAPANI GHANDRUK LANDRUK ULLERI Modi Khola BIRETHANTI DHAMPUS PHEDI

Each of the above stages (except that from Tadapani to Ghandruk) is described in detail elsewhere in this guide.

The Tatopani–Ghorepani Loop

Another variation on the theme of panoramic views and foothill villages, using clear trails and popular lodges throughout, links the hot springs village of Tatopani with the ridge-top viewpoint of Ghorepani.

Distance:	49km (30 miles)
Time:	6–7 days
Max. altitude:	3193m (10,476ft)
Start:	Beni
Finish:	Naya Pul
Trekking style:	Tea-house (lodge accommodation)

BENI marks one of the optional starts to the Pilgrim's Trail, and is reached by bus or taxi from Pokhara. From there it will take 1½ days through gorge-like narrows to reach **TATOPANI**, from where Nilgiri South shows its tremendous South Face above the Miristi Khola.

The next section of the trek is much more strenuous, but if taken over two days the climb to **GHOREPANI DEURALI** will not be too demanding for inexperienced trekkers. Described above as Section 4b of the Annapurna Circuit Trek, there's a 1560m (5118ft) ascent to be made, and views of Dhaulagiri

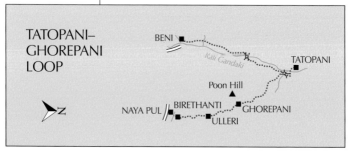

TATOPANI–
GHOREPANI
LOOP

BENI

Kali Gandaki

TATOPANI

Poon Hill

NAYA PUL   BIRETHANTI   GHOREPANI

ULLERI

demand that you keep stopping to turn around. Most visitors to Ghorepani make the pre-dawn ascent of **POON HILL** to enjoy the classic sunrise panorama before heading down the south side of the ridge to **ULLERI**, **BIRETHANTI** and **NAYA PUL** on the road to Pokhara.

The Korchon Ridge Trek

Naturally enough, Machhapuchhare is a prime focus of attention from Pokhara. Below it to the south-west, and dwarfed by the fish-tail peak, Mardi Himal is the lowest of the neighbourhood Trekking Peaks first climbed by Jimmy Roberts in 1961. A ridge runs southward from Mardi Himal over the rounded summit of Korchon and all the way down to the Pokhara valley between the valleys of the Mardi Khola on the west and Seti Khola on the east. This ridge makes a very scenic trek well away from the busy trekking routes.

Distance:	36km (22 miles)
Time:	6–7 days
Max. altitude:	3570m (11,713ft)
Start:	Pokhara (Hyangja)
Finish:	Pokhara (Hyangja)
Trekking style:	Camping

The lower part of the ridge has a confusion of trails, so you'll need a local guide to help find the way, and as there are no villages for most of the route it's essential to be self-contained. Water supplies can be a problem. It's a short, energetic trek, with several steep ascents and descents.

The Pokhara–Baglung road passes through **HYANGJA**, where a trail strikes north between rice paddies, crosses the Mardi Khola and heads along the river's east bank to **RIBBAN**, a Gurung village at the start of a long steep climb

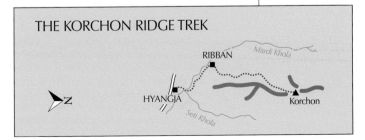

THE KORCHON RIDGE TREK

RIBBAN — Mardi Khola

N

HYANGJA — Seti Khola — Korchon

through bamboo forest that eventually comes onto the rhodo-dendron-clad Korchon ridge. The way now ascends the ridge, with several clearings from which increasingly fine views include Dhaulagiri, Annapurna I and Annapurna South, Hiunchuli, Machhapuchhare directly ahead, Annapurna IV, Lamjung Himal and, east of the Marsyangdi, Manaslu, Ngadi Chuli and Himalchuli.

It takes about 3½–4 days to reach the pastures of **KOR-CHON**, and it's worth spending at least two nights there. From it you could continue to a higher part of the ridge to gain more intimate views of Machhapuchhare. The way back to Pokhara necessarily reverses the upward route.

The Siklis Trek

North-east of Pokhara, in the foothills below Annapurnas IV and II, and Lamjung Himal, the large Gurung village of Siklis is visited by a relatively small number of commercial trekking groups using a variety of routes through sub-tropical forests and highly productive farmland. The following is just one option.

Distance:	50km (31 miles)
Time:	7 days
Max altitude:	2600m (8530ft)
Start:	Pokhara (Mardi Phul)
Finish:	Begnas Tal
Trekking style:	Camping

A short taxi ride along the Yamdi Khola's valley brings you to Mardi Phul near Hyangja, where the trek sets out to follow the Seti Khola upstream to **DHIPRANG**, near its confluence with the Sardi Khola. Along the Sardi Khola's valley the trail visits two Gurung villages before crossing the river and climbing to **GHALEKHARKA**, where there's an information centre. A steep climb through rhododendron forest brings you onto the trek's high point at a ridge to gain views of Machhapuchhare and Annapurnas IV and II. About an hour later you reach a campsite known as **NYAULKHARKA**. Next day descend to **SIKLIS**, where ACAP has its regional headquarters. A minumum of two

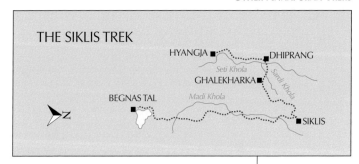

nights ought to be spent here in order to explore this interesting village and its surrounding area.

The way back to Pokhara entails descending to the Madi Khola and following the river downvalley through villages and productive farmland most of the way to **BEGNAS TAL,** where there are buses and taxis for the short road journey to Pokhara.

Begnas Tal to the Marsyangdi

Begnas Tal is the starting point for a rewarding three-day cross-country trek which joins the Annapurna Circuit at Khudi, 1½hrs from Besisahar. Useful as an approach to the Circuit trek from Pokhara, it could also be adopted as a short trek in its own right, ending with a walk downstream to Besisahar, from where it's possible to catch a bus to Kathmandu. Much of the route weaves its way through farmland, but there's a ridge to cross above Baglungpani from which an exquisite high-mountain panorama includes both the Annapurna and Manaslu himals. It's one of the finest foothill viewpoints in the whole Annapurna range.

Distance:	30km (19 miles)
Time:	3 days
Max. altitude:	1676m (5500ft)
Start:	Begnas Tal
Finish:	Khudi
Trekking style:	Camping or tea-house trekking

BEGNAS TAL TO THE MARSYANGDI

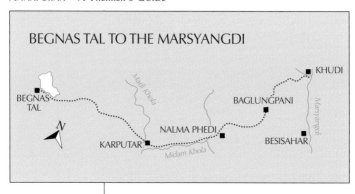

The ridge at Baglungpani provides views of both the Annapurnas and Manaslu

Begnas Tal is reached by bus in a little under an hour from Pokhara. A road continues eastward, and when this runs out trails lead to **KARPUTAR** on the east bank of the Madi Khola. The onward route is confusing, and independent trekkers would do well to have a local guide to help find the way. It roughly follows the Midim Khola upstream to a point where it is sometimes necessary to wade through the river (caution required). **NALMA PHEDI** is at the foot of a steep climb, in places on stone steps, that eventually leads to **BAGLUNGPANI** and the

wonderful ridgetop views that are the highlight of this trek. There's a good campsite on a lawn-like saddle just above the village.

On the north side of the ridge the path descends through forest to the valley of the Boran Khola and an attractive region of rice and millet fields, banana groves and ochre-painted houses. The trail edges these fields and joins the busy Annapurna Circuit trail a few minutes from **KHUDI**.

The Bara Pokhari Lekh

East of the Marsyangdi the forested Bara Pokhari Lekh is a long ridge which runs down from Himalchuli in the Manaslu Himal, almost as far as the Marsyangdi just south of Besisahar. A group of holy lakes lie high upon this ridge, and views are magnificent. It's a tough trek to reach them, and you'll need to be self-sufficient with food and camping equipment, and preferably have a local guide to show the way.

Distance:	48km (30 miles)
Time:	6–8 days
Max. altitude:	4300m (14,108ft)
Start:	Phalenksangu
Finish:	Ngadi
Trekking style:	Camping

Phalenksangu lies on the west bank of the Marsyangdi, on the road from Dumre to Besisahar. A bridge spans the river, and from the east side a trail heads alongside rice paddies, visiting a few small villages in the side-valley of the Chhamli Khola before climbing through rhododendron forest to gain the *lekh*. It will take about three days to reach the Bara Pokhari, beside the first of which stands a small Hindu shrine. The altitude of this first lake is about 3100m (10,171ft), but more are to be found further along the ridge which undulates ever higher towards Himalchuli. Not only is the Manaslu Himal seen a short distance to the north, but views stretch west along the flanks of the Annapurnas, and east to the Ganesh Himal. Go as far as you feel able, but be warned that you're likely to find

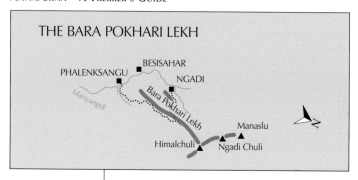

THE BARA POKHARI LEKH

snow lying on the upper reaches during the spring trekking season. As an alternative return to the Marsyangdi, locate one of several trails that descend steeply on the west flank and lead to Ngadi, a village on the Annapurna Circuit trail, a day's walk from Besisahar and the roadhead.

APPENDIX A
SUMMARY OF TREKS

TREK	START	FINISH	TIME	DISTANCE
Trek 1: The Annapurna Circuit	Besisahar	Beni or Naya Pul	15–21 days	190km (118 miles)
Trek 2: The Annapurna Sanctuary	Phedi or Naya Pul	Phedi or Naya Pul	7–12 days	84km (50 miles)
Trek 3: The Pilgrim's Trail	Beni or Naya Pul	Muktinath or Jomosom	7–9 days (+return time)	88km (54 miles) to Muktinath
Trek 4: The Ghandruk Foothill Trek	Naya Pul	Phedi	4–5 days	38km (23 miles)
Other Treks				
Upper Mustang	Jomosom	Jomosom	10-14 days	130km (80 miles)
Annapurna Panorama	Naya Pul	Phedi	5–6 days	60km (37 miles)
The Tatopani–Ghorepani loop	Beni	Naya Pul	6–7 days	49km (30 miles)
The Korchon Ridge Trek	Pokhara (Hyangja)	Pokhara (Hyangja)	6–7 days	36km (22 miles)
The Siklis Trail	Pokhara	Begnas Tal (Mardi Phul)	7 days	50km (31 miles)
Begnas Tal to the Marsyangdi	Begnas Tal	Khudi	3 days	30km (19 miles)
The Bara Pokhari Lekh	Phalenksangu	Ngadi	6–8 days	48km (30 miles)

APPENDIX B
ANNAPURNA – THE FIRST FIFTY YEARS

Of the world's 14 8000m peaks, Annapurna I was the first to be climbed (see box Annapurna – Triumph and Bitter Aftermath, Trek 3: the Pilgrims Trail, Section 2). Until 1949 the neighbouring massifs of Dhaulagiri and Annapurna had only been seen by mountaineers from a great distance, but in October that year Dr Arnold Heim from Zürich, with the backing of the Swiss Foundation for Alpine Research, gained permission to make an aerial reconnaissance of the area. However, his Indian pilot did not fly higher than 4500m (15,000ft), which was insufficient to make a useful observation, and although Heim returned with photographs and a short film, little of value in mountaineering terms had been learned. By the time Herzog's nine-man expedition from France began its approach through the Kali Gandaki in the spring of 1950, even the question of how to locate the base of Annapurna remained unanswered, thanks to errors on the Indian Survey map.

The fact that the French climbed their mountain at the first attempt, in a relatively short time and without any prior reconnaissance is a tribute to the driving force of Herzog and the mountaineering skills of his fellow climbers. Luck, too, played a large part in their success, although that luck almost ran out on the descent, and the two summiteers suffered agonies of amputation during the retreat after contracting frostbite high on the mountain. From a base at the head of the Miristi Khola, the ascent was achieved by way of the avalanche-swept North Face on 3 June, in an eight-hour climb from the top camp by Herzog and Lachenal. After this, Annapurna I was left alone for several years, although successful attempts were made elsewhere, on other summits of the massif.

In 1969 a strong German expedition conceived the ambitious plan of attacking Annapurna I by its long East Ridge, starting in the Sanctuary and first climbing Tarke Kang, then working along the ridge over Khangsar Kang to the Saddle, and on from there to Annapurna's summit. Although making good progress, violent winds on the ridge beyond Khangsar Kang defeated two separate attempts.

The second success on Annapurna I came 20 years after Herzog and Lachenal's, when a British–Nepalese Army Expedition returned to the North Face and, following the original route, put two men, Henry Day and Gerry Owens, on the top. At the same time as this expedition was taking place, Chris Bonington's team was tackling the awesome South Face which soars out of the head of the Annapurna Sanctuary. It was the most ambitious climb then attempted in the Himalaya, and when Dougal Haston and Don Whillans stood on the summit on 27 May 1970, just a week after it was vacated by Day and Owens on the north side, it heralded the dawn of a new era of Himalayan adventure.

Four years later, in April 1974, a Spanish expedition led by José Manuel Anglada reached the 8026m (26,332ft) East Summit of Annapurna I. On summit day the three climbers (Anglada, Pons and Civis) took 14hrs to ascend the North Ridge from their highest camp (at 7490m, 24,573ft), and finally reached the top at 9pm in bright moonlight.

The next truly notable achievement on Annapurna I came in 1984, when the Swiss pair Erhard Loretan and Norbert Joos completed what the Germans had attempted in 1969. Climbing the 7km long East Ridge, and reaching the East Summit only three days after leaving base, they continued over the Middle Summit to the true summit of Annapurna I, then descended the North Face to complete an amazing traverse of the mountain in alpine style.

The huge, concave Northwest Face had yet to receive its first ascent, but this came in 1985 when Reinhold Messner and Hans Kammerlander spearheaded a small expedition intent on finding a line that had not yet been tried. Other expeditions in the past had attempted this 3000m face without success, but Messner and his team discovered a route that brought the pair onto the West Ridge in swirling mist and violent winds, and they followed this right to the summit.

Apart from new lines on existing faces or ridges, that left the Northwest Pillar, a route first spotted by the French in 1950. Although an extremely difficult line, it is relatively safe from avalanche and rockfall – a rare situation on Annapurna. In the postmonsoon season of 1996, an international expedition comprising eight Polish climbers, one American and a Ukranian used 2000m of fixed rope and no less than five camps on the Pillar before putting Marciniak and Terzyul on the summit on 20 October.

By the autumn of 1999, after 50 years of mountaineering attention, Annapurna I had been summited 106 times in 120 documented expeditions, and by more routes than existed on any other 8000er. But 54 climbers had also lost their lives on this, the world's tenth highest mountain, most falling victim to rockfall or avalanche. Such an appaling loss of life makes Annapurna the second most dangerous of the 14 'big ones', and despite (or perhaps because of) its history, it has never been in fashion.

Recommended Reading

Annapurna by Maurice Herzog (Jonathan Cape, 1952)

Annapurna South Face by Chris Bonington (Cassell, 1971)

Annapurna by Reinhold Messner (The Mountaineers, 2000)

Sivalaya by Louis Baume (Gastons-West Col, 1978)

APPENDIX C
TREKKING PEAKS IN THE ANNAPURNA REGION

The term Trekking Peak, which applies to the 18 mountains included in the list drawn up by the Nepal Mountaineering Association (NMA), is something of a misnomer, for although their summits are not among the most difficult for climbers in the Himalaya, they are beyond the dreams or abilities of most trekkers. Measuring between 5500m (18,045ft) and 6600m (21,654ft) these peaks demand a certain expertise, and provide climbing adventure which slots somewhere between alpine and high-peak expeditionary mountaineering. Of course, one or two of those on the list are much easier than others, and if tackled under good conditions may seem rather 'tame' to climbers with a few epic alpine experiences behind them. However, in the Himalaya, as in the Alps, conditions can vary enormously, and what might be a straightforward four-day ascent one week can easily turn into a nightmare of life-threatening proportions the next.

Trekking Peaks, as opposed to full-scale expedition peaks, are subject to a minimum of formalities and expense. Application is made first to the NMA (PO Box 1435, Nagpokhari, Naxal, Kathmandu; e-mail: office@nma.com.np; www.nma.com.np). On completion of an application form and payment of a relatively modest fee, in foreign currency by cash or traveller's cheques, a permit for a period of one month at or above base camp is granted. An approved sirdar must then be employed to accompany the climbing party for the duration of the trek/climb. A full list of climbing rules is set out in a booklet available from the NMA at the above address.

The official list of Trekking Peaks is grouped according to height: those of 6000m and above are in Group A, while those of less than 6000m are listed in Group B. Since January 2001 the climbing fee for Trekking Peaks has been the same for both groups. The list covers a wide geographical area, but those within the region covered by this guide are given below. Bill O'Connor's book *The Trekking Peaks of Nepal* (Crowood Press, 1991) is highly recommended to anyone planning to tackle one of these peaks. It is widely available in specialist bookshops in the West as well as in those of Kathmandu. See also *Trekking & Climbing in Nepal* by Steve Razzetti (New Holland, 2000), which gives outline details of several trekking peaks in the Annapurna region.

Manang Himal
Three peaks contained in Group A are reached by a trek through the Marsyangdi valley. These are Chulu West (6419m, 21,060ft), Chulu East (6558m, 21,516ft) and Pisang Peak (6092m, 19,987ft).

In the past there was some confusion with regard to the altitude and actual location of the Chulu peaks. O'Connor pointed out that several summits forming part of the massif were not shown on maps of the region, while altitudes quoted were considered suspect. Most of the confusion over location has now been settled, although altitudes remain questionable. As an arena for climbing adventure there remains plenty of scope, with two possible summits to aim for on the **CHULU WEST** permit, and another two on that for **CHULU EAST**. Various routes are outlined in O'Connor's book. Base Camp for Chulu West is approached from Letdar above Manang, while that for Chulu East is reached by way of Braga or Humde.

PISANG PEAK is climbed by a long snow slog from a camp located on a *kharka* at about 4380m (14,370ft) high above Pisang village, from which it appears seriously foreshortened. It is a large bulk of a mountain tapering to a neat snow pyramid, and was first climbed solo in 1955 by a member of a German expedition heading for Annapurna IV. From the upper slopes a magnificent view is afforded of the Annapurna range to the south and west across the deep trench of the Marsyangdi valley. The standard route, by way of the Southwest Face/West Ridge, is graded alpine PD-. In 1994 a large German group from the DAV was avalanched below the summit, killing 10 trekkers and a Sherpa.

Annapurna Himal

Situated within the Annapurna Sanctuary, or located on its rim, four peaks are on the NMA list. Hiunchuli and Singu Chuli, both being above 6000m, are contained within Group A, while Tharpu Chuli and Mardi Himal are in Group B.

HIUNCHULI (6441m, 21,132ft) forms the western 'gatepost' of the Sanctuary. Seen from the south it appears as a large snow-bound extension of Annapurna South, while from the north it is a graceful mountain with sharply defined ridges rising to a pointed summit. It is not an easy peak; the original Southeast Face route is plagued with rockfall and avalanche potential, while the Northwest Face offers steep ice and enticing couloirs.

SINGU CHULI, otherwise known as Fluted Peak (6501m, 21,329ft), received its first ascent in 1957 from Wilfred Noyce and David Cox after their failed attempt on Machhapuchhare. It rises to the east of Annapurna I and overlooks the neighbouring trekking peak of Tharpu Chuli. An attractive mountain, it has several difficult routes and nowhere offers an easy option.

THARPU CHULI, or Tent Peak (5663m, 18,579ft), forms the southern end of a ridge projecting into the Annapurna basin from Tarke Kang (Glacier Dome). It's another fine-looking mountain whose name is easy to understand when seen from Annapurna Base Camp, but whose height is debatable. Jimmy Roberts, the first Westerner to penetrate the Sanctuary, made an attempt to climb Tharpu Chuli in 1956, but it was not until 1964 that the summit was reached by a Japanese expedition. The two 'normal routes' are: via the Northwest Ridge (alpine grade PD) and the slightly harder Southeast Ridge, graded AD.

Finally, **MARDI HIMAL** (5587m, 18,330ft) is the close south-western neighbour of Machhapuchhare and is almost completely dominated by the loftier 'fish-tail' peak. Although it is so close to the Annapurna Sanctuary (it forms part of the eastern wall of the Modi Khola's gorge), Mardi Himal is reached by a difficult five-day trek from Pokhara along a ridge that overlooks the Mardi Khola to the west and Seti Khola on the east. The actual climb, following the route of the first ascent made by Jimmy Roberts in 1961, is not difficult under normal conditions and has an alpine grade of F *(facile)*.

APPENDIX D
USEFUL ADDRESSES

1: SELECTED OVERSEAS MISSIONS OF THE NEPALESE GOVERNMENT

Embassies

UK
12a Kensington Palace Gardens
London W8 4QU
(Tel: 020 7229 1594)

USA
2131 Leroy Place NW
Washington
DC 20008
(Tel: 202 667 4550)

France
45 bis, rue des Acacias
75017 Paris
(Tel: 01 46 22 48 67)

Germany
Guerickestr. 27
10587 Berlin-Charlottenburg
(Tel: 030 3435 9920)

Consulates

USA
Suite 400
909 Montgomery St
San Francisco
CA 94133
(Tel: 415 434 1111)

Australia
PO Box 474
Edgecliff
NSW 2027
(Tel: 02 9328 7062)

Canada
Royal Bank Plaza
PO Box 33
Toronto
Ontario M5J 2J9
(Tel: 416 865 0200)

Level 7
344 Queen Street
Brisbane
Queensland 4000
(Tel: 07 3220 2007)

2: SELECTED FOREIGN MISSIONS IN NEPAL

British Embassy
Lainchaur
Kathmandu
(Tel: 410583/414588)

American Embassy
Pani Pokhari
Kathmandu
(Tel: 411179/413890)

Australian Embassy
Bansbari
Kathmandu (Tel: 371466/371076)

In addition the following **Cultural Centres** are based in Kathmandu:

The British Council
Kantipath (Tel: 211305)

French Cultural Centre
Bag Bazar (Tel: 214326)

United States Information Service
New Road (Tel: 211250)

3: CONSERVATION ORGANISATIONS IN NEPAL

Annapurna Conservation Area Project
(ACAP)
PO Box 183
Hariyo Kharka
Pokhara
Nepal
e-mail: acap@mos.com.np

King Mahendra Trust for Nature Conservation
KMTNC
PO Box 3712
Jawalakhel
Lalitpur
Nepal
e-mail: info@kmtnc.org.np
website: www.kmtnc.org.np

4: MAP SUPPLIERS

Cordee Ltd
3a De Montfort Street
Leicester
LE1 7HD

Edward Stanford Ltd
12–14 Long Acre
London
WC2E 9LP (www.stanfords.co.uk)

Adventurous Traveler Bookstore
PO Box 1468
Williston
VT 05495 USA

Bradt Enterprises Inc
95 Harvey Street
Cambridge
MA 02140 USA

Michael Chessler Books
PO Box 2436
Evergreen
CO 80439 USA

Melbourne Map Centre
PO Box 55
Holmesglen
Victoria 3148 Australia

Many bookshops in Kathmandu and Pokhara stock trekking maps for the Annapurna region. Especially useful are the Himalayan MapHouse shops, with nine outlets in Thamel, Kathmandu, and three in Pokhara. Or contact Himalayan MapHouse Pvt Ltd, GPO Box 3924 Kathmandu (e-mail:maphouse@wlink.com.np; website: www.himalayanmaphouse.com).

APPENDIX E
GLOSSARY

Whilst it would be possible to trek the main trails of Annapurna speaking only English, a little effort to communicate with Nepalis in their own language will be amply repaid. If you are trekking with an organised group, opportunities will arise to practise a few words and phrases with your crew and porters. Tea-house trekkers will find that some attempt to speak the language will be appreciated by lodge-keepers and the owners of tea-houses along the trail, while those who employ a porter-guide will discover that mutual language-exchange is a bonus to the day-to-day pleasures of the trail. Nepalis who meet and work with Europeans are keen to expand their vocabulary, and are usually very happy to offer some instruction in their own language in return for help given in English.

The following glossary lists a few words that may be useful on the trail. A few Nepali phrasebooks and dictionaries are available that would be worth consulting in addition to Stephen Bezruchka's highly recommended language tape and accompanying book, *Nepali for Trekkers* (The Mountaineers, 1991). Lonely Planet publish a small, lightweight *Nepal Phrasebook* that would sit easily in a shirt pocket for instant use on the trail.

NEPALI	ENGLISH	NEPALI	ENGLISH
aaja	today	chiso paani	cold water
baato	trail	chiyaa	tea
baayaan	left (direction)	chorten	Buddhist shrine, like an elaborate cairn
banthanti	the place in the forest		
bazaar	market	chuba	Tibetan wrap-around clothing
bhanjang	hilltop clearing		
bharal	the blue sheep	daahine	right (direction)
bhatti	traditional inn/guest-house	daal bhaat	Nepalise staple meal: rice (bhaat) with lentil sauce (daal)
bholi	tomorrow		
Bhot	Tibet	dahi	yoghurt
Bhotyia	Buddhist people of mountain Nepal	danda	ridge
		deurali	a pass on a ridge
bistaari	slowly	dhara	waterspout
chang	home-brewed beer	dharmsala	pilgrims' rest house
charpi	latrine	dokan	shop (see also pasal)
chautaara	trailside resting platform	doko	porter's conical basket
chaulki	police post	dudh	milk
chini	sugar	ghar	house

NEPALI	ENGLISH	NEPALI	ENGLISH
gompa	Buddhist temple	shaligram	ammonite
goth	herdsman's shelter	sidha	straight ahead (direction)
hijo	yesterday	sirdar	man in charge of trek crew (porters, guides, etc)
himal	snow mountain		
kani	covered archway, decorated with Buddhist motifs	stupa	large chorten
		taato paani	hot water
khaana	food	tal	lake
kharka	high pasture	Thakali	people of Thak Khola, Kali Gandaki's upper region
khola	river		
khukari	Gurkha knife (curved blade)	thanka	Buddhist scroll painting
kot	fortress	thanti	place
la	high pass	thungba	alcoholic drink
lama	Buddhist monk or priest	thukpa	noodle soup
lekh	foothill ridge	tsampa	roasted barley flour
maasu	meat	ukaalo	steep uphill
maati baato	upper trail	umaleko paani	boiled water
mani	Buddhist prayer; from the mantra 'Om mani padme hum'	yersa	summer grazing pasture

		Days of the Week	
mani wall	stone wall carved with Buddhist prayers	Aitobar	Sunday
mantra	religious incantation	Sombaar	Monday
mela	fair or market	Mangalbaar	Tuesday
naike	head porter	Budhbaar	Wednesday
namaste	traditional greeting meaning 'I salute the God within you'	Bihibaar	Thursday
		Sukrobaar	Friday
nun	salt	Sanibaar	Saturday
paani	water (see *chiso paani, taato paani* and *umaleko paani*)		
pasal	shop (see also dokan)		
phedi	literally 'the place at the foot of the hill'		
phul	egg		
pokhari	lake		
puja	religious ceremony		
rakshi	distilled spirit		
roti	bread		
sadhu	Hindu ascetic		

Days of the Week

Aitobar	Sunday
Sombaar	Monday
Mangalbaar	Tuesday
Budhbaar	Wednesday
Bihibaar	Thursday
Sukrobaar	Friday
Sanibaar	Saturday

NUMBERS

1	ek	14	chaudha	55	pachpanna
2	dui	15	pandhra	60	saathi
3	tin	16	sohra	65	paisatthi
4	char	17	satra	70	sattari
5	paanch	18	athaara	75	pachahat tar
6	chha	19	unnaais	80	asi
7	saat	20	bis	85	pachaasi
8	aath	25	pachhis	90	nabbe
9	nau	30	tis	95	pan chaanaabbe
10	das	35	paitis	100	ek sae
11	eghaara	40	chaalis	1000	ek hajaar
12	baahra	45	paitaalis		
13	tehra	50	pachaas		

APPENDIX F
USEFUL PHRASES

Nepali grammar is not very complicated, but it may take practice before it flows naturally with daily usage. One of the main rules to remember is that sentences end with the verb, for example:

Haami (We) *kukhoro* (chicken) *khaanchau* (eat).

When you ask a question, the structure is the same as that for a statement, but is differentiated by intonation. For example, if you want to ask 'Which trail is going to Manang?', the emphasis is placed on the word 'which' with your voice making a rising tone at the end of the sentence.

Manang (Manang) *jaane* (going) *baato* (trail) *kun* (<u>which</u>) *ho?* (is?).

Incidentally, it is essential to avoid asking a direct question in relation to a trail, such as 'Does this trail go to Manang?', for you will invariably receive a positive response, even if the way does not!

Emergencies and Medical Problems
Help!	*Bachaau!*
I am sick.	*Ma biraami chhu.*
I have altitude sickness.	*Lekh laagyo.*
My friend is sick.	*Mero saathi biraami bhayo.*
Please call a doctor.	*Daaktarlai bolaaunuhos.*

On the Trail
Hello/Goodbye	*Namaste*
How are you?	*Tapailai kasto chha?*
How far is Manang?	*Manang kati taada chha?*
How many hours does it take?	*Kati ghantaa laagchha?*
How much are the oranges (bananas)?	*Suntaala (keraa) kati parchha?*
I am going to the Annapurna Sanctuary.	*Annapurna Sanctuary maa jaane.*
I am lost.	*Ma baato haraayo.*
I don't know.	*Thaahaa chhaina*
I need a porter.	*Ma kulli chaainchha.*
I will stay two days.	*Dui din baschhu.*
Is it far from here?	*Yahaa bata kati taadhaa chha?*

Is the trail very steep?	*Baato dherai ukaalo chha?*
My name is	*Mero naam ...ho.*
Please give me a cup of tea.	*Ek cup chiyaa dinuhos.*
Take it slowly.	*Bistaari jaau.*
What is the name of this village?	*Yo gaaunko naam ke ho?*
What is your name?	*Tapainko naam ke ho?*
Where are you coming from?	*Kata baata?*
Where are you going?	*Tapaai kahaa jaane?*
Where have you been?	*Kata pugera aaunubhayo?*
Where is a shop?	*Pasal kahaan chha?*
Which trail goes to Manang?	*Manang jaane baato kun ho?*

BIBLIOGRAPHY

Of the numerous books on Nepal, those listed below have specific interest to trekkers concentrating on the Annapurna region. Several have wider scope, of course, but all contain information relevant to your needs. Some inevitably are out of print and unobtainable in the West, except through public libraries or internet sites. However, many bookshops in Kathmandu stock an admirable selection of new, old and reprinted volumes, and will be worth investigating if you cannot obtain what you require at home.

1: General Tourist Guides and Travelogues

Insight Guide: Nepal edited by Hans Höfer (APA Publications).
Expert contributions, both textual and photographic, give this frequently updated book an air of authority.

Nepal (Nelles Verlag/Robertson McCarta, 1990).
Gives similar coverage to the above.

Nepal: The Kingdom of the Himalayas by Toni Hagen
(Kümmerley and Frey, 1980).
Not a tourist guide as such, this large-format coffee-table book is packed with information and photographs gleaned from the author's travels throughout the country. Hagen was the first man to be given the freedom to explore the whole of Nepal, and his knowledge of the country must therefore be considered unique.

Nepal by Hugh Findlay (Lonely Planet, 5th edition, 2001).
Gives lots of practical information and advice for getting around Nepal, and includes an introduction to trekking.

Nepal – the Rough Guide by David Reed (Rough Guides, 2002).
A down-to-earth guide, largely written for budget travellers. It includes basic trekking information.

Nepal by Percival Landon (Constable, 1928 –
reprinted by Biblioteca Himalayica, New Delhi).
A popular historic overview.

The Waiting Land by Dervla Murphy (John Murray, 1967).
An entertaining travelogue of this respected travel writer's time in the mid-1960s

working with Tibetan refugees near Pokhara. As ever, the writer's observations are astute and masterfully drawn.

Travels in Nepal by Charlie Pye-Smith (Aurum Press, 1988).

Provides a thought-provoking commentary on the question of foreign-aid programmes within Nepal.

2: Trekking – Narratives and Guidebooks

The most popular trekking guides to Nepal cover many different areas, so for the trekker whose visit concentrates on just one route, or one region only, they inevitably include large passages of unused material.

Annapurna Circuit by Andrew Stevenson (Constable, 1997).

This is a highly readable narrative of one man's experiences whilst trekking around Annapurna. Read it prior to your first trek, then re-read it on your return home.

A Nepalese Journey by Andrew Stevenson (Constable, 2002).

A photographic record of several visits to the region by the author of the above book – a perfect souvenir.

Trekking in Nepal by Stephen Bezruchka
(Cordee/The Mountaineers, 7th edition, 1997).

This is the classic trekker's guide – packed with valuable information, sensitively written and frequently revised, all prospective visitors should study a copy. The author's love of the country and concern for its people is a shining example to all trekkers.

Trekking in Nepal, West Tibet & Bhutan by Hugh Swift
(Hodder & Stoughton, 1989).

Out of print, and in places out of date, this book remains one of the most inspirational on the subject. The late Hugh Swift was an avid mountain traveller with a gift for recreating the atmosphere of the Himalaya. If you can track a copy down – do so.

Trekking in the Nepal Himalaya by Stan Armington
(Lonely Planet, 8th edition, 2001).

Probably the biggest selling trekking guide to Nepal, this regularly updated book covers most regions including, of course, Annapurna. The author lives in Kathmandu and has been leading commercial treks in the Himalaya for 30 years.

Trekking and Climbing in Nepal by Steve Razzetti (New Holland, 2000).

Written and illustrated by a well-known British trek leader, the Annapurna region has good coverage, along with most other regions of mountain Nepal.

Trekking in Nepal by Toru Nakano (Springfield Books, 1990).

Brief route descriptions, regional maps and lots of colour photos in a translation of the Japanese original. The photographs will remind you to take a camera and plenty of film.

Adventure Treks: Nepal by Bill O'Connor (Cicerone Press, 1990).

Personal narratives of several treks including Annapurna Circuit and Sanctuary. Not a guidebook as such, it conveys some of the magic, as well as some of the frustrations, of trekking.

The Trekking Peaks of Nepal by Bill O'Connor (Crowood Press, 1991).

This companion volume to Adventure Treks is, perhaps, of more value, even if you have no intention of climbing any of the peaks. Brief details of major trekking routes are given, as well as outlines of the possibilities for climbing on all 18 Trekking Peaks.

Trekking in the Annapurna Region by Bryn Thomas
(Trailblazer, 3rd edition, 1999).

A useful guide covering the same treks as this book. Plenty of good pre and post trek advice.

Mustang – A Trekking Guide by Bob Gibbons and Sian Pritchard-Jones
(Tiwari's Pilgrims Book House, 1993).

A book for anyone planning to visit this region north of Kagbeni.

Trekking: Great Walks of the World by John Cleare (Unwin Hyman, 1988).

Contains a lively, well-illustrated chapter about the Annapurna Circuit.

Classic Walks of the World edited by Walt Unsworth
(Oxford Illustrated Press, 1985).

Also includes a chapter on the Annapurna Circuit.

Footloose in the Himalaya by Mike Harding (Michael Joseph, 1989).

Harding is both humorous and thoughtful as he recounts his journeys in several parts of the Himalaya, including a short trek in the Annapurna foothills.

The Trekkers' Handbook by Thomas R. Gilchrist (Cicerone Press, 1996).

Written by an experienced trek leader, this is packed with good ideas and background information for trekking virtually anywhere in the world. Recommended.

The Mountain Traveller's Handbook by Paul Deegan (BMC, 2002).

Similar to the previously mentioned volume, but with a wider remit, this is for climbers as well as trekkers, serving as a useful resource for newcomers as well as old-hands.

3: Mountains and Mountaineering

Annapurna by Maurice Herzog (Jonathan Cape, 1952).

Herzog's account of the first ascent of an 8000m peak is a true mountaineering classic, and of interest to anyone planning to tackle the Circuit or the Pilgrim's Trail. Annapurna has sold around 11 million copies, making it the biggest selling mountaineering book ever.

True Summit by David Roberts
(Simon & Schuster, New York, 2000/Constable, London, 2001).

Another view of the first ascent of Annapurna which challenges Herzog's account. But see also Messner's book below.

Annapurna by Reinhold Messner (The Mountaineers, 2000).

Perhaps the world's most successful high altitude mountaineer, Messner attempts to answer Herzog's critics (see above), and also highlights the major climbing developments on Annapurna in the fifty years since its first ascent.

Nepal Himalaya by H.W.Tilman
(Cambridge University Press 1952, now contained in a collection of The Seven Mountain Travel Books, Diadem Books/The Mountaineers 1983).

Tilman visited Manang in 1950 and made an attempt on Annapurna IV. Contains good descriptions of the Marsyangdi valley and of the peaks that wall it.

Climbing the Fish's Tail by Wilfrid Noyce
(Heinemann, 1958 – latest edition published by Book Faith India, 1998).

Account of the only expedition to climb on Machhapuchhare, it provides a stimulating picture of the Sanctuary, and also records the first ascent of Singu Chuli (Fluted Peak).

Annapurna South Face by Chris Bonington (Cassell, 1971).

Bonington's team climbed the impressive South Face in 1970, thus heralding a new era in Himalayan mountaineering. Of especial interest to those planning to trek into the Sanctuary.

Summits and Secrets by Kurt Diemberger
(George Allen & Unwin, 1971, now part of the Kurt Diemberger Omnibus published by Bâton Wicks/The Mountaineers, 1999).

Includes a brief history of attempts on, and account of the first ascent of Dhaulagiri, written in the author's highly original style.

4: Travel and Exploration

Cloud-Dwellers of the Himalayas by Windsor Chorlton (Time-Life Books, 1982).
Describes life in Nar-Phu, the remote region of Manang District.

Himalayan Pilgrimage by David Snellgrove (Shambhala Publications, 1989).
Travels through then-remote parts of Nepal in the 1950s, including the Annapurna region, by a noted Tibetan scholar. Interesting descriptions, especially of the gompa at Braga in the upper Marsyangdi valley.

Vignettes of Nepal by Harka Gurung (Sajha Prakashan, Kathmandu, 1980).
A personal account of travels in numerous parts of Nepal by a distinguished former government minister brought up in the Marsyangdi valley.

5: Anthropology and Natural History

Birds of Nepal by Fleming, Fleming and Bangdel (Avalok, 1984).
A comprehensive field guide, richly illustrated.

**A Popular Guide to the Birds and
Mammals of the Annapurna Conservation Area** (ACAP, 1989)

Concise Flowers of the Himalaya by Oleg Polunin and Adam Stainton
(Oxford University Press, 1987)

Butterflies of Nepal by Colin Smith (Tecpress, 1989)

People of Nepal by Dor Bahadur Bista (Ratna Pustak Bhandar, 5th edition, 1987).
Background information on a number of ethnic groups of Nepal.

The Festivals of Nepal by Mary M. Anderson (George Allen & Unwin, 1971)

WANT TO HELP?

Not surprisingly, many trekkers return from a trip to Nepal fired with enthusiasm for the country and its people, in the knowledge that they've had a life-changing experience. Hopefully you will too. And having received generous hospitality, care and consideration from materially-poor – but resourceful and naturally cheerful – Nepalis, there is often a desire to give something back in the way of practical help and support.

Mountaineer Doug Scott has done just that through a charity which he co-founded with the aim of improving the infrastructure of villages in the Middle Hills, through the provision of schools and health posts, training in primary health care, clean water projects and other community strengthening schemes, such as cottage industries.

Without favour towards any specific ethnic group, religion or culture, Community Action Nepal (CAN) works closely with village committees, and actively encourages local participation in each scheme in an effort to avoid donor dependency and to cultivate a sense of ownership and responsibility towards a project's success and development. CAN is currently supporting some 40 projects underway in the Middle Hills.

All money gift-aided or donated to CAN goes directly to Nepal, without any deductions to cover UK administration costs, all of which are met by Community Action Treks, Doug Scott's trekking company that supports the charity as its trading arm.

Want to help? Want to give something back?

Community Action Nepal would welcome your support. Visit www.canepal.org.uk for further information or contact:

Community Action Nepal, Warwick Mill, Warwick Bridge, Carlisle, Cumbria CA4 8RR (e-mail: info@catreks.com, Tel: 01228 564488).

Perhaps you would like to do something positive to improve the lot of **Nepalese porters**? The International Porter Protection Group (IPPG) was formed as a direct result of the tragic death of Shyam Bahadur (see the 'Porter Exploitation' box in the Introduction). Started in 1997 IPPG focuses on the provision of protective clothing, shelter and medical care for working porters, and support for injured porters and/or their dependents. By supporting IPPG you can help make a difference to the lives of the often-forgotten men and women on whose backs (literally) much of the success of a trek often depends.

For more information about the International Porter Protection Group, log on to www.ippg.net. You can forward personal accounts of trekking porters' misadventures, make suggestions or send donations to the International Coordinator, IPPG, 53 Dale Street, Ulverston, Cumbria LA12 9AR (e-mail: info@ippg.net).

LISTING OF CICERONE GUIDES